Second language learning and language teaching

VIVIAN COOK
Reader in Applied Linguistics, University of Essex

Second language learning and language teaching

SECOND EDITION

A member of the Hodder Headline Group
LONDON • NEW YORK • SYDNEY • AUCKLAND

First published in Great Britain in 1991
Second edition published in 1996 by
Arnold, a member of the Hodder Headline Group
338 Euston Road, London NW1 3BH
175 Fifth Avenue, New York, NY 10010

Distributed exclusively in the USA by
St Martin's Press Inc.,
175 Fifth Avenue,
New York, NY10010

British Library Cataloguing in Publication Data
A catalogue entry for this book is available from the British Library

Library of Congress Cataloging-in-Publication Data
Cook, V. J. (Vivian James), 1940–
    Second language learning and language teaching / Vivian Cook. —
2nd ed.
        p.   cm.
    Includes bibliographical references and index.
    ISBN 0–340–65202–0 (pbk.)
    1. Second language acquisition.   2. Language and languages—Study
and teaching.   I. Title.
P118.2.C67   1996
418'.007—dc20   95–36369
                                                           CIP

ISBN 0 340 65202 0 (Pb)

Composition by Phoenix Photosetting, Chatham, Kent
Printed and bound in Great Britain by JW Arrowsmith Ltd, Bristol

Table of contents

Acknowledgements

This book arose out of the complaints of language teachers that books on L2 learning were too academic and insufficiently linked to the classroom. The second edition has benefited from discussions and comments given by many teachers, students, colleagues and friends throughout. Like the first edition, it would never have been finished without the influence of Keith Jarrett, Mike Osborne, and Ornette Coleman, though sadly Sam was no longer able to help.

'The really important thing is less the destruction of bad old methods than a positive indication of the new ways to be followed if we are to have thoroughly efficient teaching in modern languages.'

(Otto Jespersen, 1904)

1

Second language learning and language teaching

Language is at the centre of human life. It is one of the most important ways of expressing our love or our hatred for people; it is vital to achieving many of our goals and our careers; it is a source of artistic satisfaction or simple pleasure. We use language for planning our lives and remembering our past; we exchange ideas and experiences through language; we identify ourselves with people who speak the same language. Some people are able to do some or all of this in more than one language. Knowing another language may mean: getting a job; a chance to get educated; the ability to take a fuller part in the life of one's own country or the opportunity to emigrate to another; an expansion of one's literary and cultural horizons; the expression of one's political opinions or religious beliefs. It affects people's careers and possible futures, their lives and very identities. In a world where probably more people speak two languages than speak one, language learning and language teaching are vital to the everyday lives of millions.

Since the 1970s a new academic subject has emerged, called second language (L2) learning research or second language acquisition (SLA) research, which looks at second and foreign language learning from a scientific perspective. Though still in its early stages of development, it has already produced insights from many perspectives. Most teachers have been trained to teach, not to think about second language learning. Yet everything that is achieved in the classroom depends eventually upon what goes on in the students' minds. Whether they know it or not, all teachers assume something about L2 learning; it is not that they lack a theory of language learning so much as they have a theory that they are unaware of. Without an understanding of why people need to learn other languages and of how knowledge of other languages is stored and learnt, teachers will always be less effective than they could be. Knowledge about L2 learning is a valuable complement to the teacher's other skills and knowledge.

1 The scope of this book

This book tries to convey why L2 learning research can be useful for language teaching. Its main aim is to inform those concerned with language teaching about some interesting aspects of L2 learning research and to relate them to language teaching. It is not a guide to L2 research methodology or to the merits and failings of particular research techniques, which are covered in other books (Cook, 1993; Sharwood-Smith, 1994). It is intended then for language teachers and trainee teachers.

L2 learning research provides valuable insights into teaching that will help teachers whatever their methodological slant. Partly this is at the general level of understanding; knowing what language learning consists of colours the teacher's awareness of everything that happens in the classroom and heightens the teacher's empathy with the student. Partly it is at the more specific level of the choice of teaching methods, the construction of teaching materials, or the design and execution of teaching techniques. The links between L2 learning and language teaching that are made are mostly suggestions of what *can* be done rather than accounts of what *has* been done. Some ideas presented here are based on a solid agreed foundation; others are more controversial or speculative.

Understanding how people learn language also means understanding what language *is*. So some parts of this book have to focus on the actual nature of language itself – grammar, pronunciation, vocabulary, etc. – since these are vital to understanding how people learn a second language.

The book gradually widens its scope from particular aspects of language to broader contexts and more general ideas. The first two chapters look at how people learn particular aspects of language: grammar in Chapter 2 – the area most second language acquisition research has concerned itself with; pronunciation, vocabulary, and conversational discourse in Chapter 3. The next two chapters treat learners as individuals, Chapter 4 looking at how individuals process language by listening, reading, and so on, and Chapter 5 describing how learners vary in terms of factors such as motivation and age. Next come aspects of the learning situation: Chapter 6 examines the characteristics of language teaching in classrooms, Chapter 7 puts L2 learning in the wider context of society. Finally, the research is integrated into more general ideas: Chapter 8 describes overall models of L2 learning in relationship to teaching, Chapter 9 relates teaching methods to L2 learning. Indeed, it is possible for readers who want to look first at issues of methodology rather than the research itself to start with Chapter 9, which looks at six styles of language teaching, and then to go backwards to look for the sources of the ideas involved. Readers who want to look specifically for some aspect of learning can also skip to the appropriate parts of the book.

In general, the emphasis in rewriting the new edition has been on increasing the usability of the book, based on the reactions of groups I have used it with. While some updating and correction has been carried out, the broad framework and approach of the first edition have been maintained. For example, for the benefit of those using the book with a class, most chapters include a **Focusing Questions** section near the beginning, asking some opening questions for the students to focus on, and a **Discussion Topics** section near the end, reviewing the material in the chapter.

Much of the discussion concerns the L2 learning and teaching of English, mainly because it is the chief language that has been investigated. English is, however, the language used here for exemplification rather than the subject matter itself. The teaching and learning of other modern languages are discussed when appropriate. Most sections of each chapter start with a display defining keywords and end with a boxed summary of the L2 learning area in question.

The contact with the language teaching classroom is maintained in this book chiefly through the discussion of published EFL course books. These provide a window into the classroom, even if good teachers use them only as a jumping-off point. The textbooks and syllabuses cited are taken from countries ranging from Germany to Japan to the United States, though inevitably for reasons of accessibility the bias is towards those published in England.

On the one hand, this book is highly selective in that it reports only a fraction of the research in a given area. On the other hand, it is wider than most books on second language acquisition research, which confine themselves to the acquisition of certain aspects of syntax rather than including such areas as vocabulary, listening comprehension, and pronunciation, and which take a narrow view of classroom language teaching. It covers not just current research, but also ideas from the wealth of material produced in the past twenty years.

2 What a teacher can expect from L2 learning research

Let us take three examples of the contribution L2 learning research can make to language teaching: understanding the students' contribution to learning, understanding how teaching techniques and methods work, and understanding the overall goals of language teaching.

UNDERSTANDING THE STUDENTS' CONTRIBUTION TO LEARNING

All successful teaching depends upon learning; there is no point in providing entertaining, lively, well-constructed language lessons if students do not learn. The proof of the teaching is in the learning. One crucial component in L2 learning is what the students bring with them into the classroom. With the exception of young bilingual children, L2 learners have fully formed person-alities and minds when they start learning the L2, and these have profound effects on their ways of learning and on how successful they are. L2 learning research, for example, has established that the students' diverse motivations for learning the L2 affect them powerfully. Some see learning the L2 as extending the repertoire of what they can do, others see it as a threat to their very identities. The different ways in which students tackle learning also affect their success. For instance, those who rely on getting the overall gist while listening do better than those who try to make out every word. What is happening in the class is not equally productive for all the students because their minds work in different ways. The differences between individuals do not disappear when students come in the classroom door. Students base what they do on previous experience of learning and of using language. They do not start from scratch with no backgrounds or predispositions to learn language in one way or another. Students also have much in common by virtue of possessing the same human minds. For instance, L2 learning research predicts that, however advanced they are, students will find that their memory works less well in the new language, whether they are trying to remember a phone number or the contents of an article. L2 learning research helps in understanding how apparently similar students react differently to the same teaching technique, while revealing the problems that all students share.

UNDERSTANDING HOW TEACHING METHODS AND TECHNIQUES WORK

Teaching methods usually incorporate a view of L2 learning, whether implicitly or explicitly. Grammar-translation teaching emphasizes explanations of grammatical points because this fits in with its view that L2 learning is the acquisition of conscious knowledge. Communicative teaching methods make the students talk to each other because they see L2 learning as growing out of the give and take of communication. For the most part teaching methods have developed these ideas independently from L2 learning research. They are not based, say, on L2 research into how learners use grammatical explanations or how they learn by talking to each other. More information about how learners actually learn helps the teacher to make any method more effective.

The reasons why a teaching technique works or does not work depend on many factors. A teacher who wants to use a particular technique will benefit by knowing what it implies in terms of language learning and language processing, the type of student for whom it is most appropriate, and the ways in which it fits into the classroom situation. Suppose the teacher wants to use a communicative game in the classroom, in which the students spontaneously exchange information. This implies that students are learning by communicating, that they are prepared to speak out in the classroom and that the educational context in the country allows for learning from fellow students rather than from the teacher alone. L2 learning research has something to say about all of these, as we shall see.

UNDERSTANDING THE GOALS OF LANGUAGE TEACHING

The reasons why the second language is being taught depend upon overall educational goals, which vary from one country to another and from one period to another. One avowed goal of language teaching is to help people to think better – brain-training and logical thinking; another is appreciation of serious literature; another the student's increased self-awareness and maturity; another appreciation of other cultures and races; another communication with people in other countries, and so on. Most of these have been explored in particular L2 learning research. For example, the goal of brain-training is supported by evidence that people who know two languages think more flexibly than monolinguals (Landry, 1974). Or, to take the communicative goals, it is crucial to L2 learning how the group to which the L2 learner belongs regards the group that speak the L2 (Schumann, 1978a). This information is vital when considering the viability and teaching implementation of communicative goals for a particular group of students. L2 learning research can help define the goals of language teaching, assess how achievable they may be, and contribute to their achievement.

L2 learning research is a scientific discipline that tries to describe how people learn language. It cannot decide issues that are outside its domain. While it may contribute to the understanding of teaching goals, it is itself neutral between them. It is not for the teacher, the methodologist, or any other outsider, to dictate whether a language should be taught for communication, for brain-training, or whatever, but for the society or the individual student to decide. As we shall see, one country specifies that groupwork must be used in the classroom because it encourages democracy. Another country bans any reference to English-speaking culture in textbooks because English is for international communication rather than for developing relationships with England or the USA. A third sees language teaching as a way of developing honesty and the values of good citizenship; a plenary speaker at a TESOL conference in New York proclaimed that the purpose of TESOL was to create good American citizens – to the annoyance of the British, Canadians, and other nationalities present. L2 learning research as a discipline neither commends nor denies the value of these goals, since they depend on moral or political values rather than science. But it provides suggestions how these goals may best be achieved and what their costs may be, particularly in balancing the needs of society and of the individual.

Teachers also need to see the classroom from many angles, not just from that of L2 learning research. The choice of what to do in a particular lesson depends upon the teacher's assessment of all the factors involved in teaching those students in that situation. L2 learning research shows some of the strengths and weaknesses of a particular teaching method or technique and it provides information that can influence and guide teaching. It does not provide a magic solution to all teaching problems, like a patented method with an attractive new brand-name.

3 The independence of L2 learning research

KEYWORDS

second language: 'A language acquired by a person in addition to his mother tongue'

multi-competence: the knowledge of more than one language in the same mind

the independent language assumption: the language of the L2 learner considered as a system of language in its own right rather than as a defective version of the target language (sometimes called 'interlanguage')

The establishment of L2 learning research as an independent discipline had several broad implications, which underlie much of the research to be discussed later.

L2 LEARNING IS DISTINCT FROM LANGUAGE TEACHING

Earlier approaches to L2 learning often started from language teaching and asked the question: which teaching methods give the best results? Is an oral method better than a translation method? A communicative method better than a situational one? Putting the question in this form accepts the status quo of what already happens in teaching rather than looking at underlying principles of learning. A more logical sequence is to start by investigating how people learn language and then to evaluate teaching methods in the light of what has been discovered, the order followed in this book. The first step in L2 learning research is to study learning itself and only later move on to see how teaching relates to learning.

So the teacher should be aware from the start that there is no easy link between L2 learning research and language teaching methods, despite the claims in some course books or by some researchers. The language teaching approaches of the past fifty years have by and large originated from teaching methodologists, not from second language acquisition research. The communicative approach was only remotely linked to the movements in theories of language acquisition of the 1960s and 1970s; it came chiefly out of the insight that language teaching should be tailored to students' real-world communication needs. Second language acquisition research does not provide a magic solution that can instantly be applied to the contemporary classroom so much as a set of ideas that teachers can try out for themselves to see how successful they are.

The new field did not blindly take over the concepts previously used for talking about L2 learning. Language teachers, for example, often contrast second language teaching (which takes place in a country where the L2 is widely used, say the teaching of French to immigrants in France) with foreign language teaching (which takes place in a country where it is not an everyday medium, say the teaching of French in England). While this distinction is often convenient, it cannot be taken for granted that learners in these two situations necessarily learn in two different ways without proper research evidence. Indeed we shall later look at many other dimensions to the learning situation.

So the term *L2 learning* is used in this book to include all learning of languages other than the first in whatever situation or for whatever purpose. This is the sense of *second language* defined by UNESCO: 'A language acquired by a person in addition to his mother tongue'. Nor does this book make a distinction between language 'acquisition' and language 'learning', as some writers do (e.g. Krashen, 1981a).

L2 LEARNING IS NOT NECESSARILY THE SAME AS L1 ACQUISITION

Teaching methods have often been justified in terms of how children learn their first language (L1) without investigating L2 learning directly. The 'audiolingual' method of teaching and the 'direct' method, to take two instances, were based primarily on particular views of how children learn their first language rather than on research into L2 learning, different as the methods were in themselves.

But there is no intrinsic reason why learning a second language should be the same as learning a first. Learning a first language, for example, is, in Halliday's phrase, 'learning how to mean' (Halliday, 1975) – discovering that language is used for relating to other people and for communicating ideas. People learning a second language already know how to mean. L2 learning is inevitably different in this respect from L1 learning. The similarities between learning the first and second languages have to be established by research rather than taken for granted. In some respects the two forms of learning may well be rather similar, in others quite different – after all the outcome is often very different. Evidence about how the child learns a first language has to be interpreted with caution in L2 learning and seldom in itself provides a basis for language teaching.

Second language learners in fact are different from children learning a first language since there is already one language present in their minds. There is no way that the L2 learner can become a monolingual native speaker *by definition*. So all the time we need to maintain in our minds the target of effective L2 use, not that of a pretend native speaker. The term for the knowledge of two or more languages in the same mind is 'multi-competence' (Cook, 1992).

L2 LEARNING IS MORE THAN THE TRANSFER OF THE L1

One view of L2 learning sees its crucial element as the transfer of aspects of the L1 language onto the L2. The first language helps learners when it has elements in common with the second language and hinders them when they differ. Spanish speakers may leave out the subject of the sentence when speaking English, saying 'Is raining' rather than 'It's raining', while French speakers do not. The explanation is that subjects may be omitted in Spanish, but they may not be left out in French. Nor is it usually difficult to decide from accent alone whether a foreigner speaking English comes from France, from Brazil, or from Japan.

But the importance of such transfer has to be looked at with an open mind. Various aspects of L2 learning need to be investigated before it can be decided how and when the first language is involved in the learning of the second. Though transfer from the L1 indeed turns out to be important, often in unexpected ways, its role needs to be established through properly balanced research rather than being taken for granted.

LEARNERS HAVE LANGUAGE SYSTEMS OF THEIR OWN

Suppose a student learning English says 'Me go no school'. Many teachers would see it as equivalent to the native sentence, 'I am not going to school', even if they would not draw the student's attention to it overtly. In other words, this is what the student might say if he or she were a native speaker. So this student is 'really' trying to produce a present continuous tense 'am going', a first person subject 'I', a negative 'not', and an adverbial 'to school', ending up with the native version 'I am not going to school'. But something has gone drastically wrong. Perhaps the student has not yet encountered the appropriate forms in English or perhaps he or she is transferring constructions from the first language. The assumption is that the student's sentence should be compared to one produced by a native speaker. In a way this comparison is justified, as native-like speech is often a goal for the student.

But this is where many students want to be, not where they are at the moment. It is judging the students by what they are not – native speakers. L2 learning research insists that learners have the right to be judged by the standards appropriate for them, not by those used for natives. 'Me go no school' is an example of learner language that shows what is going in their minds. 'Me' shows that they do not distinguish 'I' and 'me', unlike native English; 'no' that negation consists for them of adding a negative word after the verb, unlike its usual position before the verb; 'go' that they have no grammatical endings such as '-ing'; and so on. All of these apparent 'mistakes' conform to regular rules in the students' own knowledge of English; they are only wrong when measured against native speech. Their sentences relate to their own temporary language systems at the moment when they produce the sentence, rather than to the native's version of English.

However peculiar and limited they may be, learners' sentences can be seen as the product of those learners' own language systems; their L2 speech shows rules and patterns of its own. At each stage learners have their own language systems. The nature of these learner systems may be very different from that of the target language. While they are idiosyncratic and constantly changing, they are none the less systematic. The starting point for L2 learning research is the learner's own language system, which can be called the 'independent language assumption'. Learners are not wilfully distorting the native system but are inventing a system of their own. No one is claiming that the learner's language system takes precedence over the version of the native speaker or that learners should be content with some minimal language of their own. Ability to communicate with the native is after all the learners' goal in many cases. But finding out how students learn means starting from the curious rules and structures which they invent for themselves as they go along – their 'inter-language', as Selinker (1972) put it.

The independent language assumption had a major impact on teaching techniques in the 1970s. Teaching methods that used drills and grammatical explanations had insisted on the seriousness of the students' mistakes. A mistake in an audiolingual drill meant the student had not properly learnt the 'habit' of speaking; a mistake in a grammatical exercise meant the student had not understood the rule. The concept of the learner's own system liberated the classroom and in part paved the way for the communicative language teaching methods of the 1970s and 1980s. Learners' sentences reflect their temporary language systems rather than an imperfect grasp of the target language. If a student makes a 'mistake', it is not the fault of the teacher or the materials or even of the student, but an inevitable and natural part of the learning process. Teachers could now use teaching activities in which students talked to each other rather than to the teacher, because the students did not need the teacher's vigilant eye to spot what they were doing wrong. Their mistakes were minor irritants rather than major hazards. Hence groupwork and pairwork were now possible as the teacher did not have continuously to supervise the students' speech to pinpoint their mistakes.

IS LANGUAGE UNIQUE?

A further issue that needs to be mentioned is the dispute between those who think language is a unique property of the human mind and those who think it is the same as other aspects of the mind. Those who believe in its uniqueness take the view that the types of structures that are found in language, the kinds of meaning that they have, and the ways in which they are used are different from anything else in human beings, or indeed in other species. Language must then be learnt in unique ways, quite different from how we learn to ride a bicycle or to do arithmetic. Hence research into language learning always needs to provide evidence of its own rather than generalizing from the learning of other skills.

The opposing view is that L2 learning is a special case of general principles that apply to everything people do; there is nothing unique to it, apart from its sheer complexity. It is learnt in the same way as skills such as learning to cycle, or as cognitive processes such as learning to do multiplication. If this is accepted, L2 learning research can draw on research into all forms of learning, not just language learning. The advocates of uniqueness are mostly applied linguists, those who support non-uniqueness mostly psychologists. The argument between them is unresolved as it involves different conceptions of language, of learning, and of research methods.

But the controversy has strong implications for teaching. Uniqueness advocates insist that language teaching is unlike other school subjects and must therefore be taught in ways that are peculiar to it, differently from teaching someone physics or how to make an omelette. Many of these will in some way duplicate the 'natural' way of language acquisition as teaching methods have claimed, from the direct method through audiolingualism to the communicative approach.

Supporters of non-uniqueness emphasize that language teaching is the same in principle as other forms of training, and so language teaching can use methods employed for teaching other subjects. Hence grammatical structures or functions can be explained; they can be learnt by intensive practice; vocabulary can be memorized or learnt by conscious learning strategies – ways that are in a sense quite unnatural in that they rely on techniques found in any subject, whether geography or physics.

SECOND LANGUAGE ACQUISITION RESEARCH OFTEN DIFFERS FROM LANGUAGE TEACHING IN ITS IDEAS ABOUT LANGUAGE AND LEARNING

One issue that the reader should be aware of, which will be exemplified on most pages of this book, is that second language acquisition research often uses concepts that are substantially different from language teaching. Coming from linguistic and psychological perspectives, it takes a different view of language from that usually current in language teaching. Teachers have taken all types of grammar to heart on an almost *ad hoc* basis and have evolved a tried and true collection of grammatical ideas for teaching that are distinct from those that are used in second language acquisition research, as will be illustrated in the next chapter.

But ideas about language teaching may also be hard for the SLA person to take on board. For example, it is conventional in most language teaching to divide discussion into the four skills of listening, speaking, reading, and writing. The National Curriculum for Modern Languages, for example (HMSO, 1995), talks of encouraging pupils to 'combine two or more of the four language skills'. SLA researchers on the other hand have seldom divided up their task into the four skills, seeing each as consisting of a vast number of subskills, many of which cross boundaries between the four, or indeed rejecting the notion of skill itself as a misconception of what language is about derived from outmoded behaviourist ideas of language learning. At best the four skills seem a convenient way of categorizing teaching activities. The reader should then be on guard that the assumptions about language or language learning encountered in SLA research may be radically different from those in language teaching, let alone the actual research and its claims.

TECHNIQUE ANALYSIS

One of the bridges to make one start to think in learning terms is to practise a technique called *technique analysis*. The idea, familiar to those who have done practical criticism with literary texts, is to start from the printed page of a textbook and to take nothing else for granted – forget what the teacher's book says, ignore what you know about the method or the book. Just look at what is *there*. This may free one from all the preconceptions one has built up over the years about teaching so that one can look at what is actually going on rather than what methodologists *say* is going on.

The starting point is to take any teaching technique you have just observed in a classroom or any page of a convenient textbook and then to find out about it through the checklist of questions and explanations given below.

TECHNIQUE ANALYSIS CHECKLIST

A. What are the background assumptions of the technique?

- physical situation (equipment, group size, teacher resources)
- the students (age, motivation)
- the teacher (teaching style, training, etc.)
- joint assumptions by teacher and students (goals of teaching, classroom expectations)

B. What language input is provided?

- how much language?
- is the language discourse or fragments?
- authentic or non-authentic?
- what role does the teacher's language play?

C. What activities do the students do?

- four skills (listening, speaking, reading, writing)
- do they use communication and interaction?
- how deeply do the activities involve the students emotionally and cognitively?
- what learning strategies are the students expected to use?

First the background assumptions, which are often neglected in the discussion of language teaching. Whether or not the technique requires a blackboard or an overhead projector; whether the teacher can make photocopies; whether the students must all have copies of the book: these simple logistic factors make an immense difference. So too does the type of student. A dialogue technique in which the students play roles might not be successful with a group in which the men will not play women and the women will not speak in front of men. These variations in types of student will be looked at in Chapter 5. The assumptions that the students and the teacher bring to the situation and their previous experiences also affect the technique – do they think the L2 natives are odd? that learning a language is just a matter of memorizing lines? that the teacher is a wise being who imparts wisdom and must not be contradicted or interrupted? Do the teacher and students share the same beliefs or is the teacher an interloper from another culture? Whether these beliefs are right or wrong is beside the point if they are real to the students or the teacher and affect the technique.

The second factor is the question of language input. The most obvious necessity in teaching is that the student gets to hear the language, whether from the teacher, from tapes or books, or from other students. Without sufficient and appropriate examples of the target language, the students will get nowhere. So it is vital to consider how a teaching technique incorporates the language itself: how much new language is introduced, how interactive and communicative it is, whether it consists of whole utterances and sentences or just of fragments, phrases and words. An overall difference is between authentic language (language used by native speakers outside a classroom) and non-authentic (language specially written for teaching), as we see in Chapter 6. It is also important for teachers to be aware of what is expected from them in language terms. Are they the only ones supplying all the new language? Are they supposed to simplify their speech deliberately or to speak naturally? Are they to keep firmly to the vocabulary in the textbook or are they expected to expand it according to the individual student's requirements? This we look at in Chapter 6.

Finally, the activities the students carry out determine how they learn. There are the activities that the technique directly forces the students to do – repeat sentences, exchange ideas, memorize vocabulary, and so on. This is then the domain of teaching methodology: in Chapter 9 we shall see the main groupings of techniques into six main teaching styles. We need at least to make certain which combination of the four skills – listening, speaking, reading, writing – are being employed in the technique.

But above all learning is taking place inside the students' minds. In the privacy of their minds, they may be trying something different from what their teachers have planned; they may have switched off entirely; they may be utilizing all sorts of processes that are powerful to language learning but invisible to the teacher; they may be adopting all sorts of learning strategies, as we describe in Chapter 5. We need to see how the materials make the students' minds work and how deeply it involves their emotions, not implying that depth is necessarily either a good or a bad thing.

This is then the area that most of this book is concerned with – how our teaching activities link to the processes going on in the students' minds. Successful teaching techniques have to fit in with the particular students who are being taught and with their teachers, the particular educational context in which they are placed, and above all with the processes going on in the students' minds through which they are coming to acquire a new language.

DISCUSSION TOPICS

1. What do *you* think is going on in a student's head when they are doing, say, a fill-in exercise? Have you ever checked if this is really the case?
2. In what ways do you think textbooks are a good source of information about what is going on in a classroom, and in what ways not?
3. Do your students share the language teaching goals you are practising or do you have to persuade them that they are right? Do you have a *right* to differ from them?
4. *Why* do you believe in the teaching method you use? What evidence do you have for its success?
5. Do you think there are more similarities or dissimilarities between learning a first and a second language?
6. Can you tell the first language of L2 students from their speech alone? How about in writing?
7. What should an L2 speaker aim at if not the model of the native speaker?
8. What factors in a teaching technique do *you* think are most important?

FURTHER READING

Good technical introductions to L2 learning can be found in *The Study of Second Language Acquisition* (Ellis, 1994) and *Bilingualism* (Romaine, 1995). A general account of Technique Analysis is in 'Technique analysis: a tool for the teacher' (Cook, 1988a). An introduction to ideas about language itself can be found in *Inside Language* (Cook, 1996). Useful books with similar purposes but covering slightly different approaches to second language acquisition are: *How Languages are Learned* (Lightbown and Spada, 1993); *Language Learning* (Cohen, 1990).

2

Learning different types of grammar

Language has patterns and regularities which are used to convey meaning, some of which make up its grammar. An important part of grammar in most languages is the order of words. Any speaker of English knows that 'Ernest Hemingway likes John' does not have the same meaning as 'John likes Ernest Hemingway'. Another part of grammar consists of changes in the forms of words, more important in some languages than others – 'The cow is mad' means something different from 'The cows were mad'.

Knowledge of grammar is considered by many linguists to be the central area of the language system around which the other areas such as pronunciation and vocabulary revolve. However important the other components of language may be in themselves, they are connected to each other through grammar. Grammar is often called the 'computational system' that relates sound and meaning, trivial in itself but impossible to manage without.

Grammar is the most distinctive aspect of language and has features that do not occur with other things we store in our minds and are not found in animal languages. Furthermore, according to linguists, though often not to psychologists, they are learnt in different ways from anything else that people learn.

In some ways grammar is easier to study in L2 learners than other aspects of language because it is highly systematic and its effects are usually fairly obvious in their speech. For these reasons, much of the L2 learning research of the 1970s and 1980s concentrated on grammar. Hence it is a useful starting point from which to look at L2 learning research. This chapter first looks at different types of grammar and then selects four areas of grammatical research into L2 learning to represent the main approaches.

Focusing questions

Where do you think 'rules of grammar' come from?

- schoolbooks and teachers?
- the usage of some prestige group?

- the minds of learners?
- somewhere else?

Think of an example of a 'grammatical rule':

- what kind of meaning does it convey?
- how would you teach it?

Do you think grammar

- should be explained to the students?
- should be taught through drills?
- should be ignored?

---

1 What *is* grammar?

KEYWORDS

prescriptive grammar: grammar that 'prescribes' what people should say

traditional grammar: 'school' grammar concerned with labelling sentences with parts of speech

structural grammar: grammar concerned with how words go into phrases, phrases into sentences

grammatical (linguistic) competence: the native speaker's knowledge of language

communicative competence: the speaker's ability to put language to communicative use

pragmatic competence: the speaker's ability to use language for a range of public and private functions, including communication

To elucidate what the term 'grammar' means in the context of L2 learning, it is easiest to start by eliminating what it does *not* mean.

PRESCRIPTIVE GRAMMAR

One familiar type of grammar is the rules found in schoolbooks, for example, the warnings against final prepositions in sentences, 'This can't be put up with', or the diatribes in letters to the newspaper about split infinitives, 'To boldly go where no man has gone before'. This is called *prescriptive grammar* because it 'prescribes' what people ought to do. Modern grammarians have mostly avoided prescriptive grammar because they see their job as describing what the rules of language *are,* just as the physicist says what the laws of physics are. The grammarian has no more right to decree how people *should* speak than the physicist has to decree how electrons should move. Language is bound up with human lives in so many ways that it is easy to find reasons why some grammatical forms are 'better' than others, but these are based on criteria other than the grammar itself, mostly questions of social status. The grammarian's first task is to decide what people actually say; after this has been done, then others may decide whether it would be better to change what they say.

This type of grammar is all but irrelevant to the language teaching classroom. Since the 1960s people have believed that you should teach the language as it is, not as it ought to be. The foreign student should learn to speak the same kind of language as a native, not an artificial form that a native never uses – we all use split infinitives from time to time when the circumstances make it necessary and the non-English person will sound awkward if they try to avoid them. Mostly, however, these prescriptive do's and don't's about 'between you and me' or 'it is I' are not of sufficient importance to spend any time thinking about their implications for language teaching. The only area where prescriptive grammar still thrives is in word-processing; the program I use for writing this warns me constantly against using final prepositions and passives, common as they are in everyday English.

TRADITIONAL GRAMMAR

A second popular meaning of 'grammar' concerns the parts of speech: 'a noun is the name of a person, place or thing'. Analysing sentences means labelling the parts with their names and giving rules that explain in words how they may be combined. This is often called *traditional grammar*. In essence it goes back to the grammars of Latin, receiving its English form in the grammars of the eighteenth century. Though many grammarians today do not reject this type of grammar outright, they again feel it is unscientific. After reading the definition of a noun, we still do not know what a noun is in the way that we know what a chemical element is. And, while the concept of the parts of speech is indeed part of grammar, there are many other powerful concepts that also need to be taken into account.

Some language teaching uses forms of grammar that resemble a sophisticated form of traditional grammar. Grammar books for language teaching often present grammar through a series of visual displays and examples. For example, take Murphy (1993), *Basic Grammar in Use*. A typical unit is headed 'flower/flowers' (singular and plural). It has a display of singular and plural forms ('a flower > some flowers'), lists of idiosyncratic spellings of plurals ('babies, shelves'), words that are unexpectedly plural ('scissors'), and plurals not in -s ('mice'). It explains 'The plural of a noun is usually -s'. In other words, it assumes that students know what plural is; that it is universal as a category in all languages. But of course some languages like Chinese do not have plural forms of nouns, others like Tongan have three forms: singular, plural, and dual ('two people'). The crucial question, for linguists at any rate, is the agreement between the subject of the sentence and the verb in terms of singular or plural, which is not mentioned, though two of the four exercises that follow depend upon it.

Even mainstream textbooks often rely on the students knowing terms from traditional grammar. In the very first lesson of an EFL course for complete beginners called *Blueprint One* (Abbs and Freebairn, 1990), the 'Grammar Focus' uses the technical terms *in English* 'subject pronouns', 'possessive adjective', and 'genitive "s"'. Where the students are supposed to have learnt these terms is left to the imagination; it is certainly a constant complaint from modern language teachers in UK schools that pupils are no longer equipped with this traditional framework of grammatical terminology. And of course in countries such as Japan traditional grammar does not come from the Latin-based European traditional grammar at all.

STRUCTURAL GRAMMAR

Language teaching has also made use of *structural grammar* based on the concept of phrase structure, which shows how some words go together in the sentence and some do not. In a sentence such as 'The man fed the dog' the word 'the' seems somehow to go with 'man' but 'fed' does not seem to go with 'the'. Suppose we group the words that go together. If we put 'the' with 'man', we get one structure '(the man)', 'the' with 'dog' we get another '(the dog)'. Then these structures can be combined with each other and with the remaining words. 'Fed' belongs with '(the dog)' to get a new structure '(fed the dog)'. Now the two structures '(the man)' and '(fed the dog)' go together to assemble the whole sentence. A typical way of representing this phrase structure is through tree diagrams that show how the words build up into phrases and the phrases build up into the whole sentence (Fig. 2.1):

The man fed the dog

Fig. 2.1 An example of a phrase structure

Structural grammar describes the sentence by fitting the parts together in more and more complicated ways.

Teachers have been using this directly in substitution tables since at least the 1920s. A typical example (Fig. 2.2) can be seen in the Bulgarian course book *English for the Fifth Class* (Despotova *et al.*, 1988):

They	can draw a	black	dog
I		white	cat
You		red	rose

Fig. 2.2 A typical substitution table

Students form sentences by choosing a word from each column: 'I . . . can draw a . . . black . . . rose'. They are substituting words within a constant grammatical structure. Such exercises have long been a staple of language teaching in one guise or another. Structure drills and pattern practice are based on the same idea. Substitution tables are still common in present-day course books and grammar books, though today more as graphic displays of grammar than as teaching exercises – say the example of a 'grammar summary' in *Headway Elementary* (Soars and Soars, 1993):

Where	have	I you we they	been?
	has	she he it	

Fig. 2.3 A grammar summary

Much teaching simply uses structural or traditional grammar without realizing that there are alternative approaches.

GRAMMAR AS KNOWLEDGE

But second language acquisition research relies mainly on another meaning of 'grammar' – the knowledge of language that the speaker possesses in the mind, known as *linguistic* or *grammatical competence*. All speakers know the grammar of their language in this sense without having to study it. A speaker of English knows that 'Is John is the man who French?' is wrong without looking this up in any book – indeed few grammar books would be of much assistance. A native speaker knows the system of the language. He or she may not be able to verbalize this knowledge clearly; it is 'implicit' knowledge. Nevertheless, a single sentence of English could not be produced without knowing English grammar in this sense. A man who spontaneously says 'The girl fed the dog' shows that he knows the word order typical of English in which the subject 'The girl' comes before the verb 'fed'. He knows the ways of making irregular past tenses in English – 'fed' rather than the regular '-ed' ('feeded'); he knows that 'dog' requires an article 'the' or 'a'; and he knows that 'the' is used to talk about a dog that the listener already knows about. This is a very different type of knowledge from the ability to describe the sentence he has produced in terms of grammar, something only people who have been taught explicit 'grammar' can do.

A parallel can be found in a teaching exercise that baffles EFL students – devising instructions for everyday actions such as, 'Tell me how to put my coat on.' Everyone knows how to put a coat on in one sense but is unable to verbalize this knowledge. There is one type of knowledge in our mind which we can talk about consciously, another which is far from conscious. This view of grammar as knowledge treats it as something stored unconsciously in the mind – the native speaker's competence. The point of sentence trees, structures, rules, and so on, is ultimately that they describe the competence in our minds. One of the great dilemmas in L2 learning is the nature of the relationship between unconscious and conscious grammar, and how it can be exploited in language teaching.

As well as grammatical competence, native speakers also possess knowledge of how language is used. This is often called *communicative competence* by those who see public functions as crucial (Hymes, 1972). It is not just knowledge of the language that is important, it is how to use it appropriately for the activities in which speakers want to take part – complaining, arguing, persuading, declaring war, writing love letters, buying season tickets, and so on. Others see language as having private functions as well as public – language for dreaming or planning a day out. Hence the more general term *pragmatic competence* reflects all the possible uses of language rather than restricting them to communication (Chomsky, 1986): praying, mental arithmetic, keeping a diary, keeping a shopping list. This chapter concentrates on grammatical competence.

2 Grammatical morphemes

KEYWORDS

morpheme: the smallest unit of grammar, consisting either of a word ('toast') or part of a word ('''s' in 'John's')
grammatical morpheme: morphemes such as '-ing' and 'the' that play a greater part in structure than content words such as 'horse'
order of difficulty: how difficult particular aspects of grammar are for L2 learners

Language teaching has often distinguished 'content' words from 'structure' words. Content words have the kind of meaning that can be looked up in a dictionary and they are numbered in thousands. 'Beer' or 'palimpsest' are content words referring to definable things. A new content word can be easily invented, advertisers try to do it all the time – 'Contains the magic new ingredient kryptonite'. Structure words, on the other hand, are limited in number; they consist of words like 'the', 'to', and 'yet'. A computer program for teaching English needs about 220 structure words; the ten most common words in the COBUILD Project's analysis of 18 million words are: *the, of, and, to, a, in, that, I, it, was*, all structure words. It is easier to look up structure words in a grammar book than in a dictionary. The meaning of 'the' or 'despite' depends on the grammatical rules of the language, not on dictionary definitions. It is virtually impossible to invent a new structure word because it would mean changing the grammatical rules of the language, which are fairly rigid, rather than adding an item to the stock of words of the language. Science fiction novelists for example have a field day inventing new words for aliens, ranging from 'Alaree' to 'Vatch', new nouns for new science, ranging from 'noocyte' (artificially created intelligent cells) to 'iahklu'' (the Aldebaranian ability to influence the world through dreams); where Lewis Carroll once coined nouns like 'chortle', William Gibson now contributes 'cyberpunk' to the language. But no writer dares invent new function words, with the brave exception of Marge Piercy's non-sexist pronoun 'per'.

The smallest unit of grammar is the 'morpheme'. When the sentence is divided up in tree diagrams like the one given earlier, the whole sentence is at the top and the morphemes are at the bottom. Morphemes are studied in a branch of grammar called 'morphology'. Some words consist of a single morpheme – 'to' or 'book' or 'like' or 'black'. Some can have morphemes added to show their grammatical role in the sentence, say 'books' or 'liking' or 'blacker'. Others can be split up into several morphemes: 'mini-supermarket' might be 'mini-super-market'; 'hamburger' is seen as 'ham-burger' rather than 'Hamburg-er' leading to 'vegeburger' or 'cheeseburger' – whatever the inhabitants of Hamburg may say. The word endings such as '-ing' are usually grouped together with structure words such as 'the' under the term 'grammatical morpheme'. In many languages they are the essential clues to the structure of the sentence.

While acquiring the first language, young children use content words more easily than grammatical morphemes. Children commonly produce sentences such as 'Mummy go shop', meaning something like 'Mummy is going to the shops', where the adult sentence includes the 'missing' grammatical morphemes 'is', '-ing', 'to', 'the', and '-s'. It is as if the children know both the structure for the sentence and the content words, but either do not know the grammatical morphemes or are incapable of using them.

In the early 1970s it was discovered that English children learn these grammatical morphemes in a definite sequence (Brown, 1973). Dulay and Burt (1973) decided to see what this meant for L2 learning. They made Spanish-speaking children learning English describe pictures and checked how often the children supplied eight grammatical morphemes in the appropriate places in the sentence. Suppose that at a rudimentary level L2 learners say 'Girl go'. How do they progress from this?

1   *Plural '-s'*. The easiest morpheme for the learners was the plural '-s', getting 'Girls go'.
2   *Progressive '-ing'*. Next easiest for the learners was the word ending '-ing' in present tense forms like 'going'.
3   *Copula forms of 'be'*. Next came the use of *be* as a copula, i.e. as a main verb in the sentence ('John is happy') rather than as an auxiliary used

with another verb ('John is going'). Changing the sentence slightly gets 'Girls *are* here'.

4 *Auxiliary form of 'be'*. After this came the auxiliary forms of 'be' with '-ing', yielding 'Girls *are* going'.

5 *Definite and indefinite articles 'the' and 'a'*. Next in difficulty came the *definite and indefinite articles 'the' and 'a'*, enabling the learners to produce '*The* girls go' or '*A* girl go'.

6 *Irregular past tense*. The next morphemes were the irregular English past tenses (those that do not have a form of '-ed' ending pronounced in the usual three ways /d/, /t/ or /id/, 'played', 'learnt' and 'waited') such as 'came' and 'went', as in 'The girls *went*'.

7 *Third person '-s'*. The next in order of difficulty was the *third person '-s'* used with verbs, as in 'The girl goes'.

8 *Possessive "s'*. Most difficult was the ''s' ending used with nouns to show possession, as in 'The girl's book'.

The order of difficulty for the L2 learners is the sequence from 1 to 8. They have least difficulty with plural '-s' and most difficulty with possessive ''s'. The interesting discovery was the similarities between the L2 learners. This research with grammatical morphemes was the first to demonstrate the common factors of L2 learners so clearly. It was not just that Spanish-speaking children have a sequence of difficulty for the eight grammatical morphemes. Similar orders have been found for Japanese children and for Korean adults (Makino, 1980; Lee, 1981), though not for one Japanese child (Hakuta, 1974). The first language does not seem to make a crucial difference: all L2 learners have much the same order. Nor does it matter if the learners are children or adults; adults have roughly the same order as children (Krashen *et al.*, 1976). It did not even make much difference whether or not they were attending a language class (Larsen-Freeman, 1976)! There was a strong similarity between all L2 learners of English, whatever the explanation may be. Later researchers such as Dulay, Burt, and Krashen (1982) tend to put the morphemes into groups rather than seeing them as separate items.

There has, however, been much controversy about these sequences of grammatical morphemes. The overall problem is that while this research discovered a 'natural order' of difficulty, it did not find an explanation for this order. Without an explanation it can have only limited relevance to teaching. Another problem is over the interpretation of what a sequence is. Here we have been calling it an order of difficulty because it refers to how difficult a learner finds something at a particular moment. Sometimes, however, it has been interpreted as an order of acquisition – the sequence in which people actually acquire language. Researchers have come to realize that it is not necessarily true that things that are easy to use are learnt first and vice versa, even if in many cases this is true. An order of acquisition cannot be based solely on an order of difficulty. Lee (1981), for example, showed that the lowest and highest groups of Korean learners found auxiliary forms the easiest but they were eight out of ten for the middle group. Patsy Lightbown (1987) too found that the course of acquisition over time was far from smooth; accuracy on '-ing' for her French-speaking learners started at 69 per cent in year 1, fell to 39 per cent in year 2, and rose above 60 per cent in year 3. For this and other methodological reasons, researchers now have considerable reservations about grammatical morpheme research, although it is starting to make a comeback in some areas of psycholinguistics – some researchers claim to have found a gene for language on the basis of a family who have the speech defect of leaving them out despite being otherwise perfectly normal (Gopnik and Crago, 1991).

L2 LEARNING OF GRAMMATICAL MORPHEMES

L2 learners have a common order of difficulty for grammatical morphemes, first discovered by Dulay and Burt.

1.	Plural '-s'	'Books'
2.	Progressive '-ing'	'John going'
3.	Copula 'be'	'John is here'
4.	Auxiliary 'be'	'John is going'
5.	Articles	'The books'
6.	Irregular past tense	'John went'
7.	Third person '-s'	'John likes books'
8.	Possessive ' 's'	'John's book'

---

3 The multidimensional model

KEYWORDS

movement: a way of describing some sentences as being based on moving various elements about
development: the inevitable progression of learners through the sequence of grammatical acquisition
variation: elements which differ from one learner to another
the teachability hypothesis: 'an L2 structure can be learnt from instruction only if the learner's interlanguage is close to the point when this structure is acquired in the natural setting' (Pienemann, 1984, p. 201)

During the 1980s an attempt was made to create a broader-based sequence of development than grammatical morphemes, called the *multidimensional model*. This was first based on the speech of L2 learners of German and then expanded to include English L2 learners in Australia by Manfried Pienemann and others (Pienemann, 1986; Pienemann and Johnston, 1987).

The core idea was that some sentences are formed by moving elements in them about. English questions, for example, can be seen as moving the auxiliary or the question word to the beginning of the sentence, as was common in language teaching. So 'John is nice' becomes 'Is John nice?' by moving 'is' to the beginning, 'John is where?' becomes 'Where is John?' by moving 'where' and 'is' and 'John will go where?' becomes 'Where will John go?' by moving both 'where' and 'will' in front of 'John' (see Fig. 2.4).

Fig. 2.4 Movement in the multidimensional model

The multidimensional model takes this movement to be the main thread in the learning sequence. The learner starts with the simplest structure without movement; then gradually learns how to move the various parts around to get the final form of the sentence.

STAGE 1

First of all the learners can produce only one word at a time, like 'ticket' or 'beer', or formulas such as 'What's the time?' The learners know words, not grammar, at this stage.

STAGE 2

Next they acquire the most typical word order of the language. In both English and German this is the subject verb object (SVO) order – 'John likes beer', 'Hans liebt Bier'. The learners do not vary this word order. As well as these sentences, this stage also includes initial negatives such as 'No me live here' and intonation questions such as 'You like me?', both of which maintain the basic word order of English without any movement.

In the next stages the learner discovers how to move elements, in particular to the beginnings and ends of the sentence.

STAGE 3

First the learner concentrates on moving things to the beginning of the sentence. So the learners start to put adverbials at the beginning – 'On Tuesday

I went to London' – using wh- words at the beginning with no inversion – 'Who lives in Camden?' – and moving auxiliaries to the beginning to get Yes/No questions – 'Will you be there?' Typical learner sentences for this stage are 'Yesterday I sick', and 'Beer I like', in both of which the initial element has come from later in the sentence.

STAGE 4

At the next stage, learners discover how the preposition can be separated from its phrase in English, 'the patient he looked after' rather than 'the patient after which he looked', a phenomenon known as preposition-stranding. They also start to use the '-ing' ending – 'I'm reading a good book at the moment'. These types of movement require isolating one bit of the sentence and then moving it or finding which is the preposition and leaving it alone.

STAGE 5

Next come question-word questions such as 'Where is he going to be?', the third person grammatical morpheme '-s', 'He likes', and the dative with 'to', 'He gave his name to the receptionist'. At this stage the learners are starting to work within the sentence, not just at the beginning or end. Another new feature is the third person '-s' ending of verbs, 'He smokes'.

STAGE 6

The final stage is acquiring the order within the subordinate clause, which is sometimes different in English from that in the main clause. The question order is 'Will he go?' but the subordinate clause in reported speech is 'Jane asked if *he would go*' not 'Jane asked if *would he go*', to the despair of generations of EFL students. At this stage the learner is sorting out the more untypical orders in subordinate clauses after the ordinary sentence is learnt. In addition this stage includes structures such as 'He gave me the book' where the indirect object precedes the direct object, as opposed to 'He gave the book to me'.

The multidimensional model stresses that L2 learners have a series of interim grammars of English – interlanguages. Their first grammar uses just words; the second uses words in an SVO order; the third word order with some elements moved to the beginning or end; and so on. Like the grammatical morphemes, this sequence seems inevitable: learners go through these overall stages in the same sequence. And the reason for this sequence is quite simply the learners' limitations in processing the language: the stages of development are caused by their increasing ability to move items of the language around.

However, the multidimensional model claims that there is nevertheless variation between learners within the stages. Some learners master all the features of a particular stage, some only a few; in some ways this can be seen as a variation on the extent to which the learner tries to simplify the grammar they know. One German learner at Stage 4 may use inversion with adverbs, another may not. While they are at the same stage, they nevertheless differ in the range of forms they use. This seems to correlate with such personal details as their contacts at work or at home and their ties to the host country. There are then two dimensions to L2 learning – development, which is the same for all learners, and variation, which varies from one learner to another.

So far, in a sense, the teacher has been helpless to do much about these sequences. If all students are going to go through more or less the same sequence of morphemes, the teacher can only fit in with this. The multidimensional model is more promising in this respect since it has led to what has been called the *teachability hypothesis*: in Pienemann's own words, 'an L2 structure can be learnt from instruction only if the learner's interlanguage is close to the point when this structure is acquired in the natural setting' (Pienemann, 1984, p. 201). So teachers should teach according to the stage which their learner is at. To take some examples from the above sequence:

- Do not teach the '-s' ending of verbs in 'He likes' at early stages as it comes late.
- Concentrate in the early stages on the main word order of subject verb object, 'Cats like milk', and do not expect learners to learn the word orders of questions, 'What do cats like?', etc., until much later.
- Introduce sentence-initial adverbials, 'In summer I play tennis', as a way into the movement involved in questions, 'Do you like Brahms?'

These are three possible suggestions of many, all of which arise naturally from the research. It may be that there are good teaching reasons why they should not be taken on board, for instance, people who tried postponing questions till late found practical problems in having any type of normal language in the classroom, where questions are the life-blood. But they are nevertheless ideas that are at any rate worth considering in the sequencing of materials, whatever other factors may overrule them.

Let us compare the sequence of some elements of a typical modern EFL course with that in the multidimensional model. A typical modern course is *Flying Colours* (Garton-Sprenger and Greenall, 1990), intended for adult beginners.

Unit 1 of *Flying Colours* starts with the student looking for 'international words' such as 'bar' and 'jeans' and repeating short formulas such as 'What's your name?' and 'I don't understand'. Thus it too starts with words rather than structures, as does the multidimensional model.

Unit 2, however, plunges into questions: 'What is your phone number', 'Would you like some French onion soup?' 'What does Kenneth Hill do?' In terms of the multidimensional model these come in stages 3 and 5 and should not be attempted until the students have the main SVO structure of English fixed in their minds. Certainly this early introduction of questions is a major difference from the multidimensional model.

Unit 3 introduces the present continuous tense – 'She's wearing a jacket and jeans'. While this is already late compared to courses that introduce the present continuous in lesson 1, this is far ahead of its position in the multidimensional model sequence at stage 4.

Subordinate clauses are not mentioned in *Flying Colours*, apart from comparative clauses in Unit 6. Looking through the text, however, one finds in Unit 1 that the students have to understand sentences such as 'When he goes to a foreign country, he learns . . .' ('when' clause), 'Listen and say who is speaking' (reported speech clause), and 'Boris Becker wins after a hurricane stops the match' ('after' clause), 'The only other things I buy are a map and some postcards' (relative clause). Clearly such clauses are not seen as difficult in any way, while the multidimensional model would insist they are postponed till last of all.

Some other differences between the L2 stages and the sequences in EFL textbooks such as *Flying Colours* are then:

- The textbook collapses two L2 stages into one, for example, *Flying Colours* has several types of question in Unit 2.
- The textbook goes against some aspects of the order, for example, *Flying Colours* uses some subordinate clauses from the very beginning.
- The textbook omits some stages, for instance, the apparent omission of initial adverbs and preposition-stranding.
- Textbooks mostly have a skeleton sequence consisting of tenses and verb forms, by no means the central part of the multidimensional model or indeed of any of the sequences found in second language acquisition research.

One general issue about language teaching is very hard to resolve. Learners' interlanguages contain rules that are different from the native speaker's competence. The student may temporarily produce sentences that deviate from native correctness, say stage 2 'No me live here'. Many teaching techniques, however, assume that the point of an exercise is to get the student to produce sentences from the first lesson on that are 100 per cent correct in terms of the target language, even if they are severely restricted in terms of grammar and vocabulary. The students are not supposed to be producing sentences like 'No me live here' in the classroom. Teaching materials also only present sentences that are possible in terms of the target language, never letting learners hear sentences such as 'No me live here'. Hence they can never fully reflect the stages that interlanguages go through. There is then an implicit contradiction between the pressure on students in many classrooms to produce well-formed sentences and the natural stages that students go through. Should learners be allowed to produce these 'mistakes' in the classroom, since they are inevitable? Or should the teacher try to prevent them? The answers to this will also affect when and how the teacher will correct the student's 'mistakes'.

4 Language universals; relative clauses

KEYWORDS

accessibility hierarchy: the ease with which different types of relative clause can be formed, based upon the role of the relative element in the clause, e.g. 'The man who left was John' versus 'The man than whom I am taller is John'
statistical universals of language: aspects of grammar that are common to many, sometimes all, languages

So far in this chapter grammar has described the sentences of a single language. But grammar can also tell us what languages have in common. These common features are known as 'statistical' universals since they are established statistically by looking at as many languages as possible. An example is relative clauses such as that in 'The man *who came to tea* was Jim'. These sentences are usually seen as the combination of a main clause 'The man . . . was Jim' with a relative clause '. . . who came to tea . . .'. It was discovered by Keenan and Comrie (1977) that there were interesting similarities in how languages combine main and relative clauses together. These depended on the role that the noun phrase plays in the relative clause that was used as a link to the main clause. This concept was called the *accessibility hierarchy*, since some phrases could be 'accessed' for making relative clauses more readily than others.

Six types of relative clause make up the accessibility hierarchy. They can be thought of simply as types 1 to 6, though short grammatical explanations are given for those who want the more technical terms.

>   *Type 1.* 'The man *who left* was John' (*subject-linked clauses*). In all languages it is possible to have clauses in which the *subject* noun phrase of the relative clause is the link to the main clause, i.e. 'who' in this case.
>
>   *Type 2.* 'The car *that he crashed* was John's' (*object-linked clauses*). In most languages it is also possible to have sentences in which the grammatical *object* of the relative clause is the link to the main clause, here 'that'.
>
>   *Type 3.* 'The person *that he gave the cheque* was Tom' (*indirect object-linked clauses*). In some languages the link to the main clause is through the *indirect object* – often referring to the person who receives something. Here 'that' acts as indirect object of 'gave'.
>
>   *Type 4.* 'The person to *whom he gave the cheque* was John' (*oblique-case clauses*). In English this type of clause is effectively the same as type 3, with the addition of 'to'.
>
>   *Type 5.* 'The man *whose book I borrowed* was furious' (*possessive-linked clauses*). Next comes the relative clause linked through *possessive* words such as 'whose'.
>
>   *Type 6.* 'The man *than whom I am taller* is John' (*object of comparison-linked clauses*). Finally come relative clauses using 'than' as a link, i.e.

expressing some kind of comparison. It is difficult to find natural-sounding examples in English, though they are possible.

This is not just a list of six types of relative clause; it is arranged in a particular order – hence the name accessibility *hierarchy*. Some languages such as Malagasy have subject clauses, type 1, but not types 2–6. Others like Welsh have types 1 and 2 but not 3–6. Still others like Catalan have 1–4 but not 5–6. Many like French and German have 1-5 but not 6. English has all 6 types. The important factor is that all languages start at the top of the hierarchy with type 1, and go some way down it. No language starts at type 2 and leaves type 1 out, or has 1 and 4 but skips 2 and 3, and so on. In other words the difference between languages is how far down the hierarchy they go. The accessibility hierarchy is a general rule which all languages obey; if a language has type 1 then it may have type 2, but it cannot have type 2 without also having type 1, and so on.

How is the accessibility hierarchy relevant to L2 learning? The first language of the learner, say French, will have a certain range of relative clauses starting from type 1. The L2 of the learner, say English, may have a different range of clauses also starting from type 1. L2 learners might start with type 1, go on to learn type 2, and so on down the list. The accessibility hierarchy in this case would correspond to a sequence of acquisition. But it is also relevant to the processing of language. Popular writers use only the first few types of relative clause; intellectual writers such as Virginia Woolf use the whole range. The psychological difficulty of relative clauses varies in accordance with the hierarchy, type 1 being least difficult to understand, type 6 most difficult. It is also possible that L2 learning may be based on the L1 knowledge and the types used in the first language carried over to the second. L2 learners could start by assuming a new language has the same constructions as the first language. If the L1 has type 6 relative clauses, the learners presume the L2 has them too.

Susan Gass (1979) found that the difficulty for EFL learners indeed seemed to follow the hierarchy, with type 1 the easiest type and type 6 the most difficult (3 and 4 being collapsed into one type in her research), rather than that learners depended on the L1. There was one major exception: type 5 (possessive clauses) were much easier than expected, coming between types 1 and 2 in terms of difficulty, rather than after type 4. Other research has generally found that the L2 sequence of acquisition corresponds to the accessibility hierarchy. It should, however, be pointed out that other explanations for the phenomenon have been put forward, such as the processes of comprehension, summarized, for example, in Doughty (1991).

The question is what this means for teaching. At one level it broadens the idea of grammar. Topics such as the accessibility hierarchy need to be looked at as well as more conventional ideas. It is as important to know where the L2 fits on the hierarchy as it is to know about the passive voice or the more familiar parts of grammar. The obvious conclusion might seem to be that, everything else being equal, teaching should follow the order of the accessibility hierarchy, teaching type 1 (subject clauses) first, then type 2 (object clauses), etc. Often in some sense this has already been intuitively part of language teaching. In the elementary level textbook *English in Perspective* (Dalzell and Edgar, 1988) the first teaching page already has type 2, 'Find the thing your partner describes'; page 22 has type 1 as in 'Choose the words which interest you'; the rarer types do not appear.

But the obvious conclusion may be wrong. Given that all languages adhere to the hierarchy, learners would simply have to discover how far the language goes down it. If they know it has type 5 (possessive), they can work out it must have type 2, type 3, and so on. Suppose that all learners expect the accessibility hierarchy to be true. Then, if they know how far down the hierarchy the language comes, they can extrapolate all the other possible clauses. Eckman and his colleagues (1988) divided some EFL students into 3 groups. One group were taught type 1 (subject), a second group type 2 (object), a third group type 4 (preposition clauses), all for one hour. Then they tested how well the students knew all three types, not just the one they had been taught. The third group, who had only been taught type 4, were, not surprisingly, the best group of the three at these; but they were also the best at type 1 and type 2 clauses! In other words they had worked out the other types better than those who had started from the top of the hierarchy and worked their way down. By virtue of the common features of all languages, L2 learners can 'extrapolate' from one structure to others. The straightforward logical teaching sequence, essentially from easy to difficult, may be less effective than the reverse order. Giving the students an example of the most difficult form is sometimes useful.

L2 LEARNING OF RELATIVE CLAUSES

A. *L2 learners broadly follow the accessibility hierarchy as an order of difficulty* (Gass, 1979).

1. Subject relatives: 'The man who left was John.'
2. Possessive relatives: 'The man whose book I borrowed.'
3. Object relatives: 'The car that he crashed was John's.'
4. Object of preposition relatives: 'The person he gave the cheque to was Tom.'
5. Object of comparison relatives: 'The man than whom I am taller is John.'

B. *If L2 learners are taught clauses way down the accessibility hierarchy, they can fill in the intervening gaps* (Eckman et al., 1988). Learners taught only object of preposition clauses, 'The person he gave the cheque to was Tom', knew subject clauses, 'The car that he crashed was John's', better than those students who had been taught them directly.

5 Principles and parameters grammar

KEYWORDS

Universal Grammar: the language faculty built into the human mind consisting of principles and parameters

principles of language: aspects of human language present in all human minds, e.g. the principle of structure dependency – why you cannot say 'Is John is the man who happy?'

parameters: aspects that vary from one language to another within tightly set limits, e.g. the pro-drop parameter has two settings that distinguish pro-drop languages which do not need subjects expressed (Spanish, Chinese) and non-pro-drop languages in which they must be expressed (English, German)

So far grammar has been seen in terms of morphemes, patterns or structures, and universals spread across many languages. All of these capture some aspect of L2 learning and contribute to our knowledge of the complete process. A radically different way of looking at grammar that has become popular in recent years, however, tries to see what human languages have in common because of the nature of the human mind. This is the Universal Grammar theory associated with Noam Chomsky, for example, Chomsky (1988). Universal Grammar (UG) sees the knowledge of grammar in the mind as having two components: 'principles' that all languages have in common and 'parameters' on which they vary. All human minds are believed to possess the same language principles. They differ over the settings for the parameters for particular languages.

PRINCIPLES OF LANGUAGE

A fairly simple example of a principle is structure-dependency. How might you explain to someone how to make questions in English such as 'Is Sam the cat that is black?' One possible instruction is: 'Start from the sentence: "Sam is the cat that is black" and move the second word "is" to the beginning.'

But while this works in this instance, it obviously will not work for 'The old man is the one who's late' as it would produce 'Old the man is the one who's late?'.

To remedy this you might suggest: 'Move the copula "is" to the beginning of the sentence.' But this also does not work as it will not prevent someone mistakenly saying 'Is Sam is the cat that black?' It is important *which* 'is' is moved. The only instruction that works properly is to say: 'Move the copula "is" in the main clause to the beginning of the sentence.' This instruction depends on the listeners knowing enough of the structure of the sentence to be able to distinguish the main clause from the relative clause. In other words it presupposes that they know the structure of the sentence. This is what is meant by 'structure-dependent'. Anybody producing a question in English takes the structure of the sentence into account. Inversion questions in English, and indeed in all other languages, involve a knowledge of structure, not just of the order of the words. There is no particular reason why this should be so; computer languages, for instance, do not behave like this, nor do mathematical equations. It is just a feature of human languages that they depend on structure. In short structure-dependency is one of the language principles that is built into the human mind.

This type of grammar affects the nature of interlanguage – the knowledge of the second language in the learner's mind. As described earlier, there appeared to be few limits on how the learners' interlanguage grammars developed. Their source might be partly the learners' first languages, partly their learning strategies, partly other sources. However, the human mind always uses its built-in language principles, so interlanguages too conform to these principles. It would be literally inconceivable for the L2 learner, say, to produce questions that were *not* structure-dependent. And indeed no one has yet found sentences said by L2 learners that breach the known language principles such as structure-dependency. Interlanguages do not vary without limit but conform to the overall mould of human language since they are stored in the same human minds. Like any scientific theory, this may be proved wrong. Tomorrow someone may find a learner who has no idea of structure-dependency. But so far no one has found clear-cut examples of learners breaking universal principles.

PARAMETERS OF VARIATION

How do parameters capture the differences between languages? One variation is whether the grammatical subject of a declarative sentence has to be actually present in the sentence. In German it is possible to say 'Er spricht' (he speaks) but impossible to say 'Spricht' (speaks); declarative sentences must have subjects. The same is true for French, for English, and for a great many languages. But in Italian it is possible not only to say 'Lui parla' (he talks) but also 'Parla' (talks) without an expressed subject; declarative sentences are not required to have subjects. In Arabic and Chinese and many other languages the same is true. This variation is captured by the *pro-drop parameter* – so-called for technical reasons we will not go into here. In 'pro-drop' languages such as Italian, Chinese or Arabic the subject does not need to be actually present; in 'non-pro-drop' languages such as English or German it must always be present in declarative sentences. The pro-drop parameter variation has effects on the grammars of all languages; each of them is either pro-drop or non-pro-drop.

Children learning their first language at first start with sentences without subjects (Hyams, 1986). Then those who are learning a non-pro-drop language such as English go on to learn that subjects are compulsory. The obvious question for second language learning is whether it makes a difference if the L1 does not have subjects and the L2 does, and vice versa. Lydia White (1986) compared how English was learnt by speakers of French (a non-pro-drop language with compulsory subjects) and by speakers of Spanish (a pro-drop language with optional subjects). If the L1 setting for the pro-drop parameter has an effect, the Spanish-speaking learners should make different mistakes from the French-speaking learners. Spanish-speaking learners were much more tolerant of sentences like 'In winter snows a lot in Canada' than were the French. Oddly enough this effect does not necessarily go in the reverse direction: English learners of Spanish do not have as much difficulty with leaving the subject out as Spanish learners of English have in putting it in.

One attraction of this form of grammar is its close link to language acquisition. The parts of language that have to be learnt are the settings for the parameters on which languages vary. The parts which do not have to be learnt are the principles that all languages have in common. Learning the grammar of an L2 is not so much learning completely new structures, rules, and so on as discovering how to set the parameters for the new language.

Another attraction is that it provides a framework within which all languages can be compared, at least for the aspects of grammar that it covers. While it used to be difficult to compare grammars of different languages, say English and Japanese, because they were seen as totally different, they are now variations within a single overall scheme. Japanese can be compared to English, in its use of structure-dependency (unnecessary in Japanese questions because Japanese does not form questions by moving elements of the sentence around); in terms of the pro-drop parameter (English sentences must have subjects, Japanese do not have to); and in terms of word order parameters (Japanese phrases have the order phrase+head, for example, noun phrase followed by postposition 'Nihon ni' (Japan in), English phrases have the order head+noun phrase, for example, preposition followed by noun phrase 'in London'). This helps with the description of learners' speech, which can now be described within the same framework. Chinese, Arabic, or Spanish students all may have problems with the subject in English because of their different setting for the pro-drop parameter.

It is also important to relate this to the idea of multi-competence, the knowledge of two languages in one mind. Each L2 user's mind has two grammatical systems somewhere within it, differing only in parameter settings and vocabulary. What teachers are trying to do is create this complex state of language knowledge, never to wipe the board clean and pretend that L2 learners do not have another grammar, another group of settings for the parameters present in their minds.

The implications of this overall model for language learning and language teaching are described in greater detail in Chapter 8. For the moment we are simply concerned to point out that the study of grammar and of acquisition in recent years has been much more concerned with the development of abstract ways of looking at phenomena like pro-drop than with the conventional grammar of earlier sections. Language teaching will eventually miss out if it does not keep up with such new ideas of grammar (Cook, 1989a).

L2 LEARNING OF PRINCIPLES AND PARAMETERS GRAMMAR

1. L2 learners do not need to learn principles such as structure-dependency as they will use them automatically.
2. L2 learners need to acquire new parameter settings for parameters such as pro-drop, often starting from their L1.
3. All learners can be looked at within the same overall framework of grammar.
4. L2 learning produces a complex knowledge of languages in the mind, i.e. multi-competence.

---

6 L2 learning of grammar and L2 teaching

KEYWORDS

consciousness-raising: helping the learner by drawing attention to features of the second language
language awareness: helping the learner by raising awareness of language itself
sensitization: helping the learners by alerting them to features of the first language

Teachers are often surprised by what grammar means in L2 learning research and how much importance it is given. While the grammar used here has some resemblance to the traditional and structural grammars with which teachers are familiar – 'structures', 'rules', and so on – the perspective has changed. Grammatical morphemes cut across the teaching categories of prepositions, articles, and forms of 'be'. The accessibility hierarchy puts together information about relative clauses rather differently from most grammar books. The theory of principles and parameters puts grammar on a different plane from anything in language teaching. Hence teachers will not find any quick help with carrying out conventional grammar teaching from such forms of grammar. But they will nevertheless understand better what the students are learning and the processes through which they are going. To take two examples, sentences with missing subjects and deviant relative clauses are not only common in students' work but also can be simply explained by the pro-drop parameter and by the accessibility hierarchy. Both are insightful ways of looking at learning which teachers have not hitherto been conscious of.

Let us gather together some of the threads about grammar and teaching in this chapter. If the syllabus that the student is learning from includes grammar in some shape or form, this is not a matter of just structures and rules but of a range of highly complex phenomena, some of which have been discussed in this chapter. The L2 learning of grammar has turned out to be wider and deeper than anyone supposed. It ranges from morphemes such as 'the' to negative elements such as 'not' to universal hierarchies of relative clauses to parameters about the presence of subjects. Above all, grammar is knowledge in the mind rather than rules in a book; one crucial end-product of teaching is that students should be able to 'know' language in an unconscious sense so that they can put it to good use. Teaching has to pay attention to the internal processes and knowledge the students are building up in their minds.

Grammar is also relevant to the sequence in which elements of language are taught. Of necessity, language teaching has to present the various aspects of language in order rather than introducing them all simultaneously. The conventional solution used to be a sequence of increasing grammatical complexity, teaching the present simple first, and the past perfect continuous passive last, because the former is much 'simpler' than the latter. When language use became more important to teaching, the choice of a teaching sequence was no longer straightforward since it was aspects of communication that now had to be sequenced. For example the textbook *Opening Strategies* (Abbs and Freebairn, 1982) uses an order based on language functions:

- Lesson 1 'Ask for and say numbers'
- Lesson 2 'Ask about people's nationality'
- Lesson 4 'Say what you want'
- Lesson 11 'Give permission'
- Lesson 14 'Identify belongings', and so on.

Any function-based order runs into problems in arriving at a logical sequence; is 'requesting' simpler or more complex than 'complaining'? Hence grammar began to creep back into textbooks because it was easier to arrange in order. In addition to its functional order, *Opening Strategies* has a grammatical order, starting with the present simple tense of 'be', going on to the present tense of full verbs, then past simple of 'be', followed by present continuous, and so on. Clearly such grammatical sequencing should be related in some way to more recent ideas of the L2 learning of grammar. L2 learning research has often claimed that there are definite orders for learning language, such as the accessibility hierarchy for relative clauses, and orders of difficulty, such as the order for grammatical morphemes. What should teachers do about this? Four extreme points of view can be found:

1. Ignore the parts of grammar that have a particular L2 learning sequence, as the learner will anyway follow these automatically. Nothing teachers can do will help or hinder the student who is progressing through the grammatical morpheme order from '-ing' to 'the' and 'a'. Teachers should therefore get on with teaching the thousand and one *other* things that the student needs and let nature follow its course.

2. Follow the L2 learning order as closely as possible in the teaching. There is no point in teaching 'not' with 'any' to beginners because the students are not ready for it. Instead teachers should concentrate on sentence-external 'no', which is learnable at the first stage, 'not' which is learnable at the next, and so on. So the order of teaching should follow the order found in L2 learning as much as possible.

3. Teach the last things in an L2 learning sequence first. Relative clauses with possessive 'whose' should be taught before relative clauses using the object because the student will extrapolate from one to the other, as Eckman has shown. The students can best be helped by being given the extreme point of the sequence and having to fill in the intermediary positions for themselves.

4. Ignore grammar altogether. Some might argue that, if the students' goals are to communicate in a second language, grammar is an optional extra. Obviously this depends upon the definition of grammar: in the sense that any speaker of a language knows the grammatical system of the language then grammar is not disposable in this way but plays a part in every sentence anybody produces or comprehends for whatever communicative reason.

These positions are so simplified and extreme that no one would hold to them completely. Fuller discussion of the implications of L2 order of learning or difficulty depends on the rest of teaching. It must balance grammar against language functions, vocabulary, classroom interaction, and much else that goes on in the classroom to find the appropriate teaching for those students in that situation. Teachers do not necessarily have to choose between these alternatives once and for all. A different decision may have to be made for each area of grammar or language and each stage of acquisition. But L2 learning research is starting to provide information about sequences which will eventually prove a gold mine for teaching. In general, information on the L2 learning of grammar is often neutral between teaching techniques. It is not making claims about the experiences that learners have had so much as giving a factual description of their language development.

MAKING GRAMMAR CONSCIOUS

The question of whether grammar should be explained to the students must be raised, not for the last time. The use of explicit explanation implies that L2 learning can be quite different from L1 learning. The fact that children learn their first language without resort to conscious understanding does not mean that adults cannot learn a second language in this way. Justifying conscious understanding in L2 learning involves separating L2 learning from L1 learning with respect to whether the learners get explanations. The belief that L2 learning can potentially make use of explanation underlies distinctions such as those made by Harold Palmer (1926) between 'spontaneous capacities' for acquiring speech and 'the studial capacity' through which people study language, and by Krashen (1981a) between 'acquisition' and 'learning' (the latter being conscious and available only to older learners), and by many others. An important issue is what is learnt. I can tell you facts about languages such as Japanese or Gboudi that their native speakers could not. This does not mean I can say a single word, let alone a sentence, of Japanese or Gboudi in a comprehensible way. Conscious explanation is a way of teaching facts about the language – that is to say a form of linguistics. If this is the aim of teaching, as has indeed often been the case, conscious understanding is acceptable as a form of L2 learning.

But mostly grammatical explanation has relied on the assumption that rules that are learnt consciously can be converted into processes that are known unconsciously. The French subjunctive was explained to me at school, not just to give me academic knowledge of the facts of French but to help me to write French. After a period of absorption, this conscious rule would become part of my unconscious ability to use the language. Rutherford (1987) and others have been advocating *consciousness raising* in teaching – 'the drawing of the learner's attention to features of the target language'. This functions as an aid to help the students avoid some of the pitfalls rather than an end in itself. Unlike traditional grammar teaching, it tackles grammatical topics such as the accessibility hierarchy and the pro–drop parameter.

Stephen Krashen, however, has persistently denied that consciously acquired rules change into normal speech processes in the same way as grammar acquired unconsciously, for example in Krashen (1981a). If Krashen's view is accepted, people who are taught by conscious explanation can only produce language by laboriously checking each sentence against their conscious repertoire of rules, as many had to do with Latin at school. Or they can use it for certain 'tips' or rules of thumb such as 'i before e except after c or before g'. While not taking sides here, perhaps one should remember that many graduates of European universities who learnt English primarily by going through traditional grammars have turned into fluent and spontaneous speakers of English. This at least suggests that the conversion of conscious rules to non–conscious processes does indeed take place for some highly academic students. This 'conversion' model of L2 learning is discussed further in Chapter 8.

More indirect uses for grammar have also been put forward in recent years. One suggestion by Eric Hawkins (1984) is for *language awareness*: the learners' general awareness of language should be raised as a preliminary to L2 teaching, partly through grammar. If the students know the kind of thing to expect, they are more receptive to it. Hawkins suggests 'an exploratory approach' where the pupils investigate grammar by for example deciding where to insert 'see-through' in the sentence 'She put on her cosy, old, blue, nylon, blouse'. They invent their own labels for grammar, rather than being taught a pre-established system. As Hawkins puts it, 'grammar approached as a voyage of discovery into the patterns of the language rather than the learning of prescriptive rules, is no longer a bogey word'. It is not the teaching of particular points of grammar that matters but the overall increase in the pupil's language sensitivity. The textbook *Learning to Learn English* (Ellis and Sinclair, 1989) provides some exercises to make EFL learners more conscious of their own predilections, for instance suggesting ways for the students to discover grammatical rules themselves. Philip Riley (1985) has suggested *sensitization* of the students by using features of the L1 to help them understand the L2, say by discussing puns to help them see how speech is split up into words. Increasing awareness of language may have many educational advantages and indeed help L2 learning in a broad sense. It has, however, no particular licence from the types of grammar considered in this chapter.

DISCUSSION TOPICS

1. Take any current textbook you have to hand, and look at one or two grammar-based exercises; decide what type of grammar it employs and how successfully.
2. What aspects of grammar do you feel strongly about? For example, what things do you feel people should *not* say? Why?
3. How relevant is *any* form of grammar to language teaching today with its emphasis on communication?
4. How important do you think that grammatical morphemes are to the student? How much attention do they receive in teaching? How much should they receive?
5. Do the learners you know conform to the stages of the multi-dimensional model?
6. If you should only teach what a student is ready to receive, how do you establish what the student is actually ready for?
7. Second language acquisition research thinks that the order of acquisition is a very important aspect of teaching. How important do you think that order of presentation is to language teaching?
8. Can you conceive of other topics than relative clauses when it would be right to start by teaching the students the most difficult or most complex aspect rather than the easiest or simplest?
9. What ways of making other aspects of grammar conscious can you think of, say, pronunciation, intonation, or speech functions? Would this be a good idea?

FURTHER READING

A good overview of grammatical morphemes research is in Dulay *et al.* (1983) *Language Two*. An introduction to principles and parameters grammar can be found in Cook and Newson (1996) *Chomsky's Universal Grammar: an Introduction*. Various viewpoints on grammar and language teaching are summarized in Odlin (1994) *Pedagogical Grammar*. Otherwise the reader is referred to the books and articles cited in the text.

3

Learning the components of language

This chapter looks at some of the other components of language that are involved in L2 learning – pronunciation, vocabulary, and discourse – and presents the main trends in these areas that have potential for language teaching. While the L2 acquisition of grammar has been widely studied, these other components have been covered much more patchily and are hardly referred to in most standard introductions to L2 learning research. So, while many of the ideas are interesting for language teaching, they are only partial and may be overtaken by further, more appropriate, research. Nor, despite their obvious relevance to teaching, has much yet been done to apply them to actual teaching. While there are indeed any number of recent books on teaching vocabulary and discourse, these are usually based on language description and teaching methodology rather than on concepts from language acquisition.

Another general point is that in each of these areas it is not just that second language acquisition research has things to say about learning; it is often that it has a different idea of what students have to learn. The conventional wisdom in the teaching of pronunciation is that it consists of a set of sounds like /p/, /b/, and /g/; the usual idea of vocabulary is that it consists of a long list of words with meanings attached. A major point in this chapter is that there is far more to these areas of language than this. One of the implications of second language acquisition research is that thinking about language learning and language teaching means thinking about what language is.

Focusing questions

Think of an English sound:

- How do you think it is made by the speaker?
- How would you teach it to an L2 student?

Think of an English word:

- What is its meaning?
- How would you teach it to an L2 student?

Think of a way of starting a conversation:

- When is it used?
- How would you teach it?

---

1 Acquisition of pronunciation

KEYWORDS

phonemes: the sounds of a language that are systematically distinguished from each other, e.g. 's' from 't' in 'sin' and 'tin'

syllable structure: the way in which consonants (C) and vowels (V) may be combined into syllables in a particular language

epenthesis: padding out the syllable by adding extra vowels or consonants, e.g. 'Espain' for 'Spain'

voice onset time (VOT): the moment when voicing starts during the production of a consonant

intonation: the rise and fall in the pitch of the voice during speech

Language conveys meanings from one person to another through spoken sounds or written letters. Native speakers know how to pronounce the words, sentences and utterances of their first language. At one level they can tell the difference in pronunciation between 'drain' and 'train', the sound patterns of the language, at another the difference between 'Fine', 'Fine?', and 'Fine!', the intonation patterns in which the voice rises and falls. Languages make different use of the vast repertoire of sounds available to human beings and they structure them into syllables in different ways. Languages also differ in the ways they use intonation, hard as this may be for many learners to appreciate. It is impossible to imagine a non-handicapped speaker of a language who could not pronounce sentences in it, at least comprehensibly to others.

The study of the pronunciation system of language is known as phonology, the study of the sounds themselves being called 'phonetics'. One side of phonology is the sounds of the language that are systematically distinguished from one another – its 'phonemes'. The sound 's', for instance, is different from the sound 't' in English, so the word 'sin' means something different from 'tin'; 's' and 't' are phonemes. English needs about 45 phonemes to get all the words of the language: 'sin', 'tin', 'fin', 'son', etc.; the lack of a precise figure reflects the variation between different accents. Other languages vary in the number of phonemes from 11 to 141.

In this section the pronunciation of words is sometimes given in the conventional phonetic transcript, as the written language can often not convey the sound differences accurately. For example, the written letter 'i' is pronounced as /ai/ in 'I', /i/ in 'limit', /ə/ in 'first', and probably in other ways as well.

Pronunciation textbooks like *Ship or Sheep?* (Baker, 1981) present the student with pairs of words: 'car' /ka:/ versus 'cow' /kau/ or 'bra' /bra:/ versus 'brow' /brau/. The student learns how to tell one sound from the other and then hears and repeats sentences with a high concentration of particular phonemes such as 'I've found a mouse in the house' or 'This is the cleanest house in town', or the traditional tongue-twisters such as 'He ran from the Indies to the Andes in his undies'. The type of L2 learning implied by this technique resembles the ways of teaching structural grammar described in the last chapter in its emphasis on practice rather than communication. Pronunciation is considered a set of habits for producing sounds. The habit of producing the sound /i/ is acquired by repeating it over and over again and by being corrected when it is pronounced wrongly. Learning to pronounce a second language means building up new pronunciation habits and overcoming the bias of the first language. Only by saying 'car' /ka:/ and 'cow' /kau/ many times is the contrast between /a:/ and /au/ acquired.

These notions clash with most ideas of phonology in linguistics and language learning since the 1960s. There is no evidence that children learn the phonemes of their first language by repeating them one at a time or in pairs, as the teaching technique suggests. Instead they seem to go through stages of acquisition similar to those we saw for grammar in the last chapter.

Wilfried Wieden and William Nemser (1991) looked at the acquisition of English by Austrian schoolchildren. One interesting finding was a difference between sounds that the learners gradually improved on and sounds for which they showed no progress. The diphthong /əu/ in 'boat', for example, was perceived only 55 per cent correctly by beginners but improved over time till it was completely correct after eight years; the sound /ə/, however, at the end of 'finger' gave just as much trouble after eight years as it did at the beginning. They felt that overall the learners went through three stages:

1. *Presystemic*. At this stage learners learn the sounds in individual words but without any overall pattern.
2. *Transfer*. Now the learners start to treat the second language sounds systematically as equivalent to the sounds of their first language.
3. *Approximative*. Finally the learners realize their native sounds are not adequate and attempt to restructure the L2 sounds in a new system.

Much recent phonology does not concentrate on the phoneme so much as on abstract relationships of sounds and structures. For instance, the phoneme is regarded as consisting of a number of 'features' that are common to many phonemes. One example is the feature of 'fortis' (said with energy) versus 'lenis' (said less energetically) that separates /b/ (bit) from /p/ (pit), /d/ (den) from /t/ (ten), /z/ (zoo) from /s/ (Sue), and so on. The Austrian learners learnt this feature only gradually, Austrian German having no such distinction.

The concept of independent L2 grammars applies as much to pronunciation as to grammar. L2 learners have their own systems of pronunciation, which are not just pale shadows of the target language. German learners of English who say 'pup' /pʌp/ for 'pub' rather than /pʌb/ have devised a rule based on their first language that voicing does not matter in final consonants; so they will also say /gut/ for 'good', /gud/, /piːs/ for 'peas' /piːz/, and so on. Though some of the learners' pronunciation rules are related to their first language, they nevertheless still make up a unique temporary system – an interlanguage.

LEARNING SYLLABLE STRUCTURE

One aspect of phonology is the structure of syllables. These are made up of consonants (C), such as /t/, /s/, /p/, etc., and of vowels (V) such as /i/ or /ai/. Unlike languages like Polish, all English syllables must have a vowel, with the exception of the so-called syllabic consonants: /n/ as in /bʌtn̩/ ('button') or /l/ as in /bɒtl̩/ ('bottle'). One difficulty for the L2 learner lies in the ways in which the consonants can be combined with each other – the permissible consonant clusters. English combines /p/ with /l/ as in 'plan' /plaen/ or with /r/ as in 'pray' /prei/ but does not combine /p/ with /f/ or /z/; so there are no English words like 'pfan' or 'pzan' starting with /pf.../ or /pz.../. Aliens in Larry Niven stories, for instance, are identified by the reader because their names have non-English clusters – 'tnuctipun' /tn/ and 'ptavvs' /pt/. Even when two languages have the same consonants, they may still vary in the ways they combine them in clusters. L2 learners often try by one means or another to make English syllables fit their L1s. Examples are Koreans saying /kala:s/ for 'class', Vietnamese saying /dawait/ for 'Dwight', and Arabs saying /bilæstik/ for 'plastic'. To make English conform to Korean or Arabic, they are inserting extra vowels, a process known as 'epenthesis'. So Indian children in Yorkshire pronounce 'blue' as /bəlu/ not /blu:/, 'friend' as /fərend/ not /frend/, and 'sphere' as /səfiə/ not /sfiə/, all with epenthetic vowels (Verma et al., 1992).

The compulsory vowel in the English syllable may be preceded or followed by one or more consonants. So 'lie' /lai/, which has a consonant/vowel (CV) structure, and 'sly' /slai/, which starts with a two consonant cluster (CC), are both possible, as are 'eel' /i:l/ with VC and 'eels' /i:lz/ with VCC. Longer clusters of three or four consonants can also occur, for example, at the end of 'lengths' /leŋkθs/ or the beginning of 'splinter' /splintə/. While the English syllable can have several consonants before or after the vowel, the syllable structure of some languages allows only a **single** consonant before or after the vowel. Japanese, for instance, has no consonant clusters and most syllables end in a vowel; the English word 'strike' becomes *sutoraki* in Japanese to make it conform to the syllable structure of the language.

Some L2 learners leave consonants out of words if they are not allowed in their L1 – a process of 'simplification'. Cantonese speakers, whose L1 syllables have no final consonants, turn English 'girl' /gə:l/ into 'gir' /gə:l/ and 'Joan' /dʒəun/ into 'Joa' /dʒəu/. Arabic syllables too can be CV but not CCV, i.e. there are no two consonant clusters. 'Straw' /strɔ:/ could not be a possible syllable in Arabic because it starts with a three-consonant cluster CCC. Indian children in Yorkshire too simplify the /nd/ of 'thousand' to /d/, and the /ds/ of 'Leeds' to /d/.

Egyptian-Arabic learners of English often add an epenthetic vowel /i/ to avoid two- or three-consonant clusters. 'Children' /tʃildrən/ becomes 'childiren' /tʃildirən/ in their speech because the CC combination /dr/ is not allowed. 'Translate' /trænzleit/ comes out as 'tiransilate' /tirænzileit/ to avoid the two consonant CC sequences /tr/ and /sl/. A part of their first language is being carried over into English. The clash between the syllable structures of the L1 and L2 is resolved by the temporary expedient of adding vowels, a true interlanguage solution. It is not just the sequence of phonemes in the sentence that matters but the abstract syllable structure that governs their combinations. Hence the phonology of the syllable in the interlanguage shows effects from the L1, although it is a system of its own, which is neither L1 nor L2.

LEARNING TO VOICE CONSONANTS

Let us now jump from the structures of phonology to the actual mechanics of speech production in phonetics to see how some of the actual sounds of speech are produced. James Flege (1986) has argued that L2 learners have more problems with sounds that are similar to those in their L1 than with new sounds that are completely different. One fruitful area that bears on this is *voice onset time* (VOT). A speaker who is producing the stop consonant /g/ in the English word 'got' /gɒt/ is doing two things:

1. Blocking the back of the mouth with the tongue and then releasing this blockage, the actual 'stop'. All stop consonants such as /g/, /p/, /b/, /t/, etc. are produced by completely stopping the air coming out of the mouth for a brief moment with the tongue or the lips and then letting the air out suddenly, the 'release'.
2. Producing 'voice' by vibrating the vocal cords against each other. Voice can be felt by putting the hand against the front of the throat and feeling the vibration in /z/ and the lack of vibration in /s/. The chief, but not the sole, difference between so-called voiced sounds such as /d/ or /z/ and unvoiced sounds such as /t/ or /s/ is whether such voicing takes place.

An important aspect of stop consonants that varies from one language to another is the moment when voicing *starts* as the person produces the consonant. Voice onset time (VOT) is the name for the actual moment this occurs. In English the VOT for /g/ varies from about 88 thousandths of a second (milliseconds or msec) before the stop is released to about the same moment as the release (−21 msec). The sound /g/ is heard as voiced, so long as the speaker starts voicing within these time limits. However, in the unvoiced English sound /k/ heard in 'cot' /kɔt/, voicing starts around +80 msec *after* the stop is released. Any stop with a delay in voicing of 80 msec will be heard as unvoiced. This is shown in Figure 3.1.

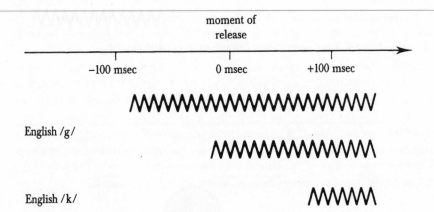

Fig. 3.1 Voice onset time in English stops /g/ and /k/

An English stop is heard as a voiced /g/ if the VOT either happens before the release or is almost simultaneous with the release. On the other hand, the stop is heard as an unvoiced /k/ if the VOT occurs after the release. This is another way of saying that English unvoiced stops are 'aspirated' – followed by a silent puff of air.

In Spanish, however, the distinction between the voiced and unvoiced sounds is made differently. A voiced sound such as /g/ has an early voice onset time of −108 msec, similar to English −88 msec. But an unvoiced sound such as /k/ has a VOT about simultaneous with the release (+29 msec) rather than much after it; there is no aspiration (Fig. 3.2). Consequently there is not the wide variation in /g/ allowable in English.

Although both languages have voiced and unvoiced stops, their systems of voicing differ. Both Spanish and English speakers agree that stop consonants with early VOT are voiced and that stops with a later VOT are unvoiced. But a Spanish speaker interprets a stop where the voicing is simultaneous with the release as a /k/, an English speaker hears it as a /g/; there is a zone in which the Spanish /g/ overlaps with the English /k/ (Fig. 3.3).

Nathan (1987) found that Spanish learners of English gradually acquire the English zero VOT for the stop /g/, something which does not actually matter for English speakers at all as −88 msec will do just as well. As Nathan puts it, 'once they have marked English voiceless stops as distinctive from voiced ones,

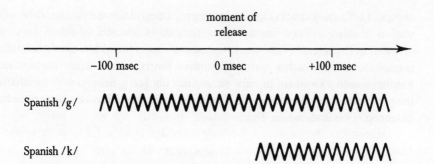

Fig. 3.2 Voice onset time in Spanish stops /g/ and /k/

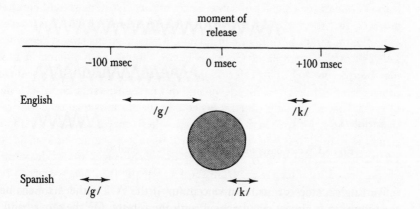

Fig. 3.3 Overlap of English /g/ and Spanish /k/

. . . it is no longer necessary to keep the voiced ones quite as distinct'. L2 learners are not just learning the major differences between phonemes; they are learning subtle differences that do not even matter to native speakers. Arabic learners similarly carry over the shorter VOTs of Arabic to English.

Voice onset time then provides a neat demonstration of the complexity of the actual production of speech and of the subtle differences between languages. It may seem to be almost unteachable. Yet in the first language it has been shown that four-month-old babies are able to distinguish /ba/ from /pa/. It seems that human babies are uniquely capable of making these minute distinctions in VOT.

An interesting question that arises is whether there are in fact two separate systems to handle the two languages or one system that covers both. French learners of English, for example, pronounce the /t/ sound in French with a longer VOT than monolinguals (Flege, 1987). Spanish/English bilinguals use more or less the same VOT in both English and Spanish (Williams, 1977). It makes no difference to their perception of stops which language is used. As

Watson (1991, p. 44) sums up, 'In both production and perception, therefore, studies of older children (and adults) suggest that bilinguals behave in ways that are at once distinct from monolinguals and very similar to them.' This reinforces the point that we should never forget: L2 students are not just imitation native speakers but are something unique – people who simultaneously possess two languages. We should not expect them to be like natives but like people who can use another language efficiently in their own right.

Research has also looked at the question of age and the L2 learning of VOT. English-speaking adults were unable to distinguish the Hindi voiced/voiceless distinction between /th/ and /dh/, while seven-month-old English babies could (Werker *et al.*, 1981).

So far the discussion has mostly been illustrating differences between L2 learners due to the transfer of some aspect of their L1. One should emphasize, however, that there are also universal processes shared by all L2 learners. For example, the simplification of consonant clusters happens almost regardless of L1. The earlier example of Germans having trouble with voicing in English may be due not to the transfer of the German equivalent but to a universal preference by all learners for 'devoicing' of final consonants. Similarly the use of CV syllables by many L2 learners could reflect a universal tendency rather than transfer from specific L1s. While epenthesis may often depend upon the structure of the L1, it is nevertheless a process that appears to be available to all L2 learners. Major (1986) claims that the early stages of L2 learning are characterized by interference from the L1, but the later stages start to reveal universal processes of acquisition common to both L1 and L2 learning; so teaching of pronunciation may have to proceed rather differently at different stages to take account of the learners' progression.

THE TEACHING OF PRONUNCIATION

What does this research show for teaching? Most language teachers use 'integrated pronunciation teaching', as Joanne Kenworthy (1987) calls it, in which pronunciation is taught as an incidental to other aspects of language. *The Pronunciation Book* (Bowen and Marks, 1992), for example, describes ways of including pronunciation work within activities primarily devoted to other activities, such as texts and dialogues. The teacher often simply corrects wrong pronunciations when they arise on an *ad hoc* basis. Such incidental correction does not probably do much good directly as it most often concentrates on a single phoneme; it may improve the students' pronunciation of a single word said in isolation. It also relies on the efficiency of correction as a teaching technique, something which has been out of fashion in other areas of language teaching for a generation. Correction may indirectly serve to raise the students' awareness of pronunciation but may also succeed in embarrassing all but the most thick-skinned of students.

One clear implication from second language acquisition research is that the learning of sounds is not just a matter of mastering the phonemes of the second language along with their predictable variants. At one level, it is learning the rules of pronunciation for the language, such as those for forming syllables; at another level, it is learning precise control over VOT. While the phonemes of the language are indeed important, pronunciation difficulties are often not to do with specific phonemes so much as with general principles – in the case of English as L2, voicing for German students, syllable structure for Arabic students, VOT for Spanish students, and so on. Language teaching should then pay more attention to such general features of pronunciation rather than the phoneme.

Learners have their own interlanguage phonologies – temporary rules of their own. The sounds of the language are not just separate items on a list to be learnt one at a time but are related in a complex system. A /p/ is different from a /b/ because it is voiced and fortis, different from a /t/ because it involves the lips, different from a /v/ because it is a stop consonant, and so on. Teaching or correcting a single phoneme may not have any effect on the students' pronunciation or may have the wrong effect. It is like taking a brick out of a wall and replacing it with another. Unless the replacement fits exactly in the structure of the whole wall, all the other bricks will move to accommodate it, or at worst the wall will fall down. Understanding how to help students' pronunciation means relating the faults first to their current interlanguage and only secondly to the target. It is not enough to compare their speech with what native speakers say and then to correct them without taking into account the two systems of the interlanguage and the target. The work with Austrian learners suggests that teachers should be aware which sounds are going to improve gradually and which are never going to improve, so that these can be treated differently. It also suggests that pronunciation teaching should relate to the particular stage the learner is at, emphasizing individual words at the beginning, relating pronunciation to the L1 for intermediates, and treating the sound system of the new language in its own right for advanced students.

All in all, the conventional teaching techniques of discrimination of sounds, correction of 'mistakes', and imitation of phonemes are only scratching the surface. They are not directly linked either to much of what the student has to learn or to the processes of learning. Pronunciation teaching has to see that pronunciation is more than the phoneme and learning is more than repetition; exercises and techniques will then start to be more widely used that reflect the way people now conceive of the sound structure of language and how it is learnt.

THE LEARNING AND TEACHING OF INTONATION

Intonation is the way that the pitch of the voice goes up and down during speech. Chinese is a 'tone' language that separates different words purely by intonation: '¯ma' with level tone means 'mother', '˅ma' with fall–rise tone means 'house'. Adult L2 learners have no problems in distinguishing Chinese tones, though with less confidence than native speakers of Chinese (Leather, 1987). Adults learning Thai, another tone language, were much worse at learning tones than children (Ioup and Tansomboon, 1987). On the other hand, research has looked at L2 learning of Portuguese and English, which are 'intonation' rather than 'tone' languages (Cruz-Ferreira, 1986). Rather than differences between words, in these languages intonation shows a variety of grammatical points (e.g. question versus statement), discourse connections (e.g. when a topic starts and finishes), and speakers' attitudes (e.g. politeness versus rudeness). In this case learners have no problems with similar intonation patterns in L1 and L2 but use strategies for unfamiliar patterns based on their idea of the range of the intonation and the extent to which they can deduce meanings from the actual words in the sentence.

Specialized intonation textbooks like my own *Active Intonation* (Cook, 1968) often present the learner with a graded set of intonation patterns for understanding and for repetition, starting, say, with the difference between rising 'Well?' and falling 'Well', and building up to more complex patterns through comprehension activities and imitation exercises. But the teaching techniques again mostly depend on ideas of practice and repetition; students learn one bit at a time, rather than having systems of their own; they repeat, they imitate, they practise, all in a very controlled way.

Some teaching methods aim simply at making the student aware of the nature of intonation rather than at improving specific aspects of it. Several examples can be found in *Teaching English Pronunciation* (Kenworthy, 1987). For instance, Kenworthy suggests getting two students to talk about holiday photographs without using any words other than 'mmm', 'ah', or 'ooo'. This makes them aware of the crucial role of intonation without necessarily teaching them any specific English intonation patterns, the objective underlying many of the communicative intonation exercises in my own textbook *Using Intonation* (Cook, 1979). This resembles the consciousness-raising approach to grammar teaching but applied to pronunciation. Dickerson (1987) made detailed studies of the usefulness of giving pronunciation rules to L2 learners, concluding that they are indeed helpful. Chapter 8 looks at such 'conversion' models in more detail.

2 Acquisition of vocabulary

KEYWORDS

components of meaning: the meaning of some words can be broken up into separate components, e.g. the word 'boy' has components 'human', 'male', and 'young'
prototype theory: words have whole meanings divided into basic level ('table'), superordinate ('furniture'), and subordinate ('coffee table')
frequency: either how many times a word occurs in speech or how often it is practised by a student

L2 LEARNING OF PRONUNCIATION

Syllable structure:

- L2 learners simplify consonant clusters and add extra 'epenthetic' vowels, often to fit the L1.

Voice onset time:

- L2 learners gradually acquire the L2 way of voicing stop consonants.
- Their L1 is affected by their knowledge of the L2.

Intonation:

- L2 learners are still capable of discriminating 'tones'.
- LS learners have strategies for dealing with 'new' intonation.

Teaching uses:

- Teachers should be aware of other aspects of pronunciation than the phoneme.
- *Ad hoc* correction of individual phonemes by the teacher may be fairly useless.
- Teaching students to be aware of pronunciation may be as beneficial as the teaching of specific points, particularly with intonation.

Grammar provides the overall patterns, vocabulary the material to put in the patterns. To understand 'Peter sat on the floor' properly the listener needs to know not only that 'sat' refers to a physical state, but also that it is usually preceded by a grammatical subject that refers to something that is alive; in other words, you cannot say 'The rock sat the man'. 'Sat' is related to other words such as 'lie' and 'stand', and it is associated in the mind with 'cat' and 'bat' and 'chair'. All of these are part of the speaker's knowledge of English vocabulary. Using 'sat' properly means not just knowing how it is defined in the dictionary, but how it relates to all the other words in the language, and how and when it may be used in sentences. Dictionaries can give a false idea that vocabulary is a list of words, each with one or more meanings attached to them. Instead words are related to each other in many ways, and this is how they are remembered and stored.

Some students still learn vocabulary lists in which each L1 word has a one-word L2 translation; English 'man' is 'homme' in French and so on. Some teachers try to get the students to associate each word with an image or an object; they hold up a picture of a man and say 'This is a man'. Both these teaching techniques imply that learning vocabulary means learning individual words one at a time. But the relationships between words are as important as the meaning of the word in isolation: how 'man' contrasts with 'woman' and with 'boy' is as important as the meaning of the word itself.

Words are not coins you exchange from one language to another according to a fixed exchange rate. Changing £5 into 35 French francs is not the same as changing 'beer' into 'bière' because the word 'beer' depends on the complex system of words for drinks in English and on the place of beer in the culture. Even the actual substance referred to can change when the word changes; 'bière' as usually served in French bars does not refer to the same substance as 'beer' as served in English pubs, being a light cool lager rather than a dark warm bitter (due to the different yeasts involved requiring different brewing and storage temperatures). Linguists sometimes claim that no word can be exactly translated into another language. Jespersen (1904) illustrated this through translations of the word 'bat' into other languages; the French 'chauvesouris' emphasizes its baldness and its resemblance to a mouse, the Latin 'vespertilio' suggests the evening when the bat is out, and the Danish 'flagermus' suggests its flapping. The word 'pub' corresponds to nothing in any country other than England, as seen by the variety of tourist bars mistakenly called pubs all over the world. A New York 'deli' again is unrecognizable in other countries. Learning the vocabulary of a second language is not just memorizing equivalent words between languages ('red' means 'rouge'), or learning the definition of the word ('red' is 'a colour typically seen in blood') or putting it in context ('Rudolph the red-nosed reindeer') but learning the meaning relationships between 'red' and all the other words in English within the full context of cultural life.

MEANING COMPONENTS

One way of analysing vocabulary is to break the meaning of a word up into smaller components. Thus the meaning of 'girl' is made up of 'female', 'human', and 'non-adult'. The meaning of 'apple' is made up of 'fruit', 'edible', 'round', and so on. Much of the dispute about gender discrimination in English comes down to whether the meaning of 'man' necessarily has the component 'male' as well as 'human' and 'adult', and whether 'girl' is made up of 'young' as well as 'female'! Breaking meaning up into components has been used in first language acquisition to study the development of words such as 'before' and 'big' in English children. At one stage they know one component of the meaning but not the other. They know 'big' and 'small' share a meaning component to do with size but think they both mean 'big'; or they know that 'before' and 'after' are to do with 'time' but do not know which one means 'prior' (Clark, 1971). L2 beginners in English indeed found it much easier to understand 'Mary talks before Susan shouts' than 'Caroline sings after Sally dances' (Cook, 1977).

A version of this components approach can be found in textbooks such as *The Words You Need* (Rudzka *et al.*, 1981). Students look at a series of 'Word Study' displays showing the different components of meaning of words. For example, a chart gives words that share the meaning 'look at/over' such as 'check', 'examine', 'inspect', 'scan', and 'scrutinize'. It shows which of them have the component of meaning 'detect errors', which 'determine that rules are observed', and so on. Students are encouraged to build up the idea of the vocabulary as consisting of such components while reading texts.

Learning a second language can literally mean seeing the world in a different way; English 'brown' does not refer to exactly the same colour as French 'brun'. This has an effect on the first language. A monolingual speaker of Korean uses the word 'paran sekj' (blue) to mean something greener and less purple than a Korean who also knows English (Caskey-Sirmons and Hickerson, 1977). Languages vary slightly in how they divide up the colours in which their speakers see the world. The same is true of the sense of taste. Speakers of Bahasa Malaysia are particularly good at distinguishing saltiness, reflected in the many expressions for salt in their language: 'masin kitchup' (salty like soy sauce), 'masin ayer laut' (salty like sea water), 'masin garam' (salty like salt), and 'masin maung' (horribly salty) (O'Mahoney and Muhiudeen, 1977). Nor is this effect confined to vocabulary. People whose first language has the word order colour + object ('black cat') tend to sort objects such as blue squares and yellow triangles out by colour while those whose language has the order object + colour ('gatto nero') tend to sort them out by shape (Hooton and Hooton, 1977).

THE PROTOTYPE THEORY OF VOCABULARY

Nevertheless many aspects of meaning cannot be split up into components but are appreciated as wholes. An influential approach of this type is Eleanor Rosch's *prototype* theory (Rosch, 1977). An English person who is asked to give an example of a typical bird is more likely to say 'sparrow' than 'penguin' or 'ostrich'; sparrows are closer to the prototype for 'birds' than penguins and ostriches. Rosch's theory suggests that, rather than components of meaning, there is an ideal of meaning in our minds – 'birdiness' in this case – from which other things depart. Speakers have a central form of a concept in their minds and the things they see and talk about correspond better or worse with this prototype.

Prototype theory also claims that children first learn words that are 'basic' because they reflect aspects of the world, prototypes, that stand out automatically from the rest of what they see. 'Sparrow' is a 'basic level' term compared to a 'superordinate level' term like 'bird', or a 'subordinate level' term like 'house sparrow'. The basic level of vocabulary is easier to use and to learn. On this foundation children build higher and lower levels of vocabulary. Some examples of the three levels of vocabulary in different areas are seen in Figure 3.4.

superordinate terms	furniture	bird	fruit
basic level terms	table, chair	sparrow	apple, strawberry
subordinate terms	coffee table, armchair	field sparrow	Golden Delicious, wild strawberry

Fig. 3.4 The three levels of vocabulary

L1 children learn the basic level terms like 'apple' before they learn the superordinate term 'fruit', or the subordinate term 'Golden Delicious'. They start with the most basic level as it is easiest for the mind to perceive. Only after this has been learnt do they go on to words that are more general or more specific. Cook (1982) showed that L2 learners first acquired basic terms such as 'table', second more general terms like 'furniture', and finally more specific terms like 'coffee table'. Rosch's levels are therefore important to L2 learning as well as to first language acquisition.

This sequence, however, is different from the usual order of presentation in language teaching in which the teacher or textbook introduces or practices a whole group of words simultaneously. For example, in Unit 9 of *Headway Elementary* by Liz and John Soars the students meet for the first time the words 'grapes', 'strawberry' and 'fruit'. According to prototype theory, this is misguided; the superordinate term 'fruit' should come only after the students have the basic level 'strawberry', not in the same exercise. The most important early words are basic level terms. The human mind automatically starts from this concrete level rather than from a more abstract level or a more specific one. Starting by teaching vocabulary items that can be easily shown in pictures fits in with the Rosch theory. A drawing can be readily recognized as a chair but is less easy to see as an armchair or as furniture. Hence prototype theory ties in with the audiovisual method of language teaching that introduces new vocabulary with a picture of what it represents, in an appropriate cultural setting. This theory has particular implications for teaching of vocabulary at the beginning stages.

We have seen then that the meaning of a word is very complex; it can be broken up into components ('boy' into 'young male adult human', say); it can be related to one central meaning ('sparrow' is the birdiest bird). Whatever learning a L2 word involves, it is not just learning a straightforward equivalence with an L1 word – 'rouge' means 'red'. And of course it does not stop there. Take word association. What is the first word that comes into your head when you think of the word 'blue'? Probably 'sky' or 'red' or 'new'. These are three types of well-known responses:

- 'blue' > 'sky'. This is called a *syntagmatic* response because it completes a syntactic structure; it is the next word in the phrase; other examples might be 'jeans' or 'bird'.

- 'blue' > 'red'. This is called a *paradigmatic* response because it chooses another word from the set of colour words (the colour paradigm); other examples might be 'black' or 'pink', etc.
- 'blue' > 'new'. This is called a *klang* response because it 'clangs' with the word as a rhyme; other examples might be 'Sue' or 'true'.

Most responses fall into these three types. The most unusual response I have had to 'blue' from a teacher was 'kind of'; you have to be a fairly dedicated jazz buff to recognize she had been listening to the classic Miles Davis album 'Kind of Blue' – presumably a syntagmatic response!

In the first language children go through a regular progression called the syntagmatic/paradigmatic shift, i.e. they start with syntagmatic 'sky' responses and move on to paradigmatic 'red' responses. In the L2 a similar shift seems apparent except that there are more of the paradigmatic 'new' responses. In the L2 then we have to build up our choice of alternative words as we do in the L1; but probably we will never have the same choice available to us as in our first language.

LEARNING AND REMEMBERING VOCABULARY

The problem lies not just in learning L2 words, but also in remembering them. Harry Bahrick (1984) investigated how well English learners remembered Spanish words eight years after they had learnt them. He found that a word that is learnt after only one or two presentations is remembered better than one that takes several presentations to learn. How well people remember something depends on how deeply they process it. Repeating words as strings of sounds is low-level processing and badly remembered; working out how words fit in the grammatical structure of the sentence is deeper and leads to better memory; using the meanings of words together within the whole meaning of the sentence is the deepest level of processing and ensures the best memory. Bahrick's research also suggested that a word is remembered best if it is practised every 30 days rather than at more frequent intervals (Bahrick and Phelps, 1987). This contradicts the belief common among teachers that every word should be practised as often as possible within a short timespan. It is *how* the word is practised that is important rather than how often.

A familiar precept of vocabulary teaching is that the most frequently used words in the target language are usually taught first. Almost all beginners books restrict the vocabulary they introduce in the first year to about a thousand of the most frequent items. The textbook *Break Into English* (Carrier *et al.*, 1985), for instance, covers 'approximately 900 lexical items'; the American course *I Love English* (Capelle *et al.*, 1985) lists about 750 words. Traditional syllabuses for language teaching usually include lists of the most frequent words. An up-to-date version of this is seen in the *COBUILD English Course I* (Willis and Willis, 1987), which was based on a vocabulary count several million words long. The first lesson teaches 91 words including 'person' and 'secretary', unlikely to be in opening lessons of other course books.

Though frequency may indeed form a logical basis for teaching, L2 learning research has little to say about it one way or another. Carter (1988) has proposed that a language has a 'core' vocabulary found in all its uses, plus 'subject' cores specific to specialist subject matters, and a non-core vocabulary. Advanced Danish university students of English tested by Dollerup *et al.* (1989) knew the high frequency 'core' words, but many also knew many low frequency words. The difference between good Danish readers and bad readers was not a straightforward matter of the better the students the rarer the words they knew. Hence a simple grading for language teaching from core frequent words to non-core infrequent words step-by-step does not seem justified.

Frequency also means how often something is repeated by the student, the implication being that to learn a word you have to use it several times. Again Bahrick's research suggests something rather different. First of all words are remembered best if they are learnt quickly with few presentations. Teachers should make the first occurrence of the word memorable rather than practising it several times. An example of this might be that students appear to have no problems in remembering swear words they have heard only once! Bahrick's approach also suggests that, if teachers want students to remember something for periods longer than a year or two, they need to space the presentations over quite long intervals of days. Overall then, while word frequency is often mentioned in language teaching and often forms part of the syllabus specification, it plays a comparatively minor role in modern ideas of vocabulary learning. Indeed it seems another one of those hangovers from the earlier days of 'behaviourist' thinking about language learning, like structural grammar and the importance of the spoken language, that have persisted because no one has questioned them.

FIRST LANGUAGE INFLUENCES ON VOCABULARY

To what does the first language vocabulary influence the learning of the second? While this influence is not so obvious as with grammar, learners may indeed fill in gaps in their knowledge of the new language with items from the first. When the languages are closely related, this may be effective – so-called 'true friends'. If you do not know the French word for 'beer', it is likely that 'Je veux un beer' will get some results. But also the ways in which the mind organizes the vocabulary of your first language have an influence on how it perceives the second. Eric Kellerman (1986) looked at how students learn words with several meanings, such as the English word 'eye', which ranges from 'potato eye', 'peacock's eye', 'electronic eye', 'human eye', 'eye of a dice', to 'eye of a needle'. The reason he chose to investigate 'eye' was that the Dutch word 'oog' happens to have the same range of meanings. So you would expect Dutch students of English to have no problems with transferring the meanings of 'oog' to English, but this was not the case. Dutch students tended to assume that the English word 'eye' could *not* have the same meanings as Dutch 'oog'. This tendency actually increased the more advanced they were. Kellerman found two causes for this. One was that the closer the meaning was to the base meaning of the word, that is to say 'human eye', the more likely it was to be transferred. A meaning such as 'eye of a dice' is remote from the base and so is thought by the students to be very unlikely in English. The other cause was how often the particular meaning of a word occurs. The more frequent a meaning the more likely the students are to transfer it. The meaning 'eye of a peacock' is infrequent and so students assume it cannot be shared by two languages even if it is not far from the base meanings. A similar example to Kellerman's is the word 'lidchot' in Hebrew (Levenston, 1979). English-speaking learners have no problems in learning the meaning 'postpone', but have the greatest difficulty in seeing that the same word can also mean 'reject'.

Many languages have words that are deceptively similar in form, particularly if the languages are closely related, English 'chair' versus French 'chaise' or English 'day' versus German 'Tag'. These are often called 'false friends' by teachers, who warn their students against their attractions. Hakan Ringbom (1982) found that Finnish learners of English in fact preferred false friends from Swedish rather than from Finnish: 'I can play pingis' for 'table-tennis' or 'This is a very beautiful stad' for 'town'. Nevertheless teachers should also be aware of the positive virtues of 'true friends'; many words do share almost the same meanings in different languages and can provide a valuable prop for the student.

A question that has often been asked by psychologists is whether the L2 user has two mental dictionaries or one. Research into the processing of semantic meaning showed that people take about the same time to say whether a 'table' is 'furniture' in their L1 as in their L2 (Caramazza and Brones, 1980). Hence they would seem to have one mental store of words. Other research has shown, however, that speed of mental access to a word is helped by hearing another word in the same language rather than a word in the speaker's other language (Kirsner *et al.*, 1980). This suggests that the two dictionaries are separate in the mind. So the simple question about one dictionary or two at the moment is unanswerable. One suggestion is that there are indeed two separate underlying stores of knowledge but that they interact during speech processing in ways that are not under the speaker's control.

VOCABULARY AND TEACHING

Teaching the complexity of word meaning

One consequence of L2 vocabulary research for teaching is that L2 learning of vocabulary is not just learning a word once and for all but learning the range of meanings that go with it. The problems associated with going from the first language to the second are not just the transfer of the actual words but also the relationships and overtones they carry in the L1. As an English speaker, I cannot conceive how 'postpone' and 'reject' could be the same word in another language. Most uses of vocabulary in textbooks imply that words have single meanings: books that have vocabulary lists usually give single word translations. The German course *English for You* (Graf, 1983), for instance, lists one translation for 'bar' (Bar) and one for 'write' (schreiben), where many might be necessary.

A traditional teaching technique was the memorizing of wordlists. A recent variant is the psychology-inspired 'mnemnotechnics' technique in which students acquire L2 words by associating them with incongruous images or sounds in the L1 – the French 'hérisson' (hedgehog) is remembered through an image of the English sound-alike 'hairy son' (Gruneberg, 1987). However, it is doubtful if many words one learns in this way will form part of one's active vocabulary. I have been waiting since school days for the opportunity to use the French word 'la jubé' (roodloft), memorized for a vocabulary test, but I have never yet seen a roodloft, let alone had anything to say about one. Teaching has, unfortunately, often counted items rather than meanings. The textbook *Break into English* (Carrier *et al.*, 1985) indeed has 900 lexical items – but how many meanings per word? Going against this tradition, the *COBUILD English Course I* (Willis and Willis, 1987) makes a point of listing a range of meanings for a word, five for 'heavy', and six for 'so', to take two words from Book 1.

Putting words in structures

An aspect of vocabulary that has become important in recent years is the position of the word in the structure of the sentence. For example, the verb 'faint' can only occur with a grammatical subject such as 'Martin' in 'Martin fainted', never with an object 'Martin fainted John'. The verb 'meet' on the other hand has to have an object 'He met John', not 'He met'. Some verbs are followed by subordinate clauses: 'I hoped Mary would go' rather than grammatical objects 'I hoped Mary'. A speaker of English knows not just what a word means and how it is pronounced but also how it fits into sentences. The Universal Grammar model of language acquisition, to be described in Chapter 8, claims that learning how each word behaves in sentences is crucial. Maurice Gross (1990) found 12,000 'simple' verbs in French of which no two could be used in exactly the same way in sentences. While there is no L2 research on the links between vocabulary and syntax of this type as yet, nevertheless teaching cannot ignore that the student has to learn not just the meaning and pronunciation of each word, but how to use it. One simple way of doing this is the traditional task of getting the students to make up sentences using particular words. For example, in *Reward* (Greenall, 1994) students are given a box containing verbs such as 'accept', 'drink' and 'sit' and are asked to 'write sentences about hospitality in your country'. The focus on a situational context makes the exercise more relevant and at the same time allows the student to use the words productively in the syntactic context of a particular sentence .

L2 LEARNING OF VOCABULARY

Components theory:

The meanings of words break up into components, which are learnt separately.

Word associations:

These fall into three types:

- klang: rhyming words, *blue > shoe*
- syntagmatic: continues a structure, *blue > sky*
- paradigmatic: chooses word from same word type, *blue > red*

Prototype theory:

Basic terms ('potato') are learnt before subordinate ('Idaho potato') and superordinate terms ('vegetable').

Depth of processing:

The type of practice counts more than frequency.

Transfer of meaning:

Transfer from the L1 is caused by two factors:

- closeness to base meaning
- frequency of occurrence

Mental dictionaries:

It is unclear whether L2 learners have one or two dictionaries in their minds.

Teaching uses:

- basic level words should be taught first
- some words may be taught through components of meaning
- it is how the word is practised not how often, that is important
- remember students transfer L1 meanings as well as the words themselves: teaching should not separate words from their structural context

---

3 Acquisition of conversational discourse

KEYWORDS

interactive discourse: spontaneous language with give-and-take
listener-related talk: language for 'chat' and maintenance of social life
information-related talk: language for transfer of information
discourse move: here used for the speaker's choice of what to do in the conversation, e.g. opening moves such as 'greeting'
adjacency pair: a pair of discourse moves that often go together, e.g. question and answer
language function: the reason why someone says something, e.g. apologizing, arguing, greeting, etc.

INTERACTION IN DISCOURSE

Normally sentences are not said in isolation but spoken in a particular situation. They do not mean much without knowing how the successive sentences are linked together, and how they relate to the situation. In one sense 'discourse' concerns how the participants influence each other while talking. They interrupt, they ask for more information, they adapt what they are saying, but they cannot take back what they have said, even if they can try and say it again. Henri Holec (1985b) calls this *interactive discourse* as there is a give-and-take between the participants. Hence interactive discourse usually occurs in speech rather than writing. But language can also consist of connected speech or writing that has been prepared and gone over, so that the sequence in which it was first devised is not the same as the sequence in which it is encountered. Usually this is written language, for instance, a set of instructions on how to work a video-recorder, but sometimes it may be prepared speech such as talks or lectures. This is 'non-interactive' discourse in Holec's terms in that the reader or listener cannot affect what happens.

A related distinction made by Gillian Brown and her colleagues (1984) is between *listener-related* talk and *information-related* talk. Listener-related talk – 'chat' – forms the basis of social life. People talk to each other to maintain social relationships. Information-related talk, however, has the purpose of transferring information from speaker to listener. It might be a doctor directing a nurse how to treat a patient, or a passenger telling a cab-driver where to go, or a teacher imparting information in a classroom. While both listener-related and information-related talk are usually interactive in Holec's terms, perhaps only information-related talk can be non-interactive.

Brown and her colleagues also draw attention to an important difference between short and long turns at speaking. Speaking at length poses quite different problems from saying one or two sentences. As they put it, 'students who are only capable of producing short turns are going to experience a lot of frustration when they try to speak the foreign language'. Native speakers too need training in various aspects of discourse. The ability to follow non-interactive discourse or to produce long turns may be vital aspects of mother-tongue teaching. The L2 teaching problems differ according to whether the students are capable of doing these in their first language or not.

This chapter deals chiefly with discourse in the interactive listener-related sense; information aspects of discourse are discussed in the next chapter, and classroom discourse in Chapter 6.

DISCOURSE MOVES IN CONVERSATION

If two people are talking, each of them has a choice of what to say and how to say it. There are certain opening moves for the conversation that can be chosen, then a choice of follow-up moves, a further choice of conversational moves linked to these, and so on until the final exchange that ends the conversation. So a conversation might start with ritualistic greetings:

A: *Hello, John.*
B: *Hello, Mary.*

Then one speaker broaches a topic of conversation, which continues for a while:

A: *Have you heard about Brian?*
B: *No? What's happened?*
A: *Oh he's gone off to Australia.*
B: *How amazing!*

The conversation continues till the speakers signal a close:

A: *Well I'd better be off now. Good-bye.*
B: *Cheerio.*

Some of these exchanges are as predictable as the steps in a waltz. If one person says a greeting – 'Hello' – the other has to say a greeting in return – 'Hello'. Other exchanges come in *adjacency pairs* with straightforward linguistic connections between the moves. A question 'What's happened?' has to be followed by an answer such as 'He's gone off to Australia'. Other connections are less obvious; a move that gives information – 'He's gone off to Australia' – calls for a polite reaction 'How amazing!' Much of conversation is made up of such pairs of moves: greeting and reply, question and answer, statement and reaction. Some psychologists such as Bruner (1983) have suggested that a child learns the first language through such routines. One example is the peekaboo game that parents play in many countries – hiding an object and then making it appear while crying 'boo'. Mothers gradually develop this routine so that the child takes part in increasingly complex sequences of moves. The child is learning how to build up structures of interaction in which language becomes steadily more important. Conversational interaction is vital for children, not just for the moves themselves that they are learning, but for the grammatical rules and lexical items they are using in the moves – for the way they learn all the components of language through interaction. The components of language are learnt through the moves of conversation.

Much of this knowledge of interaction is transferred from the first language. Knowing how to construct a conversation in one language means it can be done in another, to some extent. Languages do not differ over the moves themselves so much as over what makes up the moves. We all greet each other; we all ask questions and provide answers; but we do so differently in different languages. The main difficulty in going from one language to another is conventions over politeness. Germans prefer more direct ways of making a request than such indirect English forms as 'Could you tell me the way to the station please?' Japanese consider it polite not to disagree with the speaker.

Evelyn Hatch (1978) has advocated an approach to L2 learning based on *conversation analysis*: the analysis of conversations between native and non-native speakers. One of her examples is a telephone conversation between a native speaker and a foreign student called Pauline who is trying to get her thesis typed:

NATIVE: *Which university is it for?*
PAULINE: *Yes I have a more 100.*
NATIVE: *Pardon me?*
PAULINE: *I have more 100 pages.*
NATIVE: *Yes but is it for UCLA? Or USC?*
PAULINE: *UCLA.*
NATIVE: *I see. Well is it typed?.*

Conversation analysis sees the moves of conversation as closely linked to the topic of discussion. The prime need is for the participants to make clear what they are talking about. One opening move is *topic nomination*, when the speaker tries to establish the topic of conversation: 'Which university is it for?' The other participant has to acknowledge the topic, perhaps incorrectly: 'Yes I have a more 100'. When things go wrong, as they obviously do here, the speaker resorts to *topic clarification* to make the topic clear: 'Pardon me?' Other conversational moves are *priming*, where the non-native tries to get help from the native: 'The how you say year'; and *repairs*, where the non-native corrects herself: 'He's got a bar, a car'.

TEACHING CONVERSATIONAL DISCOURSE

The art of conversation is keeping this channel of communication open so that everyone knows what they are talking about. In native to non-native conversations the native uses more topic clarification moves than usual because of the increased unintelligibility of L2 speech. The non-native needs particular moves for stating topics unambiguously and for making certain they are continuing to be understood. While all these indeed occur from time to time in native-to-native speech, the proportions of each move inevitably change in conversations involving non-native speakers. Cook (1985) found, for instance, that non-native speakers are more formal and polite than native speakers when making requests from strangers and when thanking them. They tend to say 'Thank you very much' rather than 'Thanks', for example, regardless of whom they are speaking to. Porter (1986) compared natives and non-natives on the same discussion tasks. The non-natives had a smaller repertoire of ways of expressing themselves, for example, not using the past tense for giving their opinions, and expressing disagreement directly rather than through face-saving 'hedges'.

The fact that conversation consists of moves and the idea that learning takes place through conversational moves can come together in teaching. My own beginners book *People and Places* (Cook, 1980) used a teaching exercise called a 'conversational exchange'. The students, for example, are shown pictures of various clothes; they hear model conversations showing two conversational moves, stating opinion and reacting:

JENNY: *Joe's suit is very nice.*
EDNA: *Is it?*
JENNY: *Peter's jeans are horrible.*
EDNA: *Are they?*

Then they have to supply Edna's side of the conversation for a few exchanges, working out the appropriate answer according to their opinion of the clothes. Finally the students supply both sides of the conversation. The basic concept was indeed that learning takes place through interaction in limited exchanges: conversation is taught as linked conversational moves. As soon as possible in each exercise, the students have to choose which expression to use and have to fit it into the situation meaningfully. They are going through a learning sequence through practising a series of moves.

Conversational analysis comes close to some communicative teaching through its belief that second languages are learnt under the pressure of conversation. Interacting with other people through a series of conversational moves is not just what the learners are aiming at: it is the actual means of learning. But the concept of a 'move' outlined here is not quite the same as the idea of 'function' in most communicative teaching, which is usually concerned with functions such as 'arguing' or 'apologizing' that might occur in several different conversational moves. Topic nomination, on the other hand, is a move that may be expressed through several different functions: asking, requesting, stating, and so on. It is part of the structure of discourse rather than an isolated item to be learnt. Functions have mostly been put into lists – arguing, complaining, thanking – rather than seen as interlinked discourse moves. The teacher using a communicative method should perhaps remember that functions never occur by themselves but always in a sequence of conversational moves. However, as with the rest of this chapter, the L2 research base for interactive discourse is fairly narrow. While there are many lists of communicative functions for teaching and many accounts of the gaps that L1 children and L2 learners have in their knowledge, hardly any research has dealt with the crucial relationship between such descriptions and the actual process of L2 learning, vital as this is to its teaching application.

L2 LEARNING OF CONVERSATIONAL DISCOURSE

- L2 learners acquire language by engaging in conversations (*conversation analysis*).
- Students may transfer many aspects of this from the L1.

Teaching uses:

- Students often need to be trained to take long 'turns'.
- Students who need interactive discourse need to be taught how to take part in conversations.
- Language 'functions' should not be practised in isolation but always within the structure of discourse.

Let us draw out one particular theme, not just of this chapter but also of the last, namely the description of the language content of teaching. Most language teaching has relied on a tradition of language description all of its own, in the case of English going back to the work of Harold Palmer in grammar in the 1920s and the pronunciation work of Daniel Jones even earlier. While fashions in language teaching methodology and syllabuses come and go, the same versions of language continue to be used. One message is then that language teachers need to be aware of modern descriptions of language, whether the ideas of grammatical parameters mentioned in the last chapter or of phonological features and semantic components covered in this chapter. Teachers need to look more closely at what language *is*, not what the language teaching profession or course books *say* it is, based on no more than their say-so and the tradition of seventy years. And they should remember that, at best, the descriptions that are available are those of native speakers, not of the multicompetent user of two languages.

DISCUSSION TOPICS

1. How would *you* carry out integrated pronunciation teaching?
2. What aspects of pronunciation do you consider are (a) the most important and (b) the most teachable?

3. Take a lesson or a page from the textbook you are most familiar with: what new words are taught and how?
4. To what extent do you think that we can learn the words of another language without learning a new way of thinking to go with them?
5. How do you think the words for teaching should be selected and sequenced?
6. What is the balance between students' needs for interactive versus non-interactive discourse and for listener-related versus information-related discourse? What can the teacher do about this?
7 To what extent does the teaching of conversation you are familiar with concentrate on moves and/or functions? Should it?

FURTHER READING

Few readily accessible treatments of the areas covered in this chapter exist. Of the technical books and articles referred to, good collections on phonology and vocabulary respectively are: James and Leather (1986), *Sound Patterns In Second Language Acquisition*, Schreuder and Weltens (1993), *The Bilingual Lexicon*, and a good introduction to transfer is Odlin (1989), *Language Transfer*. Kenworthy (1987), *Teaching English Pronunciation*, provides a readable and trustworthy account of pronunciation for teachers. An interesting book with many exercises for vocabulary teaching is Lewis (1993), *The Lexical Approach*. Readers are, however, warned that most books claiming specifically to be about the teaching of vocabulary or phonology are not based on a scientific account of what native speakers actually know and have no contact with accounts of how people learn, interesting as they may be in their own right.

4

Processes in using second languages

So far this book has dealt chiefly with the learner's *knowledge* of language in various shapes and forms, that is to say, what linguists term their *competence*. This is not of much avail without the ability to understand or produce speech or writing, what linguists call *performance*. People may know they want to say something, and have the grammar, the vocabulary, and the sounds to say it with, but this knowledge is useless if they cannot actually say or comprehend anything. This chapter examines five areas of performance related to L2 learning and using. Some aspects of memory and language and cognitive processing are involved in both L1 and L2 processing, other aspects such as codeswitching between languages are unique to L2 use, some aspects such as communication strategies are the subject of dispute as to whether they are unique to L2 learning or shared.

Focusing questions

Short term memory:

1. Do you think a good memory is helpful in learning an L2?
2. How do you think memory is involved in the L2 classroom?
3. Are there any mental tasks that you feel uncomfortable with in an L2, say mental arithmetic, writing a diary, praying, etc?

Reading:

4. What do you think are the typical elements involved in going to an English restaurant?
5. What do you think are the main aims in an English academic essay?

Listening:

6. When you listen to something in an L2 do you try to work out the meaning of every word or are you content with the gist?

7. Do you believe listening comes before or after speaking in the sequence of teaching the language skills?

Codeswitching:

8. Do you consider that students should ever switch languages in mid-sentence?

Communication strategies:

9. How would you explain to someone the type of gadget you need to repair your car? Would your strategy be different in the L1 or the L2?
10. Should students have to talk about things for which they do not know the words or should they always have the vocabulary available to them?

---

1 Short-term memory processes

KEYWORDS

short-term memory (STM): the memory used for keeping information for periods of time up to a few seconds

working memory: the memory system used for holding and manipulating information while various mental tasks are carried out (Baddeley, 1986)

articulatory loop: the means by which information is kept in working memory by being audibly or silently articulated

cognitive deficit: the limitations on processing information in a second language

Memory to most people probably means remembering information for long periods. You have a good memory if you are able to recall people's names, or dates in history. However, memory plays a much wider role in language use. Anything that is stored in the mind for any length of time, whether seconds or decades, involves some form of memory. In this sense memory is involved in all aspects of the processing of the sentence.

Take a sentence: 'Unix has affected about every computer now being used.' Reading it from left to right, your eye has moved several times in getting from 'Unix' to 'used'; the earlier parts of the sentence have to be stored in your memory while you are getting to the later parts. This is even more true of the spoken language where you cannot cheat by looking back at the beginning of the sentence. Listening to: 'Once upon a time there were three bears who lived in a cottage in the forest' you have to remember the beginning 'once upon a time' while processing the middle 'three bears' before getting to the end 'in the forest'. All of the sentence has somehow to be kept in your mind in order to get at the complete meaning. Listeners remember the beginning of the sentence while processing the end, they retrieve the patterns and meanings of words from their memory and they work out the relationship of the sentence to its context from information in their memory; they store the meaning of the sentence in their memory so that they can recall it seconds or years later. The different types of information in the sentence have to be processed in different ways and at different levels of memory.

Before reading the next section, carry out a short test on yourself. Here are some phone numbers; look at each and then look away and try to remember it.

(a) 561386
(b) 206872212
(c) 01818025099

Probably you had few problems with (a) which is six digits long, slightly more problems with (b) which is nine, and may not have managed (c) at all, which is eleven. Most people can remember about seven digits in the first language, varying slightly according to the exact way in which their span is tested and according to other factors. Despite this, British Telecom has now extended the UK phone numbers so that eleven is indeed the norm, even if some of the digits in the code such as 01 are predictable.

Digit span is then a reflection of the key memory processes of short-term memory (STM): the processing of information for periods of time up to a few seconds. Information is stored in STM quite briefly, and is then usually forgotten. Can you remember any of the phone numbers now without looking back?

In a second language, memory span is reduced. Glicksberg (1963) found that L2 learners' span in English improved from 6.4 digits at the beginning of an eight-week course up to 6.7 at the end. At the end of the course the students' spans were still below those of native speakers, who scored 7.1 digits on his test. My own STM tests found that L2 learners at an early stage of English could remember 5.9 digits on average (Cook, 1977). At an advanced level, they could remember 6.7. So there was an initial shortfall of 2.1 digits from the 8 digits that natives scored on my test (Fig. 4.1).

While this difference is not very great, it is nevertheless important. L2

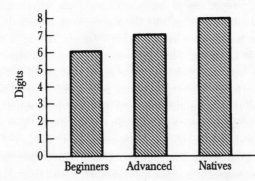

Fig. 4.1 Short-term memory spans in adult EFL learners (Cook, 1977)

learners' spans increased as their English improved, yet they were still slightly below the native speaker normal span even at advanced stages. Later research tested the STM of English schoolchildren learning French in both the L1 and the L2 (Cook, 1979). At about the age of 12 their span was 7.5 digits in English, 4.7 in French. By 14 their spans were 8.2 in English and 5.4 in French. While the students' span is improving in French, it is also improving in English. But at each stage there is a gap between their spans for English and French (Fig. 4.2).

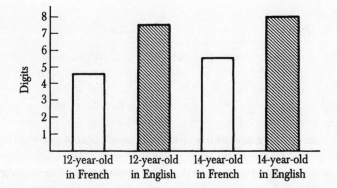

Fig. 4.2 Short-term memory spans in schoolboy French learners (Cook, 1979)

WORKING MEMORY AND THE ARTICULATORY LOOP

The question is: what stops us remembering more than seven or eight digits in our L1 and fewer than that in the L2? Gathercole and Baddeley (1993) have put forward a theory which accounts for aspects of STM called 'working memory'. This consists of a 'central executive', which controls how information is passed around the memory system in the mind, and visual and phonological 'slave systems' controlled by the executive. Working memory is used for processing information while the mind works on various tasks. The phonological system has a phonological store from which information tends to fade within a second or two. To extend its life people repeat things over and over, whether aloud or silently. They are articulating the sounds of the words, even if they do not say them. To keep the information in working memory from fading it must be constantly repeated. This continual repetition is called the articulatory loop; information is recycled back through the store to extend its life (Fig. 4.3). Whatever you are trying to remember circulates round this loop. The speed with which information travels round the loop governs how much can be remembered. That is to say, the faster a person can repeat things the more they can remember. Memory span is restricted by speed of articulation. This has several fascinating consequences for language processing. Fewer long words can be remembered than short words: it is easier to remember 'Chad, Burma, Greece, Cuba, Malta' than 'Czechoslovakia, Somaliland, Nicaragua, Afghanistan,

Fig. 4.3 Articulatory loop theory of working memory (simplified)

Yugoslavia'. Fast speakers have better spans than slow speakers, everything else being equal. Furthermore, there are differences between languages caused by the different ways they are processed in the articulatory loop: speakers of Chinese (with short digits) have better memory span than speakers of English, who in turn have better spans than speakers of Welsh (with longer digits); Chinese speakers, with a memory of 9.9 digits, are able to remember telephone numbers better than English speakers.

Working memory is not therefore an independent part of the mind but is related to pronunciation and to language use. Baddeley regards working memory as a historical by-product of the use of language. Human beings would not have an articulatory loop if they did not have language. Using an L2 means learning how to process information for a second time to the extent that working memory depends upon the first language. Gordon Brown and I found that speed of speaking in English schoolboys learning French was related to working memory span in the two languages. The causes of smaller span in an L2 might then be found in several places in the model: the central executive might be less efficient at encoding speech, as suggested by Service (1992) based on Finnish children learning English; the articulatory loop might have slower articulation so that less words can be said, as Papagno and Vallar (1992) suggest on the basis of the learning of Russian by Italians; or it may be more complex with the longer-term memory also involved, as Brown and Hulme (1992) point out.

TEACHING AND WORKING MEMORY

STM involvement in classroom activities

Working memory is involved in everyday performance in second language use and in the classroom. The restrictions on the learner's ability to speak the language are caused just as much by memory limits as by the difficulty of the syntax, vocabulary, and so on. A Cambridge university lecturer once told me that the acid test of whether a candidate deserved a scholarship in modern languages was how long a sentence he or she could repeat in the L2. If the mind cannot handle enough words, it is impossible to actually process speech. The articulatory loop theory suggests this is linked to fluency of pronunciation. Audiolingual teaching sets great store on the students' pronunciation. Communicative teaching by and large has concentrated on fluency without paying any special attention to pronunciation. Those who emphasize listening as the core skill postpone pronunciation and production in general till the student is ready for it. But training students to speak swiftly and accurately may have helpful side effects on their working memory and hence on their general ability to process language.

Ubiquitousness of working memory

The second consequence for teaching is the realization that everything the student does or says in the L2 is related in some way to STM. Even asking the students to repeat an L2 sentence is a test of their L2 memory, let alone asking them to comprehend it. So far this chapter has discussed the span for unconnected digits. Memory for sentences is restricted by factors other than the sheer number of words. Different syntactic structures place different demands on the memory processes. Baddeley (1986) showed that passive sentences take longer to understand than active sentences and that they use up more space in working memory. Part of the difficulty in comprehending L2 syntax is the load it puts on the student's memory.

The status of pronunciation

In language teaching pronunciation has been seen as having to do with sounds, as we saw in the last chapter. It has been a fairly neglected area compared to the interest in functions, grammar, etc. Provided the learner is understandable in the major phonemes of the language, there is no need to worry about finer points. The working memory theory, however, sees pronunciation as vital to language processing. If we cannot say the sounds quickly, our short-term memory span will be very restricted and consequently we will face severe difficulties with the processing of language. The neglect of pronunciation in recent years has hampered, not just the students' ability to pronounce words, but also their fundamental capacity to process the language. We should then take pronunciation much more seriously.

One entertaining, though speculative, conclusion for language teaching is that the theory predicts that performance in the language can improve according to how fast the students can speak. Hence we should try to get them to speak faster! I indeed once wrote a computer program called *Speedup* with this aim: students' L2 span and reading speed were measured; then they had to read sentences aloud from the screen, starting below their normal speed and getting faster and faster; finally they were tested to see whether their span had improved. This was intended as an entertaining computer game rather than a serious teaching exercise, yet the principle involved may well be right.

In some sense teachers have always been aware of the restrictions on working memory. Two colleagues and I had a rule of thumb for writing structure drills, which was that the student's answer should never be more than fifteen syllables long. We were putting an intuitive limit to the demands on the student's memory. Teachers giving dictation similarly split the text up into the phrases or chunks they think the students' memories can handle. Teaching that takes account of memory limitations will certainly be more effective.

COGNITIVE DEFICIT IN L2 USE

Such restrictions are examples of the more general fact that cognitive processes work less efficiently through the second language. Magiste (1979) measured how fast German-speaking children learning Swedish in Sweden carried out production tasks such as naming pictures, and comprehension tasks such as 'Mark the third letter from the left'. After a year in Sweden the comprehension tasks took about twice as long in the L2 as in the L1 and the production tasks about three times as long. Only after 4–6 years for production and 4–5 years for comprehension did the students become as quick in Swedish as in German. It thus took several years to attain the same ease in the L2 as in the L1, even though they had been living in the country where it was spoken. Younger children, however, managed this switch more quickly.

The same restrictions on cognitive processes in an L2 are found in other tasks. If L2 learners are asked to count flashes of light from a bulb for two seconds, they underestimate them more in the L2 than in the L1 (Dornic, 1969). People are worse at mental arithmetic in their second language than in their first (Marsh and Maki, 1978). The task I have tried myself with L2 learners is 'digit counting'; you get people to count from one to a hundred in their first and second language using digits, i.e. ten is 'one ough', 11 is 'one one' etc. Then you get them to count *backwards* from a hundred down to one. In the first language the few mistakes fall into a clear pattern: planning mistakes – leaving out the ten numbers 90, 80, etc. while they are planning the next ten, and phonological mistakes, leaving out numbers which repeat the same digit twice – 99, 88, 77, etc. (due to the articulatory loop getting confused). In the second language the same kinds of mistakes occur, but more of them and it takes longer. And if you try it with L2 learners you will learn some surprising facts about different languages: Japanese speakers insist on being told what they are counting and have problems with the number 4 because it has two forms, one of which unluckily is the same as the word for death; French speakers find it almost impossible to count backwards in high numbers, presumably because the normal form of the numbers is a multiplication of 20s and teens – 95 is 'quatre-vingt-quinze' (four twenties and fifteen) – which would be highly complex to do backwards.

In general then the mind is less efficient in an L2, whatever it is doing; there is an L2 'cognitive deficit', as it is sometimes called. Indeed this deficit has often been used to tell which of a bilingual's languages is dominant. Not that this deficit is enough to matter in most real-world tasks. And it is a small price to pay for the ability to use another language.

Memory is also related to the learner's age. Memory processes develop as the child matures rather than being fully present from the beginning. So the way that a child handles information in an L2 is different from that of an adult. For example STM capacity in the L1 was said earlier to be related to pronunciation and to the articulatory loop. This should have been qualified by pointing out that children under 5 do *not* use sounds in STM tasks and they do *not* repeat things to themselves in the same way as adults (Ornstein and Naus, 1978). Adult Venezuelan students of English use adult-like memory processes in English rather than child-like processes (Cook, 1981a). They carry over their adult ways of processing to a second language rather than reverting to childlike ways. Age affects the memory processes that the L2 learner can apply because the learner is at a particular stage in the development of memory; old people, for example, rely more on the articulatory loop. And the age of L2 learners varies in ways that the age of L1 children does not.

Although they are still not well understood in L2 learning, these short-term memory processes have overall implications for the classroom, even if they have been intuitively taken into account by teachers already. The things teachers ask students to do must not be beyond their cognitive capacity in the L2, which is substantially below that in their L1. I remember as a teacher asking near-beginners in English to do mental arithmetic and being shocked how bad they were at it. Cognitive deficit provides a simple explanation. Any classroom activity involves memory processes to some degree and these are restricted in the L2.

2 Reading and longer-term memory processes

KEYWORDS

schema (*pl. schemas or schemata*): the background knowledge on which the interpretation of a text depends
script: 'a predetermined stereotyped sequence of actions that defines a well-known situation' (Schank and Abelson, 1977)

Reading is also a cognitive process that is restricted in the L2. Reading, like speaking, occurs in a context rather than in isolation. The meaning of a text is

---

L2 LEARNING, SHORT-TERM MEMORY, AND WORKING MEMORY

- The span of L2 learners is more restricted in the L2 than in their L1.
- STM span increases as L2 learners develop.
- Working memory span in the L2 is related to how fast people can speak.
- L2 users have a 'cognitive deficit' which makes many of their mental processes work slightly less well in the L2.

Teaching uses:

- Remember that all teaching activities involve an STM load as well as a language load.
- Pronunciation teaching may benefit students' STM span.
- Do not expect students to cope with L2 tasks with the same ease that they can mange L1 tasks, even when these do not appear to involve language.

---

not found just in the sentences themselves, but is derived from the previous knowledge stored in the reader's mind and the processes through which the reader tackles it. I look out of my window and see an empty road, as anybody else would do sitting in the same position. However, to me the emptiness means my wife has gone out, since the family car is not there, to my son it means the bus for school has not yet arrived, to my daughter it means the postman is late. The same scene is interpreted in different ways according to our background information and predilections.

SCHEMA THEORY

A famous experiment by Bransford and Johnson (1982) asked people to read texts such as the following:

> The procedure is actually quite simple. First you arrange things into different groups depending on their makeup. Of course, one pile may be sufficient depending on how much there is to do. If you have to go somewhere else due to lack of facilities that is the next step, otherwise you are pretty well set. It is important not to overdo any particular endeavour. That is, it is better to do too few things at once than too many.

To make sense of this text a particular piece of information is required: the passage is about washing clothes. A person who does not have this information does not get much out of the text. If the topic is known, the passage is straightforward and the comprehension level is much higher. The sentences themselves do not change when we know the topic, but the interpretation they have in our minds does. The background knowledge into which a text fits, sometimes called the schema, plays a large role in how it is read.

L2 readers too need to know what the passage is about. Adams (1983) gave American students of French the same texts as Bransford and Johnson and tested whether they were better or worse at learning new vocabulary when they were told what the passage was about. Her results showed first that they were better at learning vocabulary in the first language, and second that knowing what the passage was about helped them equally in both languages. Hence this kind of background knowledge is relevant to both L1 and L2 processing. Patricia Carrell (1984) tested L2 learners of English with the same Bransford and Johnson texts to see not only whether the presence or absence of context made a difference to how much they could understand, but also the importance of whether the text had precise words like 'clothes' and 'washing machine', or vague words like 'things' and 'facilities'. Both advanced learners and natives once again found lack of context affected their comprehension. However, intermediate L2 learners also found the use of vague words was a hindrance. The provision of context varied in importance according to the stage of L2 learning. At the early stages of L2 learning, linguistic aspects of the words are as important to understanding as context. One interesting side effect of Carrell's research was that, while native speakers had a fair idea of how difficult the passages were for them to understand, non-natives did not! However, later research by Roller and Matombo (1992) interestingly did not get the same results: speakers of Shona actually remembered more of the Bransford and Johnson texts in English than in their first language.

'SCRIPTS' AND DISCOURSE

A crucial element in the understanding of discourse was given the name of *script* by Roger Schank in the 1970s (Schank and Abelson, 1977). The concept of the script came out of attempts to build computer programs that would understand human languages. The problem was that the computer did not know obvious things that human beings take for granted. Suppose a text reads, 'Bill had some hamburgers in a restaurant.' Straightforward as this sentence seems, our understanding of it relies on several unconscious assumptions about restaurants. What did Bill do with the hamburgers? He ate them, because that is what you go to restaurants for. Did he cook the hamburgers? Of course he did not. Did he fetch them himself? Probably not. Did Bill pay for them? Of course he did. In our minds there is a script for restaurants that specifies that they are places where they supply you with food that you pay for. None of this information needs to be given in the text as our minds supply it automatically. Only if the actual event does *not* conform with our background knowledge for restaurants will it be mentioned – if it is self-service, if they have run out of food, or if Bill sneaks out without paying his bill. The mind supplies such information automatically from the background script in its memory. A script is then, according to Schank and Abelson (1977), 'a predetermined, stereotyped sequence of actions that defines a well-known situation'. While in recent years Schank has developed his ideas beyond this, nevertheless the script has been a very influential view of how memory is organized.

Some scripts are virtually the same for speakers of different languages; others differ from one country to another. The script for eating-out may require all restaurants to have waitress-service, or to be takeaway, or to have cash desks by the exit or other variations. I remember once arguing that American hotels are not proper hotels because they have large entrance lobbies rather than cosy lounge areas; my British script for hotels implies lounges. Wherever there are such differences between two scripts, the L2 learners will be at a loss. They unwittingly have different expectations and they have an unpleasant shock when something turns out differently. A self-service restaurant that calls for payment in advance by naming the dishes you want can be an unpleasant trial for visitors to Italy! Or indeed the script may be totally absent; I have no script for a Finnish sauna. Many of the stereotyped problems of foreign travel that people recount show conflicts between scripts – eating sheeps' eyes, loos for mixed sexes, tipping taxidrivers, asking if food tastes good, all are absent from the scripts in particular cultures. An example can be found in the script for doctor/patient interaction (Ranney, 1993): English-speaking patients expect to ask questions of the doctor, Hmong patients do not; English speakers prefer to talk to the doctor informally, Hmong speakers prefer to show respect.

An important aspect of discourse is how the background information contributed by the script relates to the purposes of conversation. Say someone is attempting to book a plane ticket in a travel agent's. The participants have their own ideas of what they expect to get out of the conversation; the travel agent needs to know what information he needs to find out and then how to ask the customer to supply it. There is an expected framework of information necessary for the task of booking a ticket to be accomplished. The customer has to supply bits of information to fit this framework. Both participants are combining background knowledge of what goes on in a travel agent's with the specific goal of booking a ticket – almost a definition of communicative teaching!

SCRIPTS AND SCHEMA THEORY IN TEACHING

Carrell (1983) has produced a set of recommendations for language teachers, based on her own research and that of others. She points to the importance of vocabulary, revealed in her experiments with tests outlined earlier. The L2 learner needs to be supplied with the vocabulary that the native takes for granted. Carrell also sees teaching as building up the learner's background knowledge. Thus she stresses pre-reading activities that build up background knowledge, partly through providing them with appropriate vocabulary through activities such as word association practice. The techniques she suggests develop processing strategies for the text, such as flow-charting or diagramming activities. Materials should not only be interesting, but also be conceptually complete; a longer passage or an in-depth set of passages on a single topic is better than short unconnected passages.

Perhaps none of these ideas will be completely new to the practising teacher. Reading materials have after all been stressing content and background for some time. Pre-reading exercises are now standard. Communicatively oriented reading tasks meet many of her requirements. In the textbook *Reasons for Reading* (Davies and Whitney, 1979), for example, a unit on 'Persuasion' starts by setting the context firmly in a restaurant with a specimen menu and conversation and by practising vocabulary for good and bad, for food, and so on. It goes on to develop the students' interpretation of advertisements for Oxford marmalade and for Sealink ferries. All the desirable ingredients seem to be there even if the balance and overall sequence are slightly different.

The benefit for the teacher is an increased awareness of the difficulties that L2 learners face with texts. These are not just a product of the processing of the text itself but of the background information that natives automatically read into it. L2 learners have 'cognitive deficits' with reading that are not caused by lack of language ability but by difficulties with processing information in an L2. Even at advanced levels, L2 learners still cannot get as much out of a text as in their first language, even if on paper they know all the grammar and vocabulary. Cambridge university students tested by Long and Harding-Esch (1977), for example, not only remembered less information from political speeches in French than in English but also added more false information! Furthermore advanced L2 learners still read their second language much more slowly than they read their first (Favreau and Segalowitz, 1982). The problem with reading is not just the language but the whole process of getting meaning from texts.

The importance of background information through scripts and similar mental structures is much wider than the area of reading. The processing of written texts is distinctive in that the reader has to depend only on his or her own script. In speaking, someone else is usually there to help or hinder by interacting with the speaker in one way or another. As with pronunciation, reading involves important low-level processes as well as high-level comprehension. The discussion here has not been about the teaching of reading itself, i.e. literacy, but about teaching L2 students to read in a new language, which is a rather different issue. The actual literacy skills become important either when the L2 learners cannot read in their own language or when the writing system of their L1 is very different. Chinese learners of English have one type of problem in that Chinese uses characters which have no relationship to the spoken form. Greek or Russian learners of English have another set of problems in that the letters are different, rather than the system. Many other

L2 learners have problems in that English writing is further from the spoken form than that in their first languages, say Italian.

A particular problem for L2 students occurs in the use of academic language. Never mind the language problems, think of the schemas. Ruqaiya Hasan once pointed out that the crucial problem for the non-native student studying in an English setting is what counts as knowledge: one culture may prize the views of well-known authorities; another the views of the individual student. So the schema for an essay may be a collection of quotations strung together in a fairly arbitrary order; or it may be a personal argument built up from existing sources. One of the main problems for the non-native speaker of English studying in England who has previously studied in other academic systems is the nature of what an essay is, not so much the grammatical structures, vocabulary, and so on. In my own experience this is true of students coming from Greece, Iran and Hong Kong, to take a random sample.

L2 LEARNING, READING, AND MEMORY PROCESSES

- Knowledge of conventional situations (scripts) is important to L2 use.
- Background knowledge (schemata) is important to L2 learners.
- Use of 'vague words' hinders lower level learners.

Teaching uses:

- Build up students' background knowledge.
- Vocabulary should be emphasized in the teaching of texts.
- Allow for students' inherent loss of efficiency in processing the L2.

---

3 Processes in listening

KEYWORDS

parsing: the process through which the mind works out the grammatical structure and meaning of the sentence

top-down and *bottom-up*: starting from the sentence as a whole and working down to the smallest parts of it, versus starting from the smallest parts and working up

decoding versus *codebreaking*: processing language to get the 'message' versus processing language to get the 'rules'

Guides to the teaching of listening appear almost every year; some textbooks are aimed specifically at listening, others include listening components. Yet there is little L2 research concerned with the process of listening as part of the speaker's use of language. Listening does not even figure as a topic in most introductions to L2 learning. This section first looks briefly at the process of listening itself and then develops the use of listening as a vehicle for learning, the most discussed aspect in recent years. It will not discuss the actual processing of speech sounds, already mentioned in Chapter 3.

ELEMENTS OF LISTENING

Most introductions to the comprehension of speech stress three elements: access to vocabulary, parsing, and memory processes.

Access to words

At one level, in order to comprehend a sentence you have to work out what the words mean. The mind has to relate the words that are heard to the information that is stored about them in the mind – their meanings, etc. For example, a native speaker can answer the question 'Is the word "blish" English?' almost instantaneously, somehow working through many thousands of words in a few moments. Such feats show the human mind is extraordinarily efficient at organizing the storage of words and their interconnections. The context automatically makes particular meanings of words available to us. To a person reading a research article, the word 'table' means a layout of figures. To someone reading about antiques it means a piece of furniture. To someone reading a surveyor's report on a house it means the depth at which water appears in the ground, and so on. Somehow the context limits the amount of mental space that has to be searched to get the right meaning. Take the sentence 'The dog was run over by a bus.' As people listen to it, they are retrieving information about the words. They know that 'the' is an article used with certain meanings, here probably something to do with a dog that is already relevant to the conversation. Next 'dog' summons up the meanings of 'dog' important to this context, its relationships to other words such as 'bark' etc., and the probable other words that contrast with it or come in the same context, such as 'cat'. 'Run' connects in our mental dictionary with the verb 'run', with its range of meanings and its irregular past form, and to expectations that it is going to be followed by a noun phrase object, as we saw in Chapter 3. In addition there are the links between the L1 vocabulary and the L2 vocabulary; using a second language means accessing a more complicated mental dictionary.

Parsing

Parsing refers to how the mind works out the grammatical structure and meaning of the sentences it hears. Take a sentence such as 'The man ate breakfast.' To understand the sentence fully means being able to tell who is carrying out the action and what is affected by the action, and to realize that 'ate breakfast' goes together as a phrase while 'man ate' does not. Even if our minds are not consciously aware of the grammatical technicalities, nevertheless they are working out the structure of the sentence automatically. Grammar is not just in the back of our minds but is active while we are listening.

The process of parsing can be either 'bottom-up' or 'top-down'. 'Bottom-up' means building the sentence up in our minds bit by bit, putting the sounds into words, the words into phrases, the phrases into a whole sentence. So 'the' is put with 'man' to get a noun phrase 'the man'; 'ate' goes with 'breakfast' to get a verb phrase 'ate breakfast'; and the noun phrase 'the man' and the verb phrase 'ate breakfast' go together to yield the structure of the whole sentence. 'Top-down' parsing, on the other hand, means starting from the whole sentence and breaking it down into smaller and smaller bits. Given a sentence like 'The man ate breakfast' the top-down process tries to find a noun phrase, which in turn means trying to find first an article 'the' and then a noun 'man'. If it succeeds, it next tries to find a verb phrase, which means trying to find a verb 'ate' and a noun phrase 'breakfast'. If the quest to find a noun phrase and a verb phrase succeeds, it has found a sentence, complete with its structure.

In principle the mind could parse the sentence in either the bottom-up or the top-down direction. In practice listeners get the best of both worlds by using both types of process. Features such as the intonation pattern allow them to fit words and phrases within an overall structure, a top-down process. Particular words indicate the start of a phrase and allow them to build it up word by word, a bottom-up process. J. Michael O'Malley and his colleagues (1989) found that effective L2 learners used both top-down approaches of listening for intonation or phrases and bottom-up approaches of listening for words, while ineffective listeners concentrated on a bottom-up process. When parsing failed, they fell back on a range of other strategies, the least effective being translation.

Memory processes and cognition

The memory processes in listening are closely connected to those discussed earlier. All comprehension depends on the storing and processing of information by the mind. Call (1985), for instance, found that sheer memory for digits was less important to comprehension than memory for sentences. The extent of the memory restriction in an L2 depends upon how close the task is to language. Hence getting the students to do tasks that are not concerned with language may have less influence on their learning than language-related tasks, for example, comprehension activities using maps and diagrams may improve the learners' problem-solving abilities with map and diagrams but may be less successful at improving those aspects of the learners' mental processes that depend on language.

A further point that applies to listening as much as to reading is that vital aspects of the process are contributed by the listener. At the lowest level, the actual 'p' sounds of speech have to be worked out by the mind. While the actual sounds in 'pit', 'spit', and 'top' differ in terms of voice onset time, the English person nevertheless hears a /p/ in each of them; the listener's ear somehow imposes the idea of a /p/ on the sound waves it hears. The meaning of words such as 'bus' and 'breakfast' is not present in the sentence itself but is retrieved from the listener's mental dictionary to match the sequence of sounds that is heard. The sentence also has to be actively parsed by the listener to discover the phrases and constructions involved. As with reading, the listener's knowledge of the context of situation and background knowledge of the culture and society are crucial to listening comprehension. I once invited some overseas students to a party at eight o'clock; some of them asked me whether I meant eight in the morning or eight in the evening. Though it was not mentioned in my invitation, my cultural expectation was that parties take place in the evening. The scripts and schemas talked about in relation to reading are equally involved in listening. Our mental pictures of restaurants and stations come into play as soon as the appropriate situation is invoked. Any sentence listeners hear is matched against their mental models of the world as reflected in scripts and schemas. If the models of speaker and listener differ too much, they have problems in comprehending each other. O'Malley et al. (1989) found that effective listeners helped themselves by drawing on their knowledge of the world, or on their personal experiences, or by asking questions of themselves.

THE TEACHING OF LISTENING

How does this view of listening compare with that in teaching guides such as Mary Underwood's *Teaching Listening* (1989)? She recognizes three stages of teaching: *pre-listening*, where the students activate their vocabulary and their background knowledge, *while-listening*, where 'they develop the skill of eliciting messages', and *post-listening*, which consists of extensions and developments of the listening task. Some of the elements are similar. It is rightly considered important to get the students' background scripts working and the appropriate vocabulary active in their minds. What seems overlooked is parsing. Listeners do need to know the structure of the sentence in some way. Teaching has mostly ignored the process of syntactic parsing, perhaps because of its unwelcome overtones of grammar. But, as with reading, some attempt could be made to train both top-down and bottom-up parsing skills.

A development in the past ten years has been task-based teaching of listening. The students carry out a task in which they have to listen for information in a short piece of discourse and then have to fill in a diagram, check a route on a map or correct mistakes in a text. The *COBUILD English Course I* (Willis and Willis, 1987), for example, asks the students to listen to tapes of people speaking spontaneously and to work out information from them. Lesson 9 has a recording of Chris telling Philip how to get to his house in Birmingham. The students listen for factual information, such as which buses could be taken; they make a rough map of the route, and they check its accuracy against the A–Z map of Birmingham. One teaching motivation for this approach is the practical necessity for the teacher of checking that comprehension is taking place. Unfortunately in normal language use there is no visible feedback when someone has comprehended something. A visible sign of comprehension is useful to the teacher to see if the student has understood. This check can range from a straightforward question to an action based on what has happened. If you shout 'The room's on fire' and nobody moves, you assume they have not understood. Much teaching of listening comprehension has consisted of the student having to show some sign of having comprehended, whether through answering questions, carrying out tasks, or whatever.

The other motivation for task-based listening activities is that information is being transferred for a communicative purpose. Task-based listening stresses the transfer of information rather than the social dimension of language teaching. In the COBUILD example the student is practising something that resembles real world communication. It is sad, however, that the information that is transferred in such activities is usually about trivial topics or irrelevant to the students' lives. The factual information the students learn in the COBUILD exercise is how to get around in Birmingham, somewhere only a few of them are ever likely to go! Often such exercises deal with imaginary towns, or even treasure islands. Task-based exercises often neglect the educational value of the content that can be used in language teaching, although much psychological research shows that, the more important the information is to the listener, the more likely it is to be retained.

Such techniques do not so much teach listening as decorate the listening process with a few frills. They suggest that conscious attention to information will improve all the other aspects of listening, which is hardly justified by the research described here. If word access, parsing, and memory processes are improved by these activities, this is an accidental by-product. Perhaps listening cannot be trained directly and the best the teacher can do is devise amusing activities during which the natural listening processes can be automatically activated.

Another approach to listening, pioneered by Mary Underwood in the 1970s, relies on authentic tapes of people talking. After some introductory focusing activities, students were played the tape and then did follow-on comprehension activities. For instance, in *The Listening File* by Harmer and Ellsworth, a unit on 'The Historic MP, Diane Abbott' first makes the students think about the House of Commons and the problems that an MP might face. Then they listen to the tape and check whether their initial guesses were right; listen again and answer a series of detailed factual questions; they go on to follow-up activities in discussion and writing: almost literally a textbook example of Mary Underwood's three phases.

The use of authentic speech will be discussed later. Clearly one intention is to encourage top-down listening by getting the students to visualize an overall context for the speech before they hear it; they are nevertheless on second listening also doing some bottom-up processing in that they have to deal with specific pieces of information. One snag is that, building on the views of memory mentioned earlier, such types of teaching can shift over into testing memory rather than listening itself; if the students have to remember the content for any period longer than a handful of seconds they are being tested on what they can remember, not on what they actually understood. Of course this may be a very valuable skill, but it is not that used in ordinary listening. I once tried out the teaching materials I was using for the Cambridge First Certificate with native speakers and found that they did less well then my students. The explanation was that I had trained the students in the specific task of storing information from the text; the natives were untrained.

A further incidental problem comes back to the power struggle in conversat-ional discourse. An interview is a very specific type of speech; the interviewer is allowed to play the leader and ask all the questions but must remain neutral; the interviewee has to respond to whatever happens. I remember once seeing Danny Kaye being interviewed on television after he had arrived at London Airport; he interviewed the interviewer about why she had come to the airport and her life and opinions. Hilarious because it was the opposite of the usual convention. An interview is then a very specialized from of interaction. While all of us are passively familiar with interviews from the media, we are seldom called on to take part in them ourselves. One might ask whether listening materials should stress interviews so much as it is a rather untypical and unequal encounter. Better perhaps to use examples of genuine monologues, whether lectures or stand-up comedians; or perhaps real-life two-person encounters in more everyday settings – the supermarket, the library, and so on.

LISTENING-BASED METHODS OF TEACHING

So far listening has been taken as a process of *decoding* speech – working out the 'message' from the sentence you hear just as a spy decodes a secret message by using a code he or she already knows. However, the main focus in recent discussions of teaching methodology has been on listening as a way of *learning* language rather than as a way of *processing* language. Logically, L2 learners cannot learn a language if they never hear it; the sounds, the words, the structures, have to come from somewhere. This process can be called *codebreaking* – listening means working out the language code from the 'message' just as a cryptographer works out an unknown code from an intercepted message. Decoding speech has the aim of discovering the message using processes that are already known. Codebreaking speech has the aim of discovering the processes themselves from a message.

One of the first to interpret listening as codebreaking was James Asher's *total physical response method* (TPR) (Asher, 1986), which claimed that listening to commands and carrying them out was an effective way of learning a second language. A specimen TPR lesson reported by Asher (1986) consists of the teacher getting the students to respond to the commands:

> Walk to the window. Touch the window. Walk to the table. Touch the table. Juan, stand up and walk to the door. Jaime, walk to the table and sit on the table . . .

and so on. The students follow the directions the teacher gives. TPR came from psychological theories of language learning and extensive research has been carried out into it. Its unique feature is the emphasis on learning through physical actions. As Asher puts it, 'In a sense, language is orchestrated to a choreography of the human body.'

During the early 1980s there was much talk of listening-based methods, summed up under the slogan as 'Listening First' (Cook, 1986). Postovsky (1974) had described how students who were taught Russian by methods that emphasize listening were better than students taught in a conventional way. According to Gary and Gary (1981a; 1981b) the benefits of concentrating on listening are that students do not feel so embarrassed if they do not have to speak, the memory load is less if they listen without speaking, classroom equipment such as tape-recorders can be used more effectively for listening than for speaking, and so on. Classroom research has confirmed that there are distinct advantages to listening-based methods, as we see in the collection by Winitz (1981). One of the major schisms in contemporary teaching methodology is between those who require students to practise communication by both listening and speaking and those who prefer students to listen for information without speaking. This will be discussed in Chapter 9.

Krashen brings these listening-based methods together through the notion of 'comprehensible input'. He claims that 'acquisition can take place only when people understand messages in the target language' (Krashen and Terrell, 1983). Listening is motivated by the need to get messages out of what is heard. L2 learners acquire a new language by hearing it in contexts where the meaning is made plain to them. Ideally the speech they hear has enough 'old' language that the student already knows and makes enough sense in the context for the 'new' language to be understood and absorbed. How the teacher gets the message across is not particularly important. Pointing to one's nose and saying 'This is my nose', working out 'nose' from the context in 'There's a spot on your nose', looking at a photo of a face and labelling it with 'nose', 'eyes', etc., all of these are satisfactory provided that the student discovers the message in the sentence. Steve McDonough (1995) neatly summarizes the process as 'the accretion of knowledge from instances of incomprehension embedded in the comprehensible'.

Krashen claims that *all* teaching methods that work utilize the same 'fundamental pedagogical principle' of providing comprehensible input: 'if x is shown to be "good" for acquiring a second language, x helps to provide CI [comprehensible input], either directly or indirectly' (Krashen, 1981b). Krashen's codebreaking approach to listening became a strong influence on language teachers in the 1980s. It is saying essentially that L2 acquisition depends on listening: decoding *is* codebreaking. It did not, however, oddly enough, lead to a generation of published listening-based main course books.

But this theory does not say what the processes of decoding *are* and how they relate to codebreaking. The statement that teaching should be meaningful does not get us very far by itself. Most teachers have already been trying to make their lessons convey messages. Comprehensible input is too simplistic and too all-embracing a notion to produce anything but the most general guidelines on what a teacher should do. It pays little heed to the actual processes of listening or learning but promises that everything will be all right if the teacher maximizes comprehensible input. As advice this is too vague; the teacher can do anything, provided the students have to make sense of the language that is addressed to them. At least anything but make the students produce language, thus eliminating most of the 'British' communicative methods, as we see in Chapter 9.

L2 LEARNING AND LISTENING PROCESSES

- L2 listening is an active process involving background schemas, etc.
- Both 'top–down' and 'bottom–up' parsing are involved.
- Ineffective L2 students rely too much on bottom-up parsing.

Teaching uses:

- Teaching involves both decoding messages from language and codebreaking the language system from what is heard.
- Task-based listening may be dangerous if it is too task-specific.

---

4 Codeswitching by second language users

KEYWORDS

codeswitching: going from one language to the other in mid-speech when both speakers know the same two languages

The processes discussed so far are employed by all language users in one way or another. People use similar memory processes, reading processes, and listening processes in both the L1 and the L2, even if they are less efficient at using them in the L2. This section, however, looks at a process peculiar to the use of the L2, namely *codeswitching* from one language to another. To illustrate codeswitching in action, here are some sentences recorded by Zubaidah Hakim in a staffroom where Malaysian teachers of English were talking to each other. '*Suami saya dulu* slim and trim *tapi sekarang* plump like drum' (Before my husband was slim and trim but now he is plump like a drum), '*Jadi I tanya*, how can you say that when . . . *geram betul I*' *(So* I asked how can you say that when . . . I was so mad), and 'Hero you *tak datang hari ni*' (Your hero did not come today). What is happening here is a constant switching between English and Bahasa Malaysia. One moment there is a phrase or word in English, the next a phrase or word in Bahasa Malaysia. Sometimes the switch between languages occurs between sentences rather than within them. It is often hard to say which is the main language of the conversation or indeed of the sentence.

Codeswitching is found all over the world where bilingual speakers talk to each other. According to François Grosjean (1989), bilinguals have two modes of using language. One is when they speak either one language or the other, the other mode is when they codeswitch from one to the other during the course of speech. Bilingual codeswitching is neither unusual or abnormal; it is an ordinary fact of life in many multilingual societies. It is the unique feat that multicompetent speakers are capable of that no monolingual can ever achieve. The following box gives some example of codeswitching drawn from various sources, as well as some of the previous examples.

SOME EXAMPLES OF CODESWITCHING BETWEEN LANGUAGES

- Bahasa Malaysia/English: '*Suami saya dulu* slim and trim *tapi sekarang* plump like drum' (Before my husband was slim and trim but now he is plump like a drum).
- Spanish/English: '*Todos los Mexicanos* were riled up' (All the Mexicans were riled up).
- Dutch/English: '*Ik heb een kop* of tea, tea or something' (I had a cup of tea or something).
- Russian/French: '*Chustzovali, chto* le vin est tiré et qu'il faut le boire' (They felt that the wine is uncorked and it should be drunk).
- Tok Pisin/English: '*Lapun man ia cam na tok*, "oh yu poor pussiket"' (The old man came and said 'you poor pussycat').
- Japanese/English: 'She *wa* took her a month to come home *yo*'.

The interesting questions about codeswitching are why and when it happens. A common reason for switching is to report what someone has said, as in the following example where a girl who is telling a story switches from Tok Pisin (spoken in Papua New Guinea) to English to report what the man said: '*Lapun man ia cam na tok*, "oh yu poor pussiket"' (The old man came and said 'you poor pussycat'). In one sense, whenever a book cites sentences in other languages, it is a codeswitch! A second reason for switching is to use markers from one language to highlight something in another. The Japanese/English 'She *wa* took her a month to come home *yo*' uses 'wa' to indicate what is being talked about, its function in Japanese.

Another reason is that some topics are more appropriate to one language than another. Mexican Americans, for example, prefer to talk about money in English rather than in Spanish – '*La consulta èra* (the visit cost) *eight dollars.*' One of my Malaysian students told me that she could express romantic feelings in English but not in Bahasa Malaysia. Sometimes the reason for codeswitching is that the choice of language shows the speaker's role. A Kenyan man who was serving his own sister in a shop started in their own Luiyia dialect and then switched to Swahili for the rest of the conversation to signal that he was treating her as an ordinary customer. And often bilinguals use fillers and tags from one language in another, as in the Spanish/English exchange 'Well I'm glad to meet you', '*Andale pues* and do come again' (OK swell . . .). The common factor underlying these examples is that the speaker assumes the listener is fluent in the two languages. Otherwise such sentences would not be a bilingual codeswitching mode of language use but would be either interlanguage communication strategies or attempts at one-up-manship, similar to the use by some English speakers of Latin expressions such as '*ab initio* learners of Spanish' (Spanish beginners).

How does codeswitching relate to language structure? According to one set of calculations about 84 per cent of switches within the sentence are isolated words, say the English/Malaysian '*Ana* free *hari ini*' (Ana is free today), where English is switched to only for the item 'free'. About 10 per cent are phrases, as in the Russian/French '*Imela* une femme de chambre' (She had a chamber-maid). The remaining 6 per cent are switches for whole clauses, as in the German/English '*Papa, wenn du das Licht ausmachst,* then I'll be so lonely' (Daddy, if you put out the light, I'll be so lonely). But this still does not show when a switch from one language to another can take place.

The theory of codeswitching developed by Poplack (1980) claims that there are two main restrictions on where switching can happen:

1. **The 'free morpheme constraint'.** This means that the speaker may not switch language between a word and its endings unless the word is pronounced as if it were in the language of the ending. Thus an English/Spanish switch 'run*eando*' is impossible because 'run' is distinctively English in sound. But '*flip*eando' is possible because 'flip' could be a Spanish word.
2. **The 'equivalence constraint'.** This means that the switch can come at a point in the sentence where it does not violate the grammar of either language. So there are unlikely to be any French/English switches such as 'a car *americaine*' or '*une* American *voiture*', as they

would be wrong in both languages. It is possible, however, to have the French/English switch *'J'ai acheté* an American car' (I bought an American car), because both English and French share the construction in which the object follows the verb.

CODESWITCHING AND LANGUAGE TEACHING

What does codeswitching have to do with language teaching? The profile of the proficient L2 user includes the codeswitching mode of language. It is not something that is peculiar or unusual. If the bilingual knows that the listener shares the same languages, codeswitching is likely to take place for all the reasons given above. For many students the ability to go from one language to another is highly desirable; there is not much point in being multi-competent if you are restricted by the demands of a single language.

The Institute of Linguists' examinations in Languages for International Communication test whether candidates can mediate between two languages. At beginners level this may be reading an L2 travel brochure or listening to L2 answerphone messages to get information that can be used in the L1. At advanced stages it might be researching a topic through reading and conducting interviews in order to write an L1 report. In this international use of a second language the L2 learner is not becoming an imitation native speaker but is a person who can stand between the two languages, using both when appropriate. While this is not in itself codeswitching, it involves the same element of having two languages readily available rather than functioning exclusively in one or the other. One possibility is to utilize *reciprocal language teaching* in which students switch language at predetermined points (Cook, 1989b). This method pairs students who want to learn each other's languages and makes them alternate between the two languages, thus exchanging the roles of teacher and student. My own experience of this was on a summer course that paired French teachers of English with English teachers of French. For one day all the activities would take place in French, for the next day everything would be in English, and so on throughout the course. In my own case it was so effective that at the end of three weeks I was conversing with a French Inspector-General without realizing that I was using French.

But codeswitching proper can also be exploited as part of actual teaching methodology. When the teacher knows the language of the students, the classroom itself is often a codeswitching situation. The lesson starts in the L1, or the control of the class takes place through the L1, or the L1 slips in in other ways. Use of the L1 is an important indication of the extent to which the class is 'communicative', as we see in Chapter 6. Perhaps codeswitching is inevitable in the classroom if the teacher and students share the same languages and should be regarded as natural.

Rodolpho Jacobson has developed a teaching method known as the 'New Concurrent Approach' (Jacobson and Faltis, 1990), which gets teachers to balance the use of the two languages within a single lesson. The teacher is allowed to switch languages at certain key points. In a class of English taught to Spanish children, the teacher can switch to Spanish when concepts are important, when the students are getting distracted, or when the student should be praised or told off. The teacher may switch to English when revising a lesson that has already been given in Spanish.

L2 LEARNING AND CODESWITCHING

Codeswitching is the use of two languages within the same conversation, often when the speaker is:

- reporting what someone has said
- highlighting something
- discussing particular topics
- emphasizing a particular social role.

Codeswitching consists of 84 per cent single word switches, 10 per cent phrases, 6 per cent clauses.

Teachers should remember:

- The classroom is often a natural codeswitching situation.
- There is nothing wrong or peculiar about codeswitching.
- Principles exist for codeswitching in the classroom.

---

5 Communication strategies

KEYWORDS

communication strategies can be:

- mutual attempts to solve L2 communication problems by participants (Tarone 1980)
- individual solutions to psychological problems of L2 processing (Faerch and Kasper 1984)
- ways of filling vocabulary gaps in L1 or L2 (Kellerman 1990, Poulisse 1990)

L2 learners are attempting to communicate through a language that is not their own. It is different from children learning a first language where mental and social development go hand in hand with language development. Hence, unlike L1 children, L2 learners are always wanting to express things for which they do not have the means in the second language. In the 1980s there was considerable debate about the communication strategies L2 learners employ to cope with this problem. Here we shall look at three different approaches to communication strategies. The detailed lists of strategies used by these approaches are summarized in the box on page 93, which can be referred to during this section.

COMMUNICATION STRATEGIES AS SOCIAL INTERACTION

Elaine Tarone (1980) emphasizes social aspects of communication. Both participants are trying to overcome their lack of shared meaning. She sees three overall types of strategy: communication, production, and learning, the first of which we will consider here. When things go wrong, both participants try to devise a communication strategy to get out of the difficulty. One type of strategy is to paraphrase what you want to say. Typical strategies are:

- *Approximation.* Someone who is groping for a word falls back on a strategy of using a word that means approximately the same, say 'animal' for 'horse', because the listener will be able to deduce from the context what is intended.
- *Word coinage.* Another form of paraphrase is to make up a word to substitute for the unknown word – 'airball' for 'balloon'.
- *Circumlocution.* L2 learners talk their way round the word – 'when you make a container' for 'pottery'.

All these strategies rely on the speaker trying to solve the difficulty through the L2.

A second overall type of communication strategy is to fall back on the first language, known as transfer. Examples are:

- *Translation from the L1.* A German-speaking student says 'Make the door shut' rather than 'Shut the door'.
- *Language switch.* 'That's a nice tirtil' (caterpillar), distinct from the code-switching discussed above because the listener does not know the L1.
- *Appeal for assistance.* 'What is this?'
- *Mime* what you need. My daughter succeeded in getting some candles in a shop in France by singing 'Happy Birthday' in English and miming blowing out candles.

A third overall type of strategy is avoidance: do not talk about things you know are difficult in the L2, whether whole topics or individual words.

Bialystok (1990) compared some of these strategies in terms of effectiveness and found that listeners understand word coinage much better than approximation, circumlocution, or language switch, though, in terms of sheer frequency, word coinage was very rare, the commonest strategy being circumlocution.

These types of strategy are then particularly important to the teacher who is aiming to teach some form of social interaction to the students. If they are to succeed in conversing with other people through the L2 then they need at least practice in the skill of conducting conversations in which they are not capable of saying everything they want. This contrasts with some older language teaching techniques which tried to ensure that the students never found themselves doing what they had not been taught. The ability to retrieve the conversation when things go wrong is vital to using the L2. Maximally the suggestion would be that the teacher specifically teaches the strategies rather than letting them emerge out of the students' own attempts. In this case there would be specific exercises on approximation or word coinage, say, before the students had to put them together in a real conversation.

COMMUNICATION STRATEGIES AS PSYCHOLOGICAL PROBLEM-SOLVING

The approach of Faerch and Kasper (1984) concentrates on the psychological dimension of what is going on in the L2 speaker's mind. L2 learners want to express something through the second language but encounter a hitch. To get round this psychological difficulty, they resort to communication strategies. Faerch and Kasper divide these into two main groups: achievement (trying to solve the problem) and avoidance (trying to avoid it).

Achievement strategies

These subdivide into *cooperative strategies*, such as appealing to the other person for help, which are mostly similar to Tarone's list, and *non-cooperative* strategies, where the learner tries to solve the problems without recourse to others. One form of non-cooperation is to fall back on the first language when in trouble by:

- *Codeswitching.* The speaker skips language – 'Do you want to have some ah Zinsen?' (the German word for 'interest').
- *Foreignerization.* A Dane literally translating the Danish word for vegetables into English as 'green things'.

In the light of the discussion on codeswitching above these strategies seem likely to occur when the listener knows both languages, as in many research and teaching situations.

Another overall grouping is *interlanguage strategies* that are based on the learner's evolving L2 system rather than on the L1. Among these Faerch and Kasper include:

- *Substitution.* Speakers substitute one word for another, say 'if' for 'whether' if they cannot remember whether 'whether' has an 'h'.
- *Generalization.* L2 speakers use a more general word rather than a more particular one, such as 'animal' for 'rabbit'.

- *Description*. Speakers cannot remember the word for 'kettle' and so describe it as 'the thing to cook water in'.
- *Exemplification*. Speakers give an example rather than the general term, such as 'cars' for 'transport'.
- *Word coining*. That is, making up a word when a speaker does not know it, such as inventing an imaginary French word 'heurot' for 'watch'.
- *Restructuring*. The speaker has another attempt at the same sentence, as in a learner struggling to find the rare English word 'sibling': 'I have two – er – one sister and one brother'.

Avoidance strategies

These Faerch and Kasper divide into:

- *Formal avoidance*. The speaker avoids a particular linguistic form, whether in pronunciation, in morphemes, or in syntax.
- *Functional avoidance*. The speaker avoids different types of function.

Again this approach in general reminds the teacher of the processes going on in the students' minds when they are trying to speak in a new language. Practice with communication techniques such as information gap games is going to force the students to use these types of communication strategy, whether they want to or not, provided always that they have to say things that are just beyond their current level of functioning in the L2.

COMPENSATORY STRATEGIES

To some extent Tarone's social communicative strategies and Faerch and Kasper's psychological strategies are complementary ways of coping with the problems of communicating in a second language. But, as we have seen, they end up as rather long and confusing lists of strategies. Eric Kellerman and his colleagues (1987) feel that these approaches can be considerably simplified. The common factor to all communication strategies is that the L2 learner has to deal with not knowing a word in a second language; it is vocabulary lack that is crucial. The strategies exist to plug gaps in the learners' vocabulary by allowing them to refer to things for which they do not know the L2 words; a better name is then compensatory strategies – L2 learners are always having to compensate for the limited vocabulary at their disposal.

Nanda Poulisse set up an experiment in which Dutch learners of English had to carry out tasks such as retelling stories and describing geometrical shapes. She ended up with a new division of strategies into two main types, called archistrategies, each with two sub-divisions, according to the way that they coped with words they did not know.

Conceptual archistrategy

This involved solving the problem by thinking of the meaning of the word and attempting to convey it in another way:

- *Analytic strategy.* In this the learner tries to break the meaning of the word up into parts and then to convey the parts separately: so a student searching for the word 'parrot' says 'talk uh bird', taking the two parts 'bird that talks'.
- *Holistic strategy.* Here the learner thinks of the meaning of the word as a whole and tries to use a word that is the closest approximation; for example, seeking for the word 'desk', the student produces 'table', which captures all the salient features of 'desk' apart from the fact it is specifically for writing at.

Linguistic archistrategy

Here the student falls back on the language resources inside their head:

- *Morphological creativity.* One possibility is to make up a word using proper endings and hope that it works; for instance, trying to describe the act of 'ironing' the student came up with the word 'ironize'.
- *L1 transfer.* The student also has a first language on tap in their mind. It is then possible for them to transfer a word from the first to the second language, hoping that it is going to exist in the new language; thus a Dutch student trying to say 'waist' says 'middle' – the Dutch word is in fact 'middel'.

This approach led, however, to an interesting conclusion. The linguistic transfer requires knowledge of another language and hence is unique to L2 learning. However, the conceptual strategies are the same as those used in native speech when speakers cannot remember the word they want to use. Describing which parts of my car needed repairing to a mechanic, I said, 'There's oil dripping from that sort of junction in the pipe behind the engine', an analytic strategy. This not only allowed me to communicate without knowing the correct words; it also means I never need to learn them – I still do not know what this part of the car is called. Such strategies occur more frequently in L2 learners' speech only because they know fewer words than native speakers. The strategies are used by native speakers in the same way as L2 learners when they too do not know the words, as any conversation overheard in a shop selling do-it-yourself tools will confirm. Kellerman and his colleagues believe that these compensatory strategies are a part of the speaker's communicative competence that can be used in either language when needed rather than something peculiar to L2 learning (Kellerman *et al.*, 1990). Poulisse indeed showed that people had preferences for the same type of strategy when they were faced with finding a word they did not know in both the L1 and the L2; the only difference is that this situation arises far more frequently in a second language!

So it is not clear whether compensatory strategies need to be taught. L2 learners resort to these strategies in the real-world situation when they do not know words. This does not mean that it may not be beneficial for students to have their attention drawn to them so that they are reminded that these strategies can indeed be used in an L2; Zoltan Dornyei (1995), however, has demonstrated that Hungarian students who were taught communication strategies improved in their ability to define words compared to control groups. Such strategies in a sense form part of the normal repertoire of the students' communicative competence. In any teaching activity that encourages the learners to speak outside their normal vocabulary range, they are bound to occur. An exercise in the textbook *Keep Talking* (Klippel, 1984) suggests that the students describe their everyday problems such as losing their keys and not being able to remember names, and other students suggest ways of solving them. If the students do not know the word for 'key', say, they might ask the teacher (a cooperative strategy), or look it up in a dictionary (a non-cooperative strategy). Or they might attempt an analytical archistrategy: 'the thing you open doors with'. With the exception of dictionary use, these strategies can be safely ignored by the teacher. They are there if the students need them but they need not form the teaching point of an exercise. One danger with teaching activities that make the students communicate spontaneously is that sheer lack of vocabulary forces the students back onto these strategies. Hence the teacher should keep the likely vocabulary load of non-teacher-controlled activities within certain limits, ensuring that students already know enough of the vocabulary not to be forced back onto compensatory strategies for too much of the time. Or the teachers can treat them as ways of discovering and teaching the vocabulary the students lack. Further discussion of the teaching of strategies occurs in the section on learning strategies in the next chapter.

DISCUSSION TOPICS

1. How important do you now feel working memory is for the learner in the classroom?
2. Do you think that conventional techniques strain students' memory? If so what can we do about it?
3. What mental 'scripts' pose a particular problem for L2 learners? Are these covered satisfactorily in the classroom?
4. How would you go about supplying the background information students would need for a particular text?
5. To what extent do you agree that listening is a compromise between top-down and bottom-up processes?
6. Do you agree from your own experience that codebreaking and decoding are separate processes, or do you feel, like Krashen, that they are essentially the same process?

7. How do you feel about students who codeswitch between their L1 and their L2 in the classroom?
8. Do you agree that communication strategies are only for when things go wrong?
9. To what extent do you think that communication strategies should be taught?

DIFFERENT APPROACHES TO L2 COMMUNICATION STRATEGIES

Socially motivated strategies for solving mutual lack of understanding (Tarone 1980):

- paraphrase (approximation, word coinage, circumlocution)
- falling back on L1 translation, language switch, appeal for assistance, mime
- avoidance.

Psychologically motivated strategies for solving the individual's L2 problems of expression (Faerch and Kasper, 1984):

1. Achievement strategies:
   cooperative strategies (similar to list above)
   non-cooperative strategies
   codeswitching
   foreignerization
   interlanguage strategies (substitution, generalization, description, exemplification, word-coining, restructuring).
2. Avoidance strategies:
   formal (phonological, morphological, grammatical)
   functional (actional, propositional, modal).
3. Archistrategies to compensate for lack of vocabulary (Poulisse 1990):
   conceptual analytic (breaks the meaning of the word down)
   conceptual holistic (tries for a word that is closest overall in meaning)
   linguistic morphological creativity (makes up a new word by adding an appropriate ending)
   linguistic transfer (uses a word from the L1 instead).

FURTHER READING

For the areas of short-term memory processes, reading, and listening, readers are recommended to the original sources referred to in the chapter, as no book-length L2 learning treatments exist that cover the areas adequately. Code-switching is described in many books on bilingualism, particularly Romaine (1994), *Bilingualism*. One perspective on communication strategies can be found in Bialystok (1990), *Communication Strategies*. The Nijmegen communication strategies are best written up in Poulisse (1990), *The Use of Compensatory Strategies by Dutch Learners of English*.

5

Learners as individuals

So far this book has concentrated on the things that L2 learners have in common. Teachers usually have to deal with students in groups rather than as individuals; it is what all the class do that is important. However, ultimately language is not learnt by groups, but by individuals. At the end of the class, the group turns into 25 individuals who go off to use language as they will. Features of the learner's personality or mind encourage or inhibit L2 learning. The concern of the present chapter is then with how L2 learners vary as individuals.

Focusing questions

Motivation

Mark these two statements on a scale from 1–5:
Studying a foreign language is important to my students because they will be able to participate more freely in the activities of other cultural groups.

strongly agree	slightly agree	neither	slightly disagree	strongly disagree

Studying a foreign language can be important for my students because it will someday be useful in getting a good job.

strongly agree	slightly agree	neither	slightly disagree	strongly disagree

Aptitude:

- Why do you think some people are good at learning other languages?
- Do you think the same people learn a language well in the classroom as learn in a natural setting, or do these demand different qualities?

Learning strategies:

- What particular ways have you yourself found useful for learning a new language?
- How much do you value students learning from each other rather than from the teacher?

Age:

- What do you think is the best age for learning a new language? Why?
- How would your teaching of, say, the present tense, differ according to whether you were teaching children or adults?

Other individual factors:

- Do you think that girls are better than boys at second language learning?
- What personality would be best in the language classroom?

---

1 Motivation: what sort of motivation is good for L2 learning?

KEYWORDS

integrative motivation: learning the language in order to take part in the culture of its people

instrumental motivation: learning the language for a career goal or other practical reason

additive bilingualism: L2 learning that adds to the learner's capabilities

subtractive bilingualism: L2 learning that takes away from the learner's capabilities

Some L2 learners do better than others because they are better motivated. The child learning a first language cannot really be spoken about in terms of good or bad motivation. Language is one means through which all children fulfil their everyday needs, however diverse these may be. One might as well ask what the motivation is for walking or for being a human being. In these terms the second language is superfluous for many classroom learners, who can already communicate with people and use language for thinking. Their mental and social life has been formed through their first language.

The usual meaning of motivation for the teacher is probably the interest that something generates in the students. A particular exercise, a particular topic, a particular song, may make the students appear involved in the class, to the teacher's delight. Of course obvious enjoyment by the students is not necessarily a sign that learning is taking place – people probably enjoy eating ice-cream more than carrots but which has the better long-term effects? Motivation in this sense is a short-term affair from moment to moment in the class. Vital as it is to the classroom, as yet second language acquisition research has little studied it, as Crookes and Schmidt (1991) point out.

Motivation in L2 learning has, instead, chiefly been used to refer to the long-term fairly stable attitudes in the students' minds. Two types of favourable motivation have been talked about: *integrative* and *instrumental* motivation, introduced by Gardner and Lambert in a series of books and papers (Gardner and Lambert, 1972; Gardner, 1985). The integrative motivation reflects whether the student identifies with the target culture and people in some sense, or rejects them – the Focusing Questions statement 'Studying a foreign language is important to my students because they will be able to participate more freely in the activities of other cultural groups' was actually adapted from one used by Gardner for testing integrativeness. The more that a student admires the target culture – reads its literature, visits it on holiday, looks for opportunities to practise the language, and so on – the more successful the student will be in the L2 classroom.

Instrumental motivation means learning the language for an ulterior motive unrelated to its use by native speakers – to pass an examination, to get a certain kind of job, and so on; again the statement in the Focusing Questions section 'Studying a foreign language can be important for my students because it will someday be useful in getting a good job' was similarly adapted from Gardner's test battery. I learnt Latin at school because a classical language was then an entry requirement for university and for no other reason. A survey of young people in Europe found that 29 per cent wanted to learn more languages to increase their career possibilities, while 14 per cent wanted them in order to live, work, or study in the country (Commission of the European Communities 1987). The largest category, 51 per cent, however, were motivated by 'personal interest'. The last figure is a reminder that integrative and instrumental motivations are only two of the possible kinds of motivation. Gardner and Lambert (1972), for example, also recognized the possibility of 'manipulative' or 'intellectual' motivations.

L2 motivation should not therefore be considered as a forced choice between these two. Both types are important. A student might learn an L2 well with an integrative motivation or with an instrumental one, or indeed with both, for one does not rule out the other, or with other motivations. The relative importance of these has been shown to vary from one part of the world to another. In Montreal learners of French tend to be integratively motivated, in the Philippines learners of English tend to be instrumentally motivated (Gardner, 1985). Some of the different contexts of L2 learning are discussed in Chapter 7.

The distinction between integrative and instrumental motivation has been used by many researchers as a point of reference. Zoltan Dornyei (1990) argues that it is biased towards the Canadian situation where there is a particular balance between the two official languages, English and French. He therefore tested the motivation of learners of English in the typical European situation of Hungary. He found indeed that an instrumental motivation concerned with future careers was very powerful. While an integrative motivation was also relevant, it was not, as in Canada, related to actual contact with native groups but to general attitudes and stereotypes; it became more important as the learners advanced in the language. In addition he identified two factors relating to classroom learning. One was the *need for achievement* – trying to improve yourself in general, more specifically to pass an examination; the other *attributions about past failures* – whatever the learners blame their failures on.

MOTIVATION AND TEACHING

Nevertheless students will find it difficult to learn a second language in the classroom if they have neither instrumental nor integrative motivation, as is probably often the case in school language teaching. Schoolchildren have no particular contact with the foreign culture and no particular interest in it, nor do their job prospects depend on it. Only 36 per cent of pupils in England thought learning French would be useful to them, according to the Assessment of Performance Unit (1986). Teachers of French in England try to compensate for this lack by cultivating both types of motivation in their students, by stressing the career benefits that knowledge of a second language may bring, or by building up interest in the foreign culture through exchanges with French schools or samples of French food.

Otherwise teachers may have to go along with the students' motivation, or at least be sufficiently aware of the students' motivation so that any problems can be smoothed over. Course books then reflect the writer's assessment of the students' motivation. The Hungarian English course *Angol Nyelv Alapfokon* (Edina and Ivanne, 1987) uses English primarily in Hungarian scenes such as entertaining English guests, tours of Budapest for English visitors, shopping ('The oranges are 25 forints'), and letters home from sons in the army. It concentrates on jobs for which English is necessary, such as travel representatives, airline stewards, tourist guides, and journalists. It assumes that an important part of the motivation of Hungarian students is instrumental and that integration into an English-speaking culture is less important – just what Dornyei's research into Hungarian students suggested.

On the other hand, the British coursebook *Blueprint One* (Abbs and Freebairn, 1990) stresses the lifestyle of middle-class young adults in England or visiting England – booking holidays, tourist trips, living in 'typical English houses . . . with three bedrooms and a bathroom', interested in ballet, caravanning, clothes, shopping, and eating out. Again this will be valuable with students interested in this lifestyle, and alienating for those who prefer something else. *The Beginners Choice* (Mohamed and Acklam, 1992) features the lives of multi-ethnic students in England with cosmopolitan interests and worldwide contacts for house exchanges and holidays. Motivating for multilingual adult classes in the UK but less relevant for single language groups of children in other countries.

A problem teachers face is that motivations for L2 learning are deep-rooted in the students' minds and in their cultural backgrounds. This is incorporated in Gardner's socio-educational model of L2 learning, to be discussed in Chapter 8. Whatever the teacher does may be powerless against the many other influences on the students. The general issue is how the student's cultural background fits the background projected by the L2 culture. Lambert (1981, 1990) makes an important distinction between *additive* and *subtractive* bilingualism. In additive bilingualism, the learners feel they are adding something new to their skills and experience by learning a new language, without taking anything away from what they already know. In subtractive bilingualism, they feel that the learning of a new language threatens what they have already gained for themselves. Successful L2 learning takes place in additive situations; learners who see the L2 as diminishing themselves will not succeed. This relates directly to many immigrant or multi-ethnic situations; a group that feels in danger of losing its identity by learning a second language does not learn the L2 well. Chilean refugees I taught in the 1970s often lamented their lack of progress in English. However much they consciously wanted to learn English, I felt that subconsciously they saw it as committing themselves to permanent exile and thus to subtracting from themselves as Chileans. It is not motivation for learning as such which is important to teaching but motivation for learning a particular second language. Monolingual UK children in a survey conducted by the Linguistic Minorities Project (1983) showed a preference in order of popularity for learning German, Italian, Spanish and French. Young people in the European Community as a whole, however, had the order of preference English, Spanish, German, French and Italian (Commission of the European Communities, 1987).

In an ideal teacher's world, students would enter the classrooms admiring the target culture and language, wanting to get something out of the L2 learning for themselves, and thirsting for knowledge. In practice teachers have to be aware of the reservations and preconceptions of their students. What they think of the teacher, and what they think of the course, heavily affect their success. This is what teachers can influence rather than the learners' more deep-seated motivations. Motivation also goes in both directions. High motivation is one factor that causes successful learning; successful learning, however, may cause high motivation. The latter process of creating successful learning which can spur high motivation may be under the teacher's control, if not the former. The choice of teaching materials and the information content of the lesson, for example, should correspond to the motivations of the students. As Lambert (1990) puts it while talking about minority group children, 'The best way I can see to release the potential [of bilingualism] is to transform their subtractive experiences with bilingualism and biculturalism into additive ones.'

MOTIVATION AND L2 LEARNING

- Both integrative and instrumental motivations may lead to success, but lack of either causes problems.
- Motivation in this sense has great inertia.
- Short-term motivation towards the day-to-day activities in the classroom and general motivations for classroom learning are also important.

Teaching implications:

- recognize variety and nature of motivations
- work with student motivation in materials and content.

2 Aptitude: are some people better at learning a second language than others?

KEYWORDS

aptitude: usually the ability to learn the L2 in an academic classroom

Modern Language Aptitude Test (MLAT): testing phonemic coding, grammatical sensitivity, inductive language learning ability, rote learning

memory-based learners: these rely on their memory rather than grammatical sensitivity

analytic learners: these rely on grammatical sensitivity rather than memory

even learners: these rely on both grammatical sensitivity and memory

It is popularly believed that some people have a knack for learning second languages, and others are rather poor at it. Some immigrants who have been in a country for twenty years are very fluent. Others from the same background and living in the same circumstances for the same amount of time speak the language rather poorly. Given that their ages, motivations, and so on are the same, why are there such differences? As always the popular view has to be qualified to some extent. Descriptions of societies where each individual uses several languages daily, such as Central Africa or Pakistan, seldom mention people who cannot cope with the demands of a multilingual existence, other than those with academic study problems. Differences in L2 learning ability are apparently only felt in societies where L2 learning is treated as a problem rather than an everyday fact of life.

TESTS OF APTITUDE

So far the broad term 'knack' for learning languages has been used. The more usual term however is 'aptitude'; some people have more aptitude for learning second languages than others. But aptitude has almost invariably been used in connection with students in classrooms. It does not refer to the knack that some people have for learning in real-life situations but to the ability to learn from teaching. In the 1950s and 1960s considerable effort went into establishing what successful students had in common. The *Modern Languages Aptitude Test* (MLAT) broadly speaking requires the student to carry out L2 learning on a small scale. It incorporates four main factors that predict a student's success in the classroom (Carroll, 1981). These are:

- *Phonemic coding ability*: how well the student can use phonetic script to distinguish phonemes in the language.
- *Grammatical sensitivity*: whether the student can pick out grammatical functions in the sentence.
- *Inductive language learning ability*: whether the student can generalize patterns from one sentence to another.
- *Rote learning*: whether the student can remember vocabulary lists of foreign words paired with translations.

Such tests are not neutral about what happens in a classroom nor about the goals of language teaching. They assume that learning words by heart is an important part of L2 learning ability, that the spoken language is crucial, and that grammar consists of structural patterns. In short, MLAT mostly predicts how well a student will do in a course that is predominantly audiolingual in methodology rather than in a course taught by other methods. Wesche (1981) divided Canadian students according to MLAT and other tests into those who were best suited to an 'analytical' approach and those who were best suited to an 'audiovisual' approach. Half she put in the *right* type of class, half in the *wrong* (whether this is acceptable behaviour by a teacher is another question). The students in the right class 'achieved superior scores'. It is not just aptitude in general that counts but the right kind of aptitude for the particular learning situation. Predictions about success need to take into account the kind of classroom that is involved rather than being biased towards one kind or assuming there is a single factor of aptitude which applies regardless of situation.

Krashen (1981a) suggests aptitude is important for 'formal' situations such as classrooms, and attitude is important for 'informal' real-world situations. While aptitude tests are indeed more or less purpose-designed for classroom learners, this still leaves open the existence of a general knack for learning languages in real-life settings, which is different from the notion of aptitude as defined here. Horwitz (1987) anticipated that a test of cognitive level would go with communicative competence and a test of aptitude with linguistic competence. She found, however, a strong link between the two tests.

Peter Skehan (1986) argues for a slightly different set of factors. He looked at soldiers learning foreign languages and found three groups of successful learners:

1. *Memory-based* learners were usually younger and were not particularly sensitive to grammar but had good memories.
2. *Analytic* learners were a slightly older group and were poorer at memory but had good grammatical sensitivity.
3. *Even* learners were good overall.

So there seemed to be two sides of aptitude: a memory-based side and a language-based side. Lack of memory capability in older students can be compensated for by greater grammatical sensitivity. Lack of grammatical sensitivity in younger students can be compensated for by better memory. Students do well if they have both attributes but they also do well if they have either of them.

APTITUDE AND TEACHING

The problem for language teachers is what to do once the students have been tested for academic learning aptitude. There are at least three possibilities:

1. *Select students who are likely to succeed* in the classroom and bar those who are likely to fail. This would, however, be unthinkable in most settings with open access to education.
2. *Stream students into different classes* for levels of aptitude, say high-flyers, average, and below average. The Graded Objectives Movement in England, for instance, set the same overall goals for all students at each stage but allowed them different periods of time for getting there (Harding *et al.*, 1981). Aptitude is then related to the speed with which students reach the final stage. In the UK all pupils take the same GCSE (General Certificate of Secondary Education) examination in French but can choose whether to take it at General level or Extended level (Eastern Examining Board, 1986). Attitude then affects the number of aspects they are examined on at the final stage.
3. *Provide different teaching for different types of aptitude* with different teaching methods and final examinations. This might lead to varied exercises within the class, to parallel classes, or to self-directed learning. In most educational establishments this would be a luxury in terms of staffing and accommodation, however desirable.

The overall lesson is to see students in particular contexts. The student whose performance is dismal in one class may be gifted in another. Any class teaching is a compromise to suit the greatest number of students. Only in individualized or self-directed learning perhaps can this be overcome.

APTITUDE FOR L2 LEARNING

- Most aptitude tests predict success in L2 academic classrooms.
- Aptitude breaks down into different factors such as memory and grammatical sensitivity.

Teaching implications:

- Eliminating students without aptitude (if allowable on other grounds).
- Streaming students according to aptitude into fast and slow streams.
- Arranging different teaching for learners with different types of aptitude.

3 Learning strategies: how do learners vary in their approaches to L2 learning?

KEYWORDS

learning strategy: a choice that the learner makes while learning or using the second language that affects learning
good language learner strategies: the strategies employed by people known to be good at L2 learning
metacognitive strategies: these involve planning and directing learning at a general level
cognitive strategies: these involve specific conscious ways of tackling learning
social strategies: these involve interacting with other people

This section looks at the learning strategies used by L2 learners. A learning strategy here refers to a choice that the learner makes while learning or using the second language that affects learning, as distinct therefore from discourse moves (Chapter 3) or communication strategies (Chapter 4), both of which aim at language use. A summary box of the main strategy types is given on page 106.

GOOD LANGUAGE LEARNER STRATEGIES

People who are good at languages might tackle L2 learning in different ways from those who are less good or they might behave in the same way but more efficiently. One interesting theme is the *good language learner* (GLL) strategies. Naiman *et al.* (1978) tried to see what people who were known to be good at learning languages had in common. They found six broad strategies shared by GLLs as follows:

GLL strategy 1: find a learning style that suits you

Good language learners become aware of the type of L2 learning that suits them best. While they conform to the teaching situation to start with, they soon find ways of adapting or modifying it to suit themselves. Thus some GLLs supplement audiolingual or communicative language teaching by reading grammar books at home, if that is their bent. Others seek out communicative encounters to help them compensate for a classroom with an academic emphasis.

GLL strategy 2: involve yourself in the language learning process

GLLs do not passively accept what is presented to them but go out to meet it. They participate more in the classroom, whether visibly or not. They take the initiative and devise situations and language learning techniques for themselves. Some listen to the news in the L2 on the radio; others go to see films in the L2.

GLL strategy 3: develop an awareness of language both as system and as communication

GLLs are conscious not only that language is a complex system of rules but also that it is used for a purpose; they combine grammatical and pragmatic competence. In other words GLLs do not treat language solely as communication or as academic knowledge but as both. While many learn lists of vocabulary consciously, many also seek out opportunities to take part in conversations in the L2, one even driving a truck for the L2 opportunities it yielded.

GLL strategy 4: pay constant attention to expanding your language knowledge

GLLs are not content with their knowledge of a second language but are always trying to improve it. They make guesses about things they do not know; they check whether they are right or wrong by comparing their speech with the new language they hear; and they ask native speakers to correct them. Some are continually on the lookout for clues to the L2.

GLL strategy 5: develop the L2 as a separate system

GLLs try to develop their knowledge of the L2 in its own right and eventually to think in it. They do not relate everything to their first language but make the L2 a separate system. One common strategy is to engage in silent monologues to practise the L2. I have sometimes told my students to give commentaries in the L2 to themselves about the passing scene.

GLL strategy 6: take into account the demands that L2 learning imposes

GLLs realize that L2 learning can be very demanding. It seems as if you are taking on a new personality in the L2, and one which you do not particularly care for. It is painful to expose yourself in the L2 classroom by making foolish mistakes. The GLL perseveres in spite of these emotional handicaps. 'You've got to be able to laugh at your mistakes,' said one.

Some qualifications need to be made to this line of research. First of all it only describes what GLLs are aware of; this is what they *say* they do rather than what they actually do. The magic ingredient in their L2 learning may be something they are quite unaware of, and hence does not emerge from interviews. Second, the strategies are similar to what teachers probably supposed to be the case. This is partly a limitation of the original research. Most of the GLLs studied were highly educated people themselves working in education, probably rather similar to the readers of this book. The strategies are familiar because we are looking at ourselves in a mirror. As with aptitude, there may be an alternative set of strategies employed by people who are non-academic GLLs in natural settings. Third, as Steve McDonough points out, the GLL strategies are not so much strategies in the sense of a deliberate approach to solve problems as 'wholesome attitudes' that good learners have towards language learning.

TYPES OF LEARNING STRATEGIES

Extensive research that goes much deeper into learning strategies has been carried out by O'Malley and Chamot (1990) within an overall model of L2 learning based on cognitive psychology. They have defined three main types of strategy used by L2 students:

1. *Metacognitive* strategies involve planning and thinking about learning, such as planning one's learning, monitoring one's own speech or writing, and evaluating how well one has done.
2. *Cognitive* strategies involve conscious ways of tackling learning, such as note-taking, resourcing (using dictionaries and other resources), and elaboration (relating new information to old).
3. *Social* strategies mean learning by interacting with others, such as working with fellow students or asking the teacher's help.

They found that cognitive strategies accounted for the majority of those reported by ESL students, namely 53 per cent, the most important being advanced preparation – as one student put it, 'You review before you go into class' – and self-management, 'I sit in the front of the class so I can see the teacher's face clearly' (O'Malley *et al.*, 1985a). Metacognitive strategies accounted for 30 per cent, the most important being self-management and advance preparation. Social strategies made up the remaining 17 per cent, consisting about equally of cooperative efforts to work with other students and of questions to check understanding. The type of strategy varies according to the task the students are engaged in (O'Malley and Chamot, 1990). A vocabulary task calls forth the metacognitive strategies of self-monitoring and self-evaluation and the cognitive strategies of resourcing and elaboration. A listening task leads to the metacognitive strategies of selective attention and problem identification as well as self-monitoring, and to the cognitive strategies of note-taking, inferencing and summarizing as well as elaboration. The use of strategies also varied according to level: intermediate students used slightly less strategies in total but proportionately more metacognitive strategies.

LANGUAGE LEARNING STRATEGIES

The good language learner (GLL) strategies (Naiman et al., 1978):

1. Find a learning style that suits you.
2. Involve yourself in the language learning process.
3. Develop an awareness of language both as system and as communication.
4. Pay constant attention to expanding your language.
5. Develop the L2 as a separate system.
6. Take into account the demands that L2 learning imposes.

Learning strategies (O'Malley and Chamot, 1990):

- *Metacognitive strategies:* planning learning, monitoring your own speech, self-evaluation, etc.
- *Cognitive strategies*: note-taking, resourcing, elaboration, etc.
- *Social strategies*: working with fellow students or asking the teacher's help.

LEARNING STRATEGIES AND LANGUAGE TEACHING

How can teachers make use of learning strategies? The chief moral is that the students often know best. It is the learners' involvement, the learners' strategies, and the learners' ability to go their own ways that count, regardless of what the teacher is trying to do. Poor students are those who depend most on the teacher and are least able to fend for themselves. The students must be encouraged to develop independence inside and outside the classroom. Partly this can be achieved through 'learner training': equipping the students with the means to guide themselves by explaining strategies to them. The idea of learner-training shades over into self-directed learning, in which the students take on responsibility for their learning. They choose their goals; they control the teaching methods and materials; they assess how well they are doing themselves. This is dealt with further in Chapter 9.

It may not have occurred to students that they have a choice of strategies which affect their learning. Teaching can open up their options. My intermediate EFL course *Meeting People* (Cook, 1982) asked students to discuss four GLL strategies. The intention was to make them aware of different possibilities rather than specifically to train them in any strategy. A more thorough approach is seen in the textbook *Learning to Learn English* (Ellis and Sinclair, 1989), which aims 'to enable learners of English to discover the learning strategies that suit them best.' One set of activities practises metacognitive strategies. The opening questionnaire, for instance, asks the students 'Do you hate making mistakes?', 'Do you like to learn new grammar rules, words, etc. by heart?', and so on. The results divide the students into 'analytic', 'relaxed', and 'a mixture'. A second set of activities practises cognitive as well as metacognitive strategies. Teaching speaking, for instance, starts with reflection ('How do you feel about speaking English?'), knowledge about language ('What do you know about speaking English?'), and self-evaluation ('How well are you doing?'). Another guide for teachers, *Language Learning Strategies* (Oxford, 1990), provides a wealth of activities to heighten the learners' awareness of strategies and their ability to use them, for example, 'The old lady ahead of you in the bus is chastising a young man in your new language, listen to their conversation to find out exactly what she's saying to him.'

Strategy-training assumes that conscious attention to learning strategies is beneficial. This is a different proposition from claiming that the strategies themselves are beneficial. Strategy-training in a sense assumes that the strategies are teachable. While the idea that GLLs need to 'think' in the L2 may strike the students as a revelation, this does not mean they can put it into practice. They may indeed find it impossible or disturbing to try to think in the second language and so feel guilty they are not living up to the image of the GLL. For example, the GLLs studied in Canada clearly had above average intelligence; less intelligent learners may not be able to use the usual GLL strategies. Many strategies cannot be changed by the teacher or the learner, however good their intentions. Bialystok (1990) argues in favour of training that helps the students to be aware of strategies in general rather than teaches specific strategies.

Research by O'Malley and Chamot (1990) provides some encouragement for strategy-training. They taught EFL students to listen to lectures using their three strategies. One group was trained in cognitive strategies, such as note-taking, and social strategies, such as giving practice reports to fellow students. A second group was, in addition trained in metacognitive strategies, for example, paying conscious attention to discourse markers such as 'first', 'second', and so on. A third group was not taught any strategies. The metacognitive group improved most for speaking, and did better on some, but not all, listening tasks. The cognitive group was better than the control group. Given that this experiment only lasted eight 50-minute lessons spread over eight days, this seems as dramatic an improvement as could reasonably be expected. Training students to use particular learning strategies improves their language performance. But, as O'Malley and Chamot (1990) found, teachers may need to be convinced that strategy training is important, and may themselves need to be trained in how to teach strategies. However, to dampen excessive enthusiasm, it should be pointed out that there is still some doubt about how useful strategies really are: Oxford *et al.* (1990) found that Asian students of English used fewer 'good' strategies than Hispanics but improved their English more!

The learning strategies mentioned suit any academic subject. It is indeed a good idea to prepare yourself for the class, to sit near the teacher, and to take notes, whether you are studying physics, cookery, or French. Those who believe in the uniqueness of language feel language learning is handled by the mind in ways that are different from other areas. Some consciously accessible learning strategies that treat language as a thing of its own may be highly useful for L2 learning, say the social strategies. But metacognitive or cognitive strategies treat language like any other part of the human mind. Hence they may benefit students with academic leanings who want to treat language as a subject but may not help those who want to use it for its normal functions in society, that is unless of course such knowledge translates into practical ability to use the language, one of the controversies discussed in Chapter 8.

LANGUAGE TEACHING AND LEARNING STRATEGIES

- Exploit the GLL strategies that are useful to the students.
- Develop the student's independence from the teacher with 'learner training' or directed learning.
- Make students aware of the range of strategies they can adopt.
- Provide specific training in metacognitive strategies.
- Remember the similarities and differences between learning a second language and learning other school subjects.

---

4 Age: are young L2 learners better than old learners?

KEYWORDS

critical period hypothesis: the claim that human beings are only capable of learning language between the age of 2 years and the early teens

immersion teaching: teaching the whole curriculum through the second language, best known from experiments in Canada

Undoubtedly children are popularly believed to be better at learning second languages than adults. People always know one friend or acquaintance who started learning English as an adult and never managed to learn it properly and another who learnt it as a child and is indistinguishable from a native. Linguists as well as the general public often share this point of view. Chomsky (1959) has talked of the immigrant child learning a language quickly while 'the subtleties that become second nature to the child may elude his parents despite high motivation and continued practice'. My new postgraduate overseas students prove this annually. They start the year by worrying whether their children will cope with English and they end it by complaining how much better the children speak than themselves.

This belief in the superiority of young learners was enshrined in the *critical period hypothesis*: the claim that human beings are only capable of learning their first language between the age of two years and the early teens (Lenneberg, 1967). A variety of explanations have been put forward for the apparent decline in adults: physical factors such as the loss of 'plasticity' in the brain and 'lateralization' of the brain; social factors such as the different situations and relationships that children encounter compared to adults; and cognitive explanations such as the interference with natural language learning by the adult's more abstract mode of thinking (Cook, 1986). It has often been concluded that teachers should take advantage of this ease of learning by teaching the child a second language at as early an age as possible, hence the many attempts to teach a foreign language in the primary school in different countries, such as the brief-lived primary-school French programme in England. Indeed the 1990s has seen a growth in the UK in 'bilingual' playgroups teaching French to English-speaking under-fives.

EVIDENCE FOR THE EFFECTS OF AGE ON L2 LEARNING

But research evidence in favour of the superiority of young children has proved surprisingly hard to find. Much research, on the contrary, shows that age is a positive advantage. English-speaking adults and children who had gone to live in Holland were compared using a variety of tests (Snow and Hoefnagel-Höhle, 1978). At the end of three months, the older learners were better at all aspects of Dutch except pronunciation. After a year this advantage had faded and the older learners were better only at vocabulary. Studies in Scandinavia showed that Swedish children improved at learning English throughout the school years, and that Finnish-speaking children under eleven learning Swedish in Sweden were worse than those over eleven (Eckstrand, 1978). Although the total physical response method of teaching with its emphasis on physical action appears more suitable to children, when it was used for teaching Russian to adults and children the older students were consistently better (Asher and Price, 1967).

Even with the immersion techniques used in Canada in which English-speaking children are taught the curriculum substantially through French, late immersion pupils were better than early immersion students at marking number agreement on verbs, and at using 'clitic' pronouns ('le', 'me', etc.) in object verb constructions (Harley, 1986). To sum up, if children and adults are compared who are learning a second language in exactly the same way, whether as immigrants to Holland, or by the same method in the classroom, adults are better. The apparent superiority of adults in such controlled research may mean that the typical situations in which children find themselves are better suited to L2 learning than those adults encounter. Age itself is not so important as the different interactions that learners of different ages have with the situation and with other people.

However, there are many who would disagree and find age a burden for L2 learning. These chiefly base themselves on work by Johnson and Newport (1989). Their research took Chinese and Korean learners living in the United States and found that the earlier they had arrived there the better they were at detecting ungrammatical use of grammatical morphemes such as 'the' and plural '-s' and other properties of English such as wh-questions and word order; indeed those who arrived under the age of seven were no different from natives.

Usually children are thought to be better at pronunciation in particular. The claim is that an authentic accent cannot be acquired if the second language is learnt after a particular age, say the early teens. For instance, the best age for Cuban immigrants to come to the United States so far as pronunciation is concerned is under six, the worst over thirteen (Asher and Garcia, 1969). Ramsey and Wright (1974) found younger immigrants to Canada had less foreign accent than older ones. But the evidence mostly is not clear-cut. Indeed Ramsey and Wright's evidence has been challenged by Cummins (1981). Other research shows that, when the teaching situation is the same, older children are better than younger children even at pronunciation. An experiment with the learning of Dutch by English children and adults found imitation was more successful with older learners (Snow and Hoefnagel-Höhle, 1977). Neufeld (1978) trained adults with a pronunciation technique that moved them gradually from listening to speaking. After eighteen hours of teaching, nine out of twenty students convinced listeners they were native speakers of Japanese, eight out of twenty that they were native Chinese speakers.

It has become common to distinguish short-term benefits of youth from long-term disadvantages of age. David Singleton (1989) sums up his authoritative review of age with the statement:

> The one interpretation of the evidence which does not appear to run into contradictory data is that in naturalistic situations those whose exposure to a second language begins in childhood in general eventually surpass those whose exposure begins in adulthood, even though the latter usually show some initial advantage over the former.

Adults start more quickly and then slow down. Though children start more slowly, they finish up at a higher level. My own view is that much of the research is still open to other interpretations (Cook, 1986). The studies that show long-term disadvantages mostly use different methodologies and different types of learners from those conducted into short-term learning. In particular the long-term research has by coincidence mostly used immigrants, particularly to the United States, but the short-term research has used learners in educational systems elsewhere. Hence factors such as immigration cannot at present be disentangled from age.

JOSEPH CONRAD

Let us digress for a moment onto the famous case of Joseph Conrad. Philip Lieberman (1984, p. 95) claims that 'whenever I get into an argument with my learned colleagues who claim that anyone can learn to speak five languages without an accent, I fall back on Joseph Conrad, who is my staff, my support'. Conrad was born in Poland, went to live in Marseille at seventeen where he improved the French he had started learning as a child, and then started English at twenty while a seaman on a Polish ship, passing the British second mate's examination in spoken and written English two years later; he then became one of the leading novelists in English of his time. But Ford Madox Ford claimed that 'speaking English he had so strong a French accent that few who did not know him well could understand him at first'. Norman Page (1986) does not feel Ford is a reliable witness: 'like many of Ford's statements this needs to be viewed with some scepticism'. Virginia Woolf, however, claimed that Conrad was 'a foreigner, talking broken English'; Paul Valéry that his English was 'horrible'; H.G. Wells that 'he spoke English strangely'; Bertrand Russell that he 'spoke English with a very strong foreign accent'. Lady Ottoline Morell had perhaps the only kind words for his English: 'He talked English with a strong accent as if he tasted his words in his mouth before pronouncing them; he talked extremely well, though he had always the talk and manner of a foreigner.' Indeed there is a counterclaim that Conrad spoke English with a strong accent to forestall unwelcome invitations to give talks. Certainly the memoirs by his wife and sons make no mention of his odd English.

So it might seem that there is indeed a Conrad effect: people cannot manage to learn a second language efficiently after their teens. But, if we are talking about Conrad as an L2 learner, we should not forget that English was in fact his *third* language. His French was spoken with 'elegance' according to one witness, with 'general ease and no trace of an accent' according to another; he conversed with Henry James in French by preference. By all accounts his French was native-like. And acquired after the age of seventeen. So it seems unfair to hold him up to ridicule as an unsuccessful learner on account of his accent in his third language.

Conrad was, nevertheless, famous for the quality of his written English, the language he chose to write in. He himself claimed to have great difficulties and said he was 'a coal-miner in his pit quarrying all my English sentences out of a black night'. How many fluent native speakers of English, however, could write a sentence as vivid as this? Could Ford Madox Ford, Lady Ottoline Morell, or, dare one say it, Virginia Woolf? In other words, his command of English was in the front rank of English writers; critics have spent years trying to find clear 'mistakes' in his grammar (though, to give Ford Madox Ford some due, some editing by others may have taken place). One of the most successful writers of the century is dismissed as a failure because he spoke with an accent in this third language. If only all our learners were half as successful as Conrad (except of course for his accent!).

AGE AND LANGUAGE TEACHING

How should a language teacher take the student's age into account? One question is when L2 teaching should start. This also involves how long the learners are going to be studying. If they are intending to spend many years learning the L2, they might as well start as children rather than as adults since they will probably end up better speakers. If they are going to learn the L2 for a few years and then drop it, like the majority of learners perhaps, there is an advantage for adults, who would reach a higher standard during the same period. But, as Bernard Spolsky (1989a) points out, 'Educational systems usually arrive first at a decision of optimal learning age on political or economic grounds and then seek justification for their decision.' When to teach children a second language is usually not decided by language teachers or L2 learning experts.

The other question is whether the use of teaching methods should vary according to the age of the students. At particular ages students prefer particular methods. Teenagers may dislike any technique that exposes them in public; role-play and simulation are in conflict with their adolescent anxieties. Adults can feel they are not learning properly in play-like situations and prefer a conventional formal style of teaching. These are not factors that affect L2 learning directly. Adults learn better than children from the 'childish' activities of total physical response – if you can get them to join in! Age is by no means crucial to L2 learning itself. Spolsky (1989a) describes three conditions for L2 learning related to age:

1. 'Formal' classroom learning requires 'skills of abstraction and analysis'. That is to say, if the teaching method entails sophisticated understanding and reasoning by the student, as for instance a traditional grammar-translation method, then it is better for the student to be older.
2. The child is more open to L2 learning in informal situations. Hence children are easier to teach through an informal approach.
3. The natural L2 situation may favour children. The teaching of adults requires the creation of language situations in the classroom that in some ways compensate for this lack. An important characteristic of

language spoken to small children is that it is concerned with the 'here and now' rather than with the absent objects or the abstract topics that are talked about in adult conversation – adults do not even talk about the weather much to a two-year-old child! That is to say, ordinary speech spoken by adults to adults is too sophisticated for L2 learning. Restricting the language spoken to the beginning L2 learner to make it reflect the here-and-now could be of benefit. This is reminiscent of the audiovisual and situational teaching methods, which stress the provision of concrete visual information through physical objects or pictures in the early stages of L2 learning. But it may go against the idea that the content of teaching should be relevant and should not be trivial, to be discussed in the next chapter.

Most adaptation to the age of the learner in textbooks probably concerns the presentation of material and topics. Taking *The Beginners Choice* (Mohamed and Acklam, 1992), the first lesson starts with photographs of people aged between about eighteen and twenty-five dressed in denim, and looking lively – listening to a Walkman or a ghetto-blaster, reading magazines – all in colourfully glossy photographs; the topics in the book include holidays and divorce – what age would you say this was aimed at? The opening lesson of *Hotline* (Hutchinson, 1992) has a photo-strip story of two young men going along a street, one in a suit, the other with trainers and a purple backpack; topics include soap operas such as *Neighbours* and demos against roadworks – what age is this for? The answers from the blurb are 'adults' and 'teenagers' respectively. But as always with published materials they have to aim at an 'average' student; many teenagers may scorn soap operas, many adults have no interest in discussing holidays yet again.

AGE IN L2 LEARNING

- To be older leads to better learning in the short term, other things being equal.
- Some research still favours child superiority at pronunciation, but not reliably.
- Children get to a higher level of proficiency in the long term than those who start L2 learning while older, perhaps because adults slow down.

Teaching uses:

- deciding when to teach the L2.
- varying methods according to the student's age.

5 Are other personality traits important to L2 learning?

KEYWORDS

cognitive style: a person's typical ways of thinking, seen as a continuum between field-dependent (FD) cognitive style, in which thinking relates to context, and field-independent (FI) style, in which it is independent of context

extrovert and introvert: people's personalities vary between those who relate to objects outside themselves (extroverts) and those who relate to the contents of their own minds (introverts)

Though there has been research into how other variations between L2 learners contribute to their final success, it has produced a mass of conflicting answers. Mostly, isolated areas have been looked at rather than the learner as a whole. Much of the research is based on the non-uniqueness view of language and so assumes that L2 learning varies in the same way as other types of learning, say learning to drive or to type. One piece of research shows that something is beneficial; a second piece of research following up the same issue shows it is harmful. Presumably this conflict demonstrates the complexity of the learning process and the varieties of situation in which L2 learning occurs. But this is slender consolation to teachers, who want a straight answer.

COGNITIVE STYLE

This term refers to a technical psychological distinction between typical ways of thinking. Imagine standing in a room that is slowly leaning to one side without the people inside it knowing. Some people attempt to stand upright, others lean so that they are parallel to the walls. Those who lean have a *field-dependent* (FD) cognitive style; that is to say, their thinking relates to their surroundings. Those who stand upright have a *field-independent* (FI) style; they think independently of their surroundings. The usual test for cognitive style is less dramatic, relying on distinguishing shapes in pictures and is thus called the Embedded Figures Test. Those who can pick out shapes despite confusing backgrounds are field-independent, those who cannot are field-dependent. My own informal check is whether a person adjusts pictures that are hanging crookedly or does not. Obviously these are tendencies rather than absolutes; any individual is somewhere on the continuum between the poles of FI and FD.

A difference in cognitive style might well make a difference to success in L2 learning – another aspect of aptitude. Most researchers have found that a tendency towards FI (field independence) helps the student with conventional classroom learning (Alptekin and Atakan, 1990). This seems in a sense obvious in that formal education in the West successively pushes students up the rungs of a ladder of abstraction away from the concrete (Donaldson, 1978). Hansen and Stansfield (1981) used three tests with L2 learners: those that measured the ability to communicate, those that measured linguistic knowledge, and those that measured both together. FI learners had slight advantages for communicative tasks, greater advantages for academic tasks, and greatest for the combined tasks. However, since then Bacon (1987) found no differences between FD and FI students in terms of how much they spoke and how well they spoke. This illustrates again the interaction between student and teaching method; not all methods suit all students.

Cognitive style varies to some extent from one culture to another. There are variations between learners on different islands in the Pacific and between different sexes, though field-independence tends to go with good scores on a cloze test (Hansen, 1984). Of course there is no general reason why FI people in general are better or worse at cognitive functioning than those who are FD. FI and FD are simply two styles of thinking. A challenge has been posed to the use of FI/FD in second language acquisition by Roger Griffiths and Ronald Sheen (1992), who argue that the concept has not been sufficiently well defined in the research and is no longer of much interest within the discipline of psychology, from which it came.

PERSONALITY

Perhaps an outgoing, sociable person learns an L2 better than a reserved, shy, person. Again, the connection is not usually so straightforward. Some researchers have investigated the familiar division between extrovert and introvert personalities. In Jungian psychology the distinction applies to two tendencies in the way that people interact with the world. Some people relate to objects outside them, some to the interior world. Rossier (1976) found a link between extroversion and oral fluency. There would seem a fairly obvious connection to language teaching methods. The introverts might be expected to prefer academic teaching that emphasizes individual learning and language knowledge; the extroverts audiolingual or communicative teaching that emphasizes group participation and social know-how.

OTHER INDIVIDUAL VARIATION

What else? Many other variations in the individual's mental make-up have been checked against L2 success.

Intelligence, for example, has some connection with school performance. There are links between intelligence and aptitude in classrooms as might be expected (Genesee, 1976).

Sex differences have also been investigated. The UK Assessment of Performance Unit (1986) found English girls were better at French than English boys in all skills except speaking. In my experience of talking with teachers it is true in every country that second languages are more popular school subjects among girls. Only one in four undergraduates studying in the Languages and Linguistics department at Essex is a man.

Level of first language is also relevant. Some studies support the common teacher's view that children who are more advanced in their L1 are better at their L2 (Skehan, 1988).

Empathy. Those students who are able to empathize with the feelings of others are better at learning L2 pronunciation, though this depends to some extent on the language the students are acquiring (Guiora *et al.*, 1972).

Of course all teachers have their own pet belief about factors that are crucial to L2 learning. One of my own suspicions is that the time of year when the student was born makes a difference, due in England, not to astrological sign, but to the extra schooling children get if they are born at certain times. But my own checks with the university computer cannot seem to prove this.

Many of the factors in this chapter cannot be affected by the teacher. Age is unchangeable, as are aptitude, intelligence, and most areas of personality. As teachers cannot change them, they have to live with them. In other words, teaching has to recognize the differences between learners. At a gross level this means catering for the factors that a class have in common, say age and type of motivation. At a finer level the teacher has to cater for the differences between individuals in the class by providing opportunities for each of them to benefit in their own way; ideally this would be what I have called 'ambiguous teaching': the same teaching can be taken in different ways by different students. To some teachers this is not sufficient; nothing will do but complete individualization so that each student has his or her own unique course. For class teaching the aspects in which students are different have to be balanced against those that they share. Much L2 learning is common ground whatever the individual differences between learners may be.

DISCUSSION TOPICS

1. Give three ways in which you would increase (a) positive short-term motivation and (b) integrative motivation in your students.
2. Is it really possible to change the students' underlying motivation, as opposed to simply increasing it?
3. What should be done with students who have a low aptitude for L2 learning?
4. Which learning strategies have you employed yourself? Which would you recommend to students?
5. How could you train learning strategies in your students?
6. When do you think is the best age to learn a foreign language?
7. Name two teaching techniques that would work best with adults, two with children.
8. How can you cater for different personality types in the same classroom?
9. If girls are in fact better at L2 learning than boys, why should this be the case?

FURTHER READING

Main sources for this chapter are: Skehan (1989), *Individual Differences in Second-Language Learning*; O'Malley and Chamot (1990), *Learning Strategies in Second Language Acquisition*; Singleton (1989), *Language Acquisition: The Age Factor*. A useful and clear guide to strategies is McDonough (1995), *Strategy and Skill in Learning a Foreign Language*.

6

Language and input in the L2 classroom

The question that has sometimes been asked is 'Can second languages be taught?' Or, as Michael Long (1983) puts it less contentiously, 'Does second language instruction make a difference?' Though a fair amount of discussion of this question has taken place, it is in a sense like asking a doctor if medical treatment benefits the patient. When the students are studying for educational benefit or for personal profit in places where the L2 has no function in the society, the question is beside the point, since teaching is the chief or indeed only source of the second language. Whatever they know, whatever they can say or understand, is an effect of teaching. Perhaps Greeks learning English in Athens might learn it better if they lived in London, or English people learn Chinese better if they lived in Beijing, but, as they do not have the chance, the comparison is hypothetical so far as practical implications for language teaching are concerned. There is no other choice than the classroom.

In societies where the second language is in actual use, L2 learning in the world outside can more meaningfully be compared with L2 learning inside the classroom. The issue of whether one is better than the other hardly arises since few L2 learners have the option of deciding between learning in a classroom or a street; it is their circumstances that decide. It is a different question to ask whether the doctor's treatment was successful – to consider whether the students would have done better if they had been taught differently – but this involves the comparison of different teaching methods, not a dismissal of teaching. Perhaps one should point out, to the relief of teachers, that Long's survey of research concluded that instruction *does* in fact make a difference – supported more recently by work by Catherine Doughty (1991), who showed that learners were helped to learn English relative clauses by particular forms of teaching compared to other students.

Focusing questions

- Do you think people would learn English best inside or outside a classroom?

- Do you think of the classroom as a real situation of its own or as something artificial?
- How much of the class time do you think the teacher speaks? How much should they speak?
- How and why do you think language should be simplified for use in the classroom?
- If you walked through the door of a strange classroom, how would you be able to tell that a communicative method of language teaching was being used?
- In what way do you adapt your speech to children? to foreigners?
- When you were at school did you think of your teachers as wise superior beings or as helpful equals?

---

1 L2 learning inside the classroom

KEYWORDS

leader and follower: in some types of conversation one person has the right to lead the conversation while the others follow his or her lead
teacher-talk: the amount of speech supplied by the teacher rather than the students
initiation: the opening move by the teacher
response: the student's response to the teacher's opening move
feedback: teacher evaluation of the student response
authentic speech: 'an authentic text is a text that was created to fulfil some social purpose in the language community in which it was produced' (Little *et al.*, 1988)

L2 LEARNING INSIDE AND OUTSIDE CLASSROOMS

It is perfectly natural and proper to ask whether L2 learning is the same inside the classroom as outside. One extreme point of view sees the L2 classroom as a world of its own. Whatever it is that the students are doing, it is quite different from the 'natural' ways of learning language. Thus some teaching methods exploit deliberately 'unnatural' L2 learning. Grammar-translation teaching, for instance, is exploiting the other faculties the mind has available for L2 learning rather than making use of the 'natural' processes of the language faculty. At the opposite extreme is the view that all L2 learning, or indeed all language learning of L1 or L2, is the same. The classroom at best exploits this natural learning, at worst puts barriers in its way, as argued in the Krashen model (Krashen 1981a) developed in Chapter 8.

What evidence is there one way or the other? Some areas of grammar have been investigated in classrooms as well as in the world outside. Learners appear to go through the same sequence of acquisition in both situations. The order of acquisition for grammatical forms such as negation and questions was substantially the same for German children learning English at school as for those learning naturally (Felix, 1981). Three children learning English as a second language in London over a period of time started by producing 'no' by itself or 'anaphoric' 'no' with a separate sentence 'Red, no' (Ellis, 1986). Sentences with external negation 'No play baseball' were said before those with internal negation 'I'm no drawing chair.' This happened slowly over the period of a year, only one child producing a single sentence with an auxiliary within the sentence 'This man can't read.' The children were going through the usual stages in the acquisition of negation despite the fact that they were actually being taught negation during the course of the year. So it appears that much of the time students in classrooms learn second languages in the same way as learners who never go near them.

THE LANGUAGE OF CLASSROOMS IN GENERAL

Let us start with the language interaction that occurs in all classrooms. Most face-to-face conversation is interactive and listener related. Some situations, however, give one participant a more directive role than the others; one person can be called the 'leader' who takes the initiative, the other are 'followers' who respond to it. For example, an interviewer has the right to guide the conversation and to ask questions that would be out of place in other situations. 'How old are you?' addressed to an adult is unthinkable except in an interview. In the classroom this overall 'leader' role falls to the teacher. The exchange of turns between listeners and speakers is under the teacher's overall guidance, overtly or covertly. So, not surprisingly, about 70 per cent of the utterances in most classrooms come from the teacher.

So far this resembles the child learning the first language in that adults often assume the same basic right to direct the conversation when talking to children. 'How old are you?' is a frequent question from adults to children. The difference between the classroom and other leader-directed conversations lies in the way that the turns are structured. Let us take a short classroom exchange from Sinclair and Coulthard (1975):

TEACHER: Can you tell me why you eat all that food? Yes.
PUPIL: To keep you strong.
TEACHER: To keep you strong. Yes. To keep you strong. Why do you want to be strong? . . .

This exchange has three main moves:

1. *Initiation.* The teacher takes the initiative by requiring something of the student, say through a question such as 'Can you tell me why you eat all that food?' The move starts off the exchange; the teacher acts as leader.

2. *Response*. Then the student does whatever is required, here answering the question by saying 'To keep you strong'. So the move responds to the teacher's initiation; the student acts as follower.

3. *Feedback*. The teacher does not go straight on to the next initiation but announces whether the student is right or wrong, 'To keep you strong. Yes.' The teacher evaluates the student's behaviour and comments on it in a way that would be impossible outside the classroom and unlikely even from many parents speaking to children.

This three-move structure of initiation, response, and feedback – or IRF as it is known – is very frequent in teaching. Even in lectures teachers sometimes attempt feedback moves with comments such as 'That was a good question.' Language teaching styles such as the academic or audiolingual rely heavily on this classroom structure. IRF was after all the format of the classic language laboratory drill. Other styles of teaching such as the communicative may discourage it because it is restricted to classroom language rather than being generally applicable. Nor is IRF the only characteristic of such exchanges. One common feature, illustrated by the 'Yes' in 'Can you tell me why you eat all that food? Yes', is that the teacher selects and approves who is to speak next, a feature common to all leader/follower situations ranging from chairpeople at committee meetings to Congressional committees of investigation.

LANGUAGE IN THE LANGUAGE TEACHING CLASSROOM

Are language teaching classrooms any different from other classrooms? Craig Chaudron (1988) cites figures from various sources about teacher talk: teacher talk takes up 77 per cent of the time in bilingual classrooms in Canada, 69 per cent in immersion classes, and 61 per cent in foreign language classrooms. Werner Hullen (1989) found 75 per cent of the utterances in German classrooms came from the teacher. A massive amount of the language the student hears is provided by the teacher.

The uniqueness of the L2 teaching classroom is that language is involved in two different ways. First of all, the organization and control of the classroom take place through language; second, language is the actual subject matter that is being taught. A school subject like physics does not turn the academic subject back on itself. Physics is not taught through physics in the same way that language is taught through language. This twofold involvement of language creates a unique problem for L2 teaching. The students and teachers are interacting through language in the classroom, using the strategies and moves that form part of their normal classroom behaviour. But at the same time the L2 strategies and moves are the behaviour the learner is aiming at, the objectives of the teaching. The teacher has to be able to manage the class through one type of language at the same time as getting the student to acquire another type. There is a falseness about much language teaching that does not exist in other school subjects because language has to fulfil its normal classroom role as well as be the content of the class. N.S. Prabhu (1987) suggests dealing with this problem by treating the classroom solely as a classroom: 'learners' responses arose from their role as learners, not from assumed roles in simulated situations or from their individual lives outside the classroom'; the real language of the classroom is classroom language.

The teacher's language is particularly important to language teaching. Teachers of physics adapt their speech to suit the level of comprehension of their pupils, but this is only indirectly connected to their subject matter. The students are not literally learning the teacher's language. Teachers of languages who adapt their speech directly affect the subject matter: language itself. Like most teachers, I have felt while teaching that I was adapting the grammatical structures and the vocabulary to what the students could take.

But is this subjective feeling right? Do teachers really change their speech for the level of learner or do they simply believe they do so? What is more, do such changes actually benefit the students? Observation of teachers confirms there is indeed adaptation of several kinds. Steven Gaies (1979) recorded student-teachers teaching EFL in the classroom. At each of four levels from beginners to advanced their speech increased in syntactic complexity. Even at the advanced level it was still less complicated than their speech to their fellow students. Craig Chaudron (1983) compared a teacher lecturing on the same topic to native and non-native speakers. He found considerable simplification and rephrasing in vocabulary: 'clinging' became 'holding in tightly', and 'ironic' became 'funny'. He felt that the teacher's compulsion to express complex content simply often led to 'ambiguous over-simplification on the one hand and confusingly redundant over-elaboration on the other'. Hullen (1989) found the feedback move was prominent with about 30 per cent of teacher's remarks consisting of 'right', 'ah', 'okay', and so on.

What does this high proportion of teacher-talk mean for L2 teaching? Several teaching methods have tried to maximize the amount of speaking by the student. The audiolingual method approved of the language laboratory precisely because it increased each student's share of speaking time. Communicative methods support pairwork and groupwork partly because they give each student the chance to talk as much as possible. Other methods do not share this opinion that teacher-talk should be minimized. Conventional academic teaching emphasizes factual information coming from the teacher. Listening-based teaching sees most value in the students extracting information from what they hear rather than in speaking themselves. One argument for less speech by the students is that at least the sentences that the students hear will be correct examples of the target language, not samples of the interlanguages of their fellow students.

AUTHENTIC AND NON-AUTHENTIC LANGUAGE

A further distinction is between authentic and non-authentic language. Here is a typical textbook dialogue taken from *Flying Colours I* (Garton-Sprenger and Greenall, 1990):

NICOLA: Do you like this music?
ROGER: Not very much. I don't like jazz.
NICOLA: What kind of music do you like?
ROGER: I like classical music . . .

This is *non-authentic* language specially constructed for its teaching potential. People in real-life conversations do not answer questions so explicitly, do not speak in full grammatical sentences, and do not keep to a clear sequence of turns. Instead they speak like these two people, who were recorded while talking about ghosts for the course book *English Topics* (Cook, 1975):

MRS BAGG: Oh, how extraordinary.
JENNY DREW: So . . . 'cos quite a quite a lot of things like that.
MRS BAGG: I mean were they frightened? 'Cos I think if I actually . . .
JENNY DREW: No.
MRS BAGG: . . . saw a ghost because I don't believe in them really, I would be frightened, you know to think that I was completely wrong.

This is then an example of *authentic* language, defined by Little *et al.* (1988) as 'created to fulfil some social purpose in the language community in which it was produced'. Until recently teaching provided the students with specially adapted language, not only simplified in terms of syntax and confined in vocabulary but also tidied up in terms of discourse structure. The belief was that such non-authentic language was vital to L2 learning.

With the advent of methods that looked at the communicative situation the students were going to encounter, it began to seem that the students were handicapped by never hearing authentic speech in all its richness and diversity. Hence exercises and courses have proliferated that turn away from specially constructed classroom language to any pieces of language that have been really used by native speakers, whether tapes of conversations, advertisements from magazines, train timetables, or a thousand and one other sources. Indeed in most countries it is possible to use authentic texts based on local circumstances taken from local English-language newspapers such as the *Jerusalem Post*, or the *Buenos Aires Herald*.

Two justifications for the use of authentic text in communicative teaching are put forward by Little *et al.* (1988):

1. *Motivation and interest.* Students will be better motivated by texts that have served a real communicative purpose.
2. *Acquisition-promoting content.* Authentic texts provide a rich source of natural language for the learner to acquire language from.

An additional reason put forward by Cook (1981b) is:

> 3. *Filling-in gaps.* Designers of course books and syllabuses may miss some of the aspects of language used in real-life situations; we often do not know what people actually say in railway stations or offices. This lack can be filled most easily by giving students the appropriate real-life language taken from situations appropriate to their needs.

The fact that the language is authentic does not in itself make it more difficult than specially written language. Difficulty depends partly upon the amount of material that is used. Take two beginners examples. A BBC Russian course simply recorded people on the streets of Moscow saying 'Zdravstvujte' ('Hello') to the cameraman – totally authentic but no problem for the students. The recording or text does not have to consist of many words to be authentic: 'EXIT', 'This door is alarmed', 'Ladies', to take three authentic written signs. Difficulty also depends upon the task that is used with the material. You can play two philosophers discussing the nature of the universe to beginners provided all you ask them to do is identify which is a man, which a woman, or who is angry, who is calm, or indeed who said 'well' most often.

It is a decision for the teacher whether authentic language should be used in the classroom or whether non-authentic language reflects a legitimate way into the language. In other words the choice is between decoding and codebreaking: are the processes of learning similar to those of use, so that authentic language is needed, or are they distinct, so that appropriate non-authentic language is helpful? Other factors involved in this decision will be the goals of the students and the other constraints of the teaching situation. And of course it must not be forgotten that the classroom is a classroom; authentic language by definition is not normal classroom language and is being used for purposes quite other than those of its original speakers, however well intentioned the teacher.

LANGUAGE IN CLASSROOM L2 LEARNING

- Teacher-talk makes up around 70 per cent of classroom language.
- Language teaching classrooms are different from other subjects because language is not just the medium but also the content.
- Authentic speech may motivate and help communicative goals, if decoding equates with codebreaking.
- Non-authentic speech may be specially tailored to students' learning needs if codebreaking is seen as different from decoding.

2 Language in the communicative classroom

KEYWORDS

Communicative Orientation of Language Teaching: the COLT scheme devised at OISE describes the activities that occur in communicative classrooms

Let us now look more closely at the nature of the language classroom. A scheme for describing what goes on in language teaching has been developed at OISE (Ontario Institute for Studies in Education) in Toronto, known as COLT – Communicative Orientation of Language Teaching (Fröhlich *et al.*, 1985; Allen *et al.*, 1990). COLT measures the extent to which the activities of a classroom represent communicative teaching. An outline of the whole scheme is given on page 128. COLT has two parts: A, *Classroom events*, categorizes the activities that take place in the classroom; B, *Communicative features*, looks at what the actual activities consist of. The researchers sat in on four types of classes in Ontario: 'core French' classes, which were ordinary foreign language classes, 'extended French' classes, which, in addition, used French for teaching one or more other school subjects, 'French immersion' classes, which used French for most school activities, and English as a Second Language (ESL) classes, where non-English speaking students spent most of their day.

COLT PART A CLASSROOM EVENTS

The types of classroom events considered in COLT are:

(a) *What type of activity occurs?* These are not categorized in any particular way.

(b) *How do the teachers and students participate in the activity? Is teaching to the whole class, in small groups, or to individuals?* The ESL classes had the most individual work, the extended French classes had the most teacher-talk.

(c) *What content is talked about in the activity?* This is divided roughly into classroom management, discussion of language, discussion of other topics, and who controls the choice of topic. Classroom management took up less then 10 per cent of the time; language as a topic ranged from 66 per cent in an ESL class to 14 per cent in a French immersion class.

(d) *Which skills or combination of skills are being used?* The combinations of Listening-Speaking and Listening-Speaking-Reading were the most common rather than single skill activities.

(e) *What materials are being used?* This is seen in terms of the type (text, audio, or visual), the source (specially constructed teaching materials or natural language), and the extent to which the materials control the teaching. Texts are divided into 'minimal' and 'extended', i.e.

individual or connected sentences. Text materials predominated in the classroom. The French immersion made the highest use of extended text, the core French the lowest; the source was usually specially constructed materials.

Part A of COLT draws out the salient features of the classroom and distinguishes one class from another. This brings some surprises, such as the concentration on form in the ESL class. The devisers of COLT decided that a communicative class would probably have more groupwork, would focus on meaning, and the participants would choose the topics; the texts would be extended, and the language would be authentic rather than specially constructed. On this scale of 'communicativeness' the core French classes were least communicative, the French immersion most communicative.

COLT PART B COMMUNICATIVE FEATURES

Part B of COLT looks at how the participants in the classroom interact with each other, in particular:

(a) *Which language is used, L1 or L2?*

(b) *Is there is an information gap?* Do the students have to exchange real pieces of information? Two overall categories are: requesting information and giving information.

(c) *How long are the utterances?* Does an utterance last for more than a sentence or two?

(d) *Reaction to code or message.* This reflects whether the teachers draw attention to language mistakes.

(e) *Does what one person says take account of what the others say?*

(f) *Who initiates an exchange?* teacher or student?

(g) *How restricted are the linguistic forms?* This ranges from the use of only single linguistic forms to the free use of any form.

While the teachers concerned mostly used the L1, the amount of sustained speech by teachers varied from 28 per cent in the core French classes to 61 per cent in the ESL. As with the communication strategies outlined in Chapter 4, perhaps the crucial decision is whether to use the L1 or the L2 for solving communicative tasks. In the Canadian classrooms, while teachers often commented 'Good', etc., as an evaluation, they rarely followed up the content of the student's response. Students had the minimal amount of sustained speech in the core French class, the most in French immersion and ESL.

COLT does then bring out some interesting sidelights on the classroom. The supposedly communicative class is often less different from the conventional class than might be supposed. When Allen *et al.* (1990) looked only at the core French classes, they found that the students in more communicative classes appeared to achieve much the same proficiency as those in less communicative ones.

COLT confirms the impression that many teachers still think of an L2 class as language practice above all else. If the student's answer leads away from the language point that is being pursued, it is ignored, however promising the discussion might seem. Seldom does genuine communication take place in which the students and teacher develop a communicative exchange leading away from the language teaching point. Yet one of the early claims of the Direct Method pioneers was that genuine interchange of ideas was possible. Lambert Sauveur boasted that he could give a beginners class on any topic, and, when challenged to give a class on God, succeeded brilliantly (Howatt, 1984). The IRF exchange, and the evaluation move by the teacher in particular, is a constant reminder to the students that they are engaged in language practice, not in 'real' communication.

The approach exemplified by COLT looks at the language used in actual classrooms through the filter imposed by a particular scheme of analysis. Many such schemes for analysing classrooms have been devised, usually known by a set of initials such as FLint, FOCUS, or ECS, to take three of the better known, described, for example, in Allwright (1988). COLT has the advantage that it is deliberately oriented towards a teaching approach that is current and that it looks at relevant aspects of the teaching process. Often information yielded by these schemes ends up as a mass of figures that either show the obvious – teachers talk more than students – or the obscure. Such research tends to intimidate teachers through the sheer complexity it reveals about the classroom. However *any* situation analysed in this fashion would seem as complex. The title of a book on discourse was *The First Five Minutes* (Pittenger *et al.*, 1960), and this accurately described the entire content: analysis of the first five minutes of a single interview. Most results from these schemes at present seem remote from most teachers' practical concerns.

3 Language input and language learning

KEYWORDS

baby talk, motherese, foreigner talk: forms of language specially designed for listeners without full competence
postfigurative: a culture in which people learn from older wiser guardians of knowledge
cofigurative: a culture in which people learn from their equals
prefigurative: a culture in which people learn from their juniors

The language of the language teaching classroom is distinctive because it is designed for language learning to take place. All languages have special varieties for talking to speakers who are believed not to speak very well. For example, 'baby talk' or 'motherese' are used when talking to babies. These have similar

---

COMMUNICATIVE ORIENTATION OF LANGUAGE TEACHING (COLT)

Part A: Classroom events:

- What type of activity occurs?
- How do the teachers and students participate in the activity?
- What content is talked about in the activity?
- Which skills or combination of skills are being used?
- What materials are being used?

Part B: Communicative features:

- Which language is used, L1 or L2?
- Is there is an information gap?
- How long are the utterances?
- Reaction to code or message?
- Does what one person says take account of what the others say?
- Who initiates an exchange?
- How restricted are the linguistic forms?

---

characteristics in many languages: exaggerated changes of pitch, louder volume, 'simpler' grammar, special words such as 'bow-wow', or 'walkies!', and so on.

Barbara Freed (1980) found that 'foreigner talk' addressed to non-native speakers also had simple grammar and a high proportion of questions with 'unmoved' question words, e.g. 'You will return to your country when?' rather than 'When will you return to your country?' But the functions of language in foreigner talk were more directed at the exchange of information than at controlling the person's behaviour, as in baby talk. Most teachers rarely fall totally into this style of speech. Nevertheless experienced teachers have a distinct type of speech and gesture when speaking to foreigners.

But the fact that baby talk exists does not prove that it has any effect on learning. After all people have been talking to animals for years without any of them learning to speak. In other words, baby talk and foreigner talk varieties of language reflect what people believe less proficient speakers need – but their beliefs may be wrong. Many child language researchers feel that acquiring the first language does not depend upon some special aspect of the language that the child hears. The effects of baby talk on children's first language development have so far been impossible to prove. It may well be that its characteristics are beneficial but this is chiefly a matter of belief, given the many children who acquire the first language in far from optimal conditions. Some further aspects of input in language learning are discussed in relation to the Universal Grammar (UG) model in Chapter 8.

TEACHING AND LANGUAGE INPUT

L2 learning differs from L1 learning in that the majority of students fall by the wayside before they get to a level equivalent to an L1 learner. An important element in L2 success appears to be how learners are treated: the teaching method used with them, the language they hear, and the environment in which they are learning. The purpose of language teaching in a sense is to provide optimal samples of language for the learner to profit from – the best 'input' to the process of language learning. Everything the teacher does provides the learner with opportunities for encountering the language.

At this point the mostly British-based communicative method of teaching parts company with the mostly American listening-based methods. The communicative methods have emphasized the learners' dual roles as listeners and as speakers. A typical exercise requires students to take both roles in a conversation and not only to understand the information they are listening to but also to try to express it themselves. They are receiving input not only from the teacher but also from their peers in the class. The listening-based methods, however, confine the student to the role of listener. In a technique such as total physical response the students listen and carry out commands but they do not have to speak. Hence the input they receive is totally controlled by the teacher. An example from Krashen and Terrell *The Natural Approach* (1983) consists of showing the students pictures and getting them to choose between them according to the teacher's description: 'There are two men in this picture. They are young. They are boxing.' This approach was encapsulated in the slogan 'Maximize comprehensible input' discussed in Chapter 4.

Communicative teaching methods have often felt that it is beneficial to students to listen to authentic language consisting of judiciously chosen samples of unexpurgated native speech, as we have seen. Authentic speech evidently needs to be made comprehensible by one method or another if it is to be useful to the learner. Its deliberate avoidance of any concession to the learner needs to be compensated for in some way.

IMPLICATIONS FOR TEACHING

One overall moral is that there is no such thing as *the* classroom. Classrooms vary in many ways. Some students have been hypnotized, some have studied in their sleep, some have seen Lego blocks built into sentences, some have had the world of meaning reduced to a set of coloured sticks, some have sat in groups and bared their souls, others have sat in language laboratories repeating after the tape. The classroom is a variable, not a constant. Teachers can adapt it in whatever way suits their students and their aims. Nor should we forget that instruction does not only take place in classrooms. The self-motivated autonomous student can learn as efficiently as any taught in a class.

What advice can be given about input in the classroom?

1. *Be aware of the two levels at which language enters into the classroom.* Using the L1 for classroom management and instructions deprives the students of genuine examples of language use and sets a tone for the class that influences much that happens in the L2 activities. Overusing the 'leader' pattern of IRF teacher-talk undermines a communicative classroom by destroying the usual give-and-take of interaction outside the classroom.

2. *Be aware of the different sources of input.* Language may come first from the teacher, second from the textbook or teaching materials, and third from the other students, not to mention sources outside the classroom. All of these provide different types of language: the teacher the genuine language of the classroom, the textbook purpose-designed non-authentic language or authentic language taken out of its usual context, the other students 'interlanguage' full of non-native-like forms but at the same time genuine communicative interaction.

3. *The input that the students are getting is far more than just the sentences they encounter.* The whole context provides language; this includes the patterns of interaction between teacher and class and between students in the class, down to the actual gestures used. Many teachers ostensibly encourage spontaneous natural interaction from the students but they still betray that they are teachers controlling a class in every physical gesture they make.

4. *Students learn what they are taught.* This truism has often been applied to language classrooms: in general, students taught by listening methods turn out to be better at listening; students taught through reading are better at reading. The major source of language available to many learners is what they encounter in the classroom. This biases their knowledge in particular ways. A teacher I observed was insisting that the students used the present continuous; hardly surprisingly his students were later saying things like 'I'm catching the bus every morning.' The teacher's responsibility is to make certain that the language input that is provided is sufficient for the student to gain the appropriate type of language knowledge and does not distort it in crucial ways. While in many respects L2 learners go their own way in developmental sequences, etc., their classroom input affects their language in broad terms.

Much of what we have seen so far implies that language itself is the most important ingredient in the classroom, the core of the syllabus, the basis for the teaching technique and the underlying skeleton of the class whether considered as conversational interaction, authentic or non-authentic, simplified grammatical structures, or whatever. This has been challenged by those who see the classroom as a unique situation with its own rationale.

Prabhu (1987), for example, talked of how the classroom consisted of particular processes and activities; his celebrated work in Bangalore organized language teaching around the activities that could be done in the classroom: interpreting information in tables, working out distances and so on. More recently Michael Long and Graham Crookes (1993) have been evolving a system of language teaching arranged around pedagogic tasks 'which provide a vehicle for the presentation of appropriate language samples to learners'. A task has an objective and has to be based on tasks that the students need in their lives. Language is by no means the sole factor in the language teaching classroom and the students will suffer if all the teacher's attention goes on organizing language content and interaction.

CULTURE AND THE CLASSROOM

Two links with other areas must be made. One concerns the individual in the classroom, the other the classroom as part of the society. The individual's attitudes to the classroom form an important component in L2 learning. The student's attitudes towards the learning situation as measured by feelings about the classroom teacher and level of anxiety about the classroom contribute towards the student's motivation. This is discussed further in Chapter 8. But there may also be a sharp opposition between different teachers. Adrian Holliday (1994) describes the difference between the social context of the expatriate EFL teacher and the non-native teacher who lives in that country. These may have very different interpretations of the same classroom, the one based on the West-dominated 'professionalism' of the EFL tradition, the other on the local educational system. Holliday tells of an encounter in Egypt between Beatrice, an expatriate lecturer, and Dr Anwar, a local member of an EFL project. To the expatriate it was discussion among equals about their experiences in the language laboratory, to Dr Anwar it was a waste of his expert time. Teachers may then inhabit different cultures of their own, as well as the differences between the cultures of the student and the target language.

So far as the society is concerned, the expectations of the students and teachers about the classroom depend upon their culture. Margaret Mead (1970) makes a useful division between *postfigurative* societies, in which people learn from wise elders, *cofigurative* societies, in which they learn from their equals, and *prefigurative* societies, in which they learn from their juniors. Many cultures view education as postfigurative. The classroom to them is a place in which the wise teacher imparts knowledge to the students. Hence they naturally favour teaching methods that transfer knowledge explicitly from the teacher to the student, such as academic teaching methods. Other cultures see education cofiguratively. The teacher designs opportunities for the students to learn from each other. Hence they prefer teaching methods that encourage groupwork and pairwork. Mead feels that modern technological societies are often prefigurative, as witness the ease with which teenagers master computers, compared to their parents. There is not to my knowledge a language teaching parallel to this last type, unless in certain 'alternative' methods.

So certain teaching methods will be dangerous to handle in particular societies. Whatever the merits of the communicative method, its attempts to promote non-teacher-controlled activities in China were at first perceived as insults to the Confucian ethos of the classroom, which emphasized the benefits of learning texts by heart (Sampson, 1984). In Mead's terms a cofigurative method was being used in a postfigurative classroom. A teaching method has to suit the beliefs of the society about what activities are proper for classrooms. It usually goes far beyond the language teacher's brief to decide on the overall concept of the classroom in a society. The different links between L2 learning and societies are followed up in the next chapter.

CLASSROOM INPUT AND LANGUAGE TEACHING

Everything the teacher does provides the learner with opportunities for encountering the language.

- Be aware of the two levels at which language enters into the classroom.
- Be aware of the different sources of input.
- The input that the students are getting is far more than just the sentences they encounter.
- Students learn what they are taught (in some sense).
- What works in the classroom in one cultural milieu will not work in another.

DISCUSSION TOPICS

1. To what extent can and should the classroom duplicate the language of the world outside?
2. Should teachers feel guilty if they talk for most of the time in a lesson? Or would students be disappointed if they did not?
3. What kinds of authentic speech can you envisage using in a specific classroom? How would you use them?
4. How successful do you think COLT would be at measuring the classrooms you are familiar with?
5. Do you now feel that you should simplify your speech while teaching or not?
6. Have you encountered yourself the gulf between the expatriate and the local teacher?
7. How would you see your teaching in terms of prefigurative, cofigurative, and postfigurative?

FURTHER READING

Two books that give a wealth of information on the language teaching classroom are: Chaudron (1988), *Second Language Classrooms: Research on Teaching and Learning*; and Ellis (1990), *Instructed Second Language Acquisition*. The use of authentic texts in teaching is described in Little *et al.* (1988), *Authentic Texts in Foreign Language Teaching: Theory and Practice*.

7

Multilingual societies and the goals of language teaching

To most people in England it seems remarkable that someone can use more than one language in their everyday life; to most people in the Cameroon there is nothing surprising in using four or five languages in the course of a day. To some acquiring a second language is a difficult feat; to others it is ordinary and unexceptionable. Probably more people in the world are like the typical Cameroonian than the typical Englishman. Harding and Riley (1986) point out 'there are 3000–5000 languages in the world but only about 150 countries to fit them all into'. The Commission of the European Communities survey (1987) into young people found that 83 per cent of 20–24 year olds in Europe had studied a second language. Knowing a second language is a normal part of human existence; it may well be unusual to know only one language. This chapter looks at some of the roles that second languages play in people's lives and sees how they can be interpreted as goals of language teaching. It goes outside the second language acquisition research area proper to explore ideas about bilingualism and multilingualism that are crucial for the language teacher.

Focusing questions

Second languages in society

- How many languages do you know? How many do you use in a day?
- Would you bring up your children to speak two languages? Why?
- In the area where you live, how many languages are spoken?

Goals of language teaching

- Do you think people who come to live in another country should *either* learn the majority language and forget their own *or* adopt the majority language for some everyday purposes *or* try to keep both the majority language and their L1 going?

- What goals do you or your students have for the second language outside their own country? Careers? Education? Access to information? Travel?

---

1 The different roles of second languages in societies

KEYWORDS

élite bilingualism: either the choice by parents of bringing up children through two languages, or societies in which members of a ruling group speak a second language
official language: language(s) recognized by a country for official purposes
multilingualism: countries where more than one language is used for everyday purposes
linguistic imperialism: means by which a 'Centre' country dominates 'Periphery' countries by making them use its language

Perhaps this section should start by disposing of one myth that used to bedevil bilingualism – that somehow bilingualism in itself had a bad effect on children. The older view can be typified by Thompson (1952): 'There can be no doubt that the child reared in a bilingual environment is handicapped in his language growth.' This view is still around; see, for example, the advice in a pamphlet for parents of Down syndrome children *I Can Talk* (Streets, 1976, reprinted 1991): 'Bilingual families: for any child this is confusing – one language should be the main one to avoid confusion.'

Since the 1960s research has pointed unequivocally to the advantages of bilingualism: children who know a second language are better at separating semantic from phonetic aspects of words, at tasks involving classification, and at tests of creativity; they have sharper awareness of language, as we see below; a brief list of bilingual writers such as Nabakov and Conrad soon confirms this. As for confusion, Einstein used more than one language (and was also a late speaker as a child!). Diaz in 1985 typifies the modern view: 'growing up with two languages is, indeed, an asset to children's intellectual development.' Much of the earlier belief in the deficiencies of the bilingual was due to not separating bilingualism out from the problems of poverty and isolation of immigrant groups.

BILINGUALISM BY CHOICE

Some people speak two languages because their parents decided to bring them up bilingually in the home. This so-called 'élite' bilingualism is not forced on the parents by society or by the educational system but is their free choice. Often one of the languages is the majority language of the country, the other a minority language spoken as a native by one parent. Sometimes both parents speak a minority language themselves but feel the majority language should also be used in the home. However, Saunders (1982) describes how he and his wife decided to bring up their children in German in Australia though neither of them was a native speaker of German. Others have three languages in the family; Philip Riley's children speak English and Swedish at home and French at school.

This choice by the parents also extends in some countries to educating their children through a second language – for example, in the International School movement across Europe, or in the English language boarding schools that exist in countries from Kenya to India to Chile. Attending such schools usually depends upon having money or upon being an expatriate; it is mostly a preserve of the middle classes. While L2 learning is often considered a 'problem' in the education of lower-status people, it is seen as a mark of distinction in higher-status people. Bilingualism by choice mostly takes place outside the main educational contexts of L2 teaching, according to a variety of approaches depending on the parents' wishes; accounts of these will be found in the self-help manuals written for parents by Arnberg (1987), by de Jong (1986), and by Harding and Riley (1986).

SECOND LANGUAGES FOR RELIGIOUS USE

Some people speak a second language because of their religious beliefs. For centuries after its decline as an international language, Latin functioned as a religious language of the Catholic Church. Muslims read the Koran in Arabic, regardless of whether they live in an Arabic-speaking country like Saudi Arabia, or in a country like Malaysia where Arabic has only a religious function. Jews outside Israel continue to learn Hebrew so that they can pray in it and study the Bible and other sacred texts. In parts of India, Christianity is identified with English, in Ethiopia with Aramaic. Though the language of religious observances is specialized, it is nevertheless a form of second language use. Again this type of L2 learning is distinct from most classroom situations and will not be discussed further here.

OFFICIAL LANGUAGES AND L2 LEARNING

According to Laponce (1987) there are 32 countries that recognize more than one language for official purposes. Switzerland has four languages (German, French, Italian, Romansh), and uses Latin on its stamps ('Helvetia'). The Singapore government uses English, Mandarin, Malay, and Tamil. Canada is officially bilingual in English and French. But the fact that a country has several official languages does not mean that any individual person speaks more than one; the communities may be entirely separate. Mackey (1967) claims that 'there are fewer bilingual people in the bilingual countries than there are in the so-called unilingual countries'. Few Canadians for instance use both English and French in daily life. Instead, the French and English speakers live predominantly in different parts of the country, as do the German, French and Italian speakers in Switzerland, and the French and Dutch speakers in Belgium. It is necessary in many of these countries to teach speakers of one official language to use another official language; Afrikaans-speaking civil servants in South Africa need English, their English-speaking counterparts in Canada need French. This does not necessarily mean that each official language is equally favoured; few Swiss would bother to learn Romansh as a second language. Nor does it mean that the official language learnt is actually the version used in the country; in Switzerland again, French-speaking children learn High German, not the Swiss German mostly spoken there, so that they can in a sense speak with Germans better than they can with their own countrymen.

Sometimes a language can become an official language with at first few, if any, native speakers. Hebrew was revived by a popular movement in Israel long before being adopted by the new state. The teaching of Hebrew in Israel did not just educate one group in the language of another but created a group of people who spoke a second language that would become the first language of their children. In some countries an official language is selected that has, at least to start with, a small proportion of native speakers, for example, Swahili in Tanzania, where only 10 per cent of the population are native speakers. Another pattern is found in Zaïre, where French is the official language but there are four 'national languages', Kiswahili, Ciluba, Lingala, and Kikongo, which are used as lingua franca among speakers of different mother tongues. To take a final example, in Pakistan four languages are spoken in different provinces: Pashto, Punjabi, Balochi, and Sindi; Urdu is used all over the country, as is Arabic for religious purposes; in addition English is an official language.

MULTILINGUALISM AND L2 LEARNING

Regardless of whether they have more than one official language, most countries contain large numbers of people who use other languages. England uses one language for official purposes; nevertheless the Linguistic Minorities Project (1983) found that 30.7 per cent of children in the London Borough of Haringey spoke languages other than English at home. Some countries, however, consist almost entirely of speakers of a single language: 99.3 per cent of the inhabitants of Japan speak Japanese (Grosjean, 1982). Others conceal a variety of languages under one official language. France has an estimated nine million people who are bilingual in other indigenous languages, not taking into account two million migrant workers from Portugal and North Africa (Valdman, 1976; Harding and Riley, 1986); it may well be that more bilinguals in Toronto speak English alongside Chinese, Japanese, or Italian than do French, despite English and French being the official language. In the United

States the population in 1976 included nearly 28 million, or one in six of those over fourteen who had a non-English mother tongue, most of whom were born in the USA (Wardhaugh, 1987); this has led to a worry about the continuing status and importance of English.

Mobility also plays a part in multilingualism. Some countries, for one historical reason or other, have of course included static populations of speakers of different languages, sometimes called 'internal colonies'. The UK has had speakers of Welsh, Gaelic, and English for many centuries. In Central Africa some 285 languages are spoken in Cameroon and 212 in Zaïre. In many cases this may reflect the arbitrary borders imposed on various countries in modern times. But much multilingualism seems to be based on movement of people or conquest; the empires of Islam and France led to Algeria having French, Arabic, and Berber speakers; the consequences of the British Empire and trade led to Malaysia having speakers of Bahasa Malaysia, Chinese, Indian languages, and various indigenous languages. Recent changes in such groups have sometimes consisted of people going back to their homeland; ethnic Germans returning to Germany, Turkish-speaking Bulgarians returning to Turkey, and so on. A balance between the languages in one country has often been arrived at, though not necessarily with the consent or approval of the speakers of the minority languages: children were forbidden to speak Basque in Spain, Navajo in the USA, or Kurdish in Turkey; Koreans in Japanese-occupied territories had to adopt Japanese names; the Turkish minority in Bulgaria had to use Bulgarian names. Indeed deaf children have often been made to sit on their hands in class to prevent them using sign language, a type of language that people often forget about when considering multilingualism.

The past few decades seem to have accelerated movements of people from one country to another, as refugees, such as the Vietnamese, as immigrants, such as Algerians in France, or as migrant workers such as Moroccans in Germany. This has created a vast new multilingualism. New York is said to be the biggest Gujerati-speaking city outside the Indian subcontinent, Melbourne the largest Maltese-speaking city in the world. An Indian student of mine born in Uganda said that the first Indian city she had lived in was the London suburb of Southall. A wealth of languages are spoken in every European town today regardless of the official language of the country; Turkish is spoken in London or in Berlin or in Amsterdam, Arabic can be heard from Paris to Brussels to Berlin. In some cases these people are temporary birds of passage intending to return to their country once the political or economic situation changes. In other cases they are permanent citizens of the country with the same rights as any other citizen, like Finnish-speaking citizens of Sweden or Bengali-speaking citizens of England.

In many cases such multilingualism is bound to be short-lived. Paulston (1986) describes how immigrants to the United States from Greece and Italy become native speakers of English over three or four generations. She feels that such a shift from minority to majority language is prevented only when there are strong boundaries around the group, whether social or geographical (Gaelic in the Hebrides) or self-imposed (the Amish in the USA), or when there is a clear separation in social use of the two languages ('diglossia'), as in Standard Arabic versus local versions of Arabic in North Africa. Having one's own ethnic culture as a minority group means speaking the language of that culture, usually different from the majority language, but not necessarily so – as in the use of English by many Scottish nationalists. Language is then often part of ethnicity, and hence associated with political movements for the rights of particular groups.

INTERNATIONALISM AND SECOND LANGUAGES

But for many students the L2 has no real role within the society itself; English is not learnt in China because it is used inside China. Instead the L2 is taught in the educational system because of the benefits it brings from outside the home country. Any language may of course be taught with the aim of promoting relationships with other countries that use it. Most obviously this applies to languages used for international purposes across many countries. Historically such international languages have been the legacy of empires: the Roman Empire bequeathed Latin as an international language of scholarship so that Marvell, Milton, and Newton would use it well over a thousand years after the Romans left England. French, English and Spanish similarly functioned as the languages of colonialism but continued as languages of international communication.

So a particular country, or indeed a particular individual, may decide to learn a second language for a purpose outside their own society, whether to be able to do business with other countries, to gain access to a scientific literature or to a cultural heritage, or to be able to work in other countries. In Israel, English is taught in schools as the language for wider communication and for access to world commerce and culture, although it also serves as the language of English-speaking immigrants and for communicating with English-speaking tourists. Such use of an international language does not necessarily entail any acceptance of the values of the society from which it originates. Steve Biko justified English as the language of the Black People's Convention in South Africa because it acted as a lingua franca and it was 'an alytical' (Biko, 1978). Anti-British graffiti in Belfast are written in English not Irish. The speaker's attitudes to the target culture are marginal to such uses.

Sometimes as a legacy of colonialism the original speakers of an international language feel that they have the right to say what it should be or how it should be taught. The best French is still thought of as spoken in France; the Alliance Française in London advertises its courses with the slogan 'Learn French from the French'. While the aims of the UK GCSE syllabus for French refer to 'French-speaking countries', this is automatically taken to be France, as a student from the Ivory Coast bitterly pointed out to me. French is also often presented as the language of civilization and culture. Tougas is quoted in

Wardhaugh (1987) as saying 'La culture française . . . répond aux aspirations profondes de l'âme noire' (French culture . . . responds to the deep aspirations of the black soul).

English has been treated more as a commercial property to be sold to particular countries as a means of communication and development (Wardhaugh, 1987). However, setting aside political or commercial motivations, the responsibility for international languages has passed out of the hands of the original owners. Furthermore, the right to say how something should be taught is even less a right of the native speaker than the right to say how something should be said. An Englishman or an American has no more right to tell an Egyptian how to teach English than does a Japanese; the only one who can say what is right for Egypt is the Egyptian: as a spokesman said in China, 'For China we need a Chinese method.' Whether an idea or an approach in language teaching is useful does not intrinsically depend on which country it comes from. Its merits have to be accepted or rejected by the experts on the situation – the teachers and students who live and work there.

As we have seen in this section, language is not politically neutral. Deciding which language should be used in a particular country or which other language should be taught affects the economic and cultural life not only of the country itself but also of the country from which the language comes. Take the example of English. There is the situation of Singapore, whose decision to make English its 'first' language must have played a significant part in its economic success. Then there is the situation of the UK itself, which, by promoting English as a Foreign Language, can try to keep economic links with many parts of the world – with rather less economic success of late than Singapore! Not to mention the vast sums of money involved in the language teaching operation itself, whether in the sales of British books or the students coming to UK language schools.

Robert Phillipson (1992) calls this 'linguistic imperialism' and sees it as a special case of Galtung's (1980) concept of 'a dominant Centre (the powerful western countries) and a dominated Periphery (the under-developed countries)'. The Centre of the world can exert this domination in part by forcing the Periphery to use its languages. So English as a Centre language is used for business purposes of trading between Periphery countries and the Centre. However, this use was so successful that it escaped the hands of its originators and allowed Periphery countries to do business with each other rather than with the UK itself!

In addition, educational systems in the Periphery emphasize English and indeed have instruction through English, particularly at university; the University of Gaza, for example, uses English as the means of instruction for all subjects, as do universities in Egypt and Botswana. Above all English is a requirement for scientific writing and reading: few scientists can make a proper contribution to their field without having access to English, either in person or through translation of one kind or another. Eighty-six per cent of research papers in Biology are written in English and 97 per cent of those on cross-cultural psychology. While the teaching of scientific English may be of vital importance to the individual learners, the pressure to use English for science is a form of linguistic imperialism. Publication in scientific journals depends on getting over an additional hurdle that native speakers do not have to meet; journals that come from the Centre are not going to value independent views from people outside this area. Even in the second language acquisition research area we are dealing with, this is apparent; it is dominated by literature *in* English which is biased towards accounts of acquisition *of* English mostly in highly developed countries. As a member of an editorial board for a journal on second language acquisition, I have found it hard to evaluate contributions fairly; an original piece of research from outside the Centre is very often not up-to-date in the literature or methodology of the field and the English may be less cogently worded; should it be published in preference to a less original paper written by a native speaker at a UK university with all the latest techniques and information in polished prose? Academics who live in Centre countries naturally feel they cannot compromise academic standards – but it is the standards of the Centre that are continually perpetuated, not the potentially infinite richness of scientific exploration possible through different cultures and approaches.

Indeed the influence of the Centre is not just on the choice of language that other countries need to learn but on the very means of teaching them. French Audiovisualism is exported to Francophone Africa; British communicative teaching to almost everywhere on the globe. Holliday (1994) points to the permanent guilt feelings of the local teacher never able to apply the Centre-approved methods to their own satisfaction, basically because they were not of course designed specifically for the needs of any local situation.

2 The goals of language teaching

KEYWORDS

assimilationist teaching: teaching that expects people to give up their native languages and to become speakers of the majority language of the country
transitional L2 teaching: teaching that allows people to function in a majority language, without necessarily losing or devaluing the first language
language maintenance and bilingual language teaching: these teach or maintain the minority language within its group
submersion teaching: extreme sink-or-swim form of assimilationist teaching in which minority language children are simply put in majority language classes

What does this mean for L2 learning and teaching? We can make a broad division between local goals which foster the L2 within the country, international goals which foster it for use outside the country, and individual goals which aim at developing the potential of the individual learner.

LOCAL GOALS OF TEACHING

The local goals of language teaching are those that serve the needs of the society within itself, particularly the need for different groups to interact with each other. They can be seen as having three broad divisions, drawing on the distinctions made in *Bilingualism or Not* (Skutnabb-Kangas, 1981): assimilationist, transitional, and language maintenance. All of these are concerned with the position of minority language children relative to the majority language.

Assimilationist language teaching

Assimilationist teaching accepts that society has the right to expect people to give up their native languages and to become speakers of the majority language of the country; they are assimilated into the rest of the country. One example has been the five-month courses teaching Hebrew to new immigrants to Israel. Here the motivation was to unify people coming from many parts of the world within a single cultural heritage, though this is now changing more into vocationally relevant teaching of the type described below. An extreme form of assimilationist teaching is so-called 'submersion' teaching – the 'sink or swim' method of putting minority language children in a majority language classroom and usually forbidding them to use their own language. According to Skutnabb-Kangas (1981), 'This model is used almost exclusively in Denmark, Norway, France, Great Britain, Holland etc.'

Transitional language teaching

The aim of transitional L2 teaching is to allow people to function in the majority language of the country, without necessarily losing or devaluing their first language. While resembling assimilationist teaching, the motivation is different. To use Lambert's terms, assimilationist teaching is 'subtractive' in that the learners feel their first language is being taken away from them; transitional teaching is 'additive' in that it adds the ability to function in the majority language without displacing the first language. With transitional language teaching the minority language speaker still has the right to function in his or her own language except when communicating with the majority groups.

The educational system is one aspect of this. In many countries education takes place almost exclusively through the main official language: English in England, French in France. Hence those who do not speak the language of the school need help in acquiring it. Often there are special classes to enable children to acquire the majority language for the classroom. The Bilingual Education Act in the United States, for example, required the child to have English teaching as an aid in the transition to the ordinary classroom. Grosjean

(1982) says of such classes, 'For a few years at least the children can be in a transitory haven before being "swallowed up" by the regular system.' Ironically such schemes are now difficult in the UK following the Calderdale report finding that separate provision contravenes laws against racial discrimination (Commission for Racial Equality, 1986).

Employment is another aspect of this. Schemes are set up to help the worker who does not know the language of the workplace; adult immigrants to Sweden, for example, are entitled to 600–700 hours of instruction in Swedish. Or the needs of the new adult immigrant are sometimes taken care of by special initial programmes. The aim of such transitional teaching is, not to suppress the first language in the minority language speakers, but to enable them to use the majority language sufficiently for their own educational or employment needs. They still keep the values of their first language for all functions except those directly involving speakers of the majority language.

Language maintenance and bilingual language teaching

The aim of language maintenance or 'heritage' teaching is to teach minority languages to speakers of the minority language. Many ethnic groups want to keep their own language alive in their children. One possibility is the bilingualism by choice of bringing up children with two languages in the home. Many groups also collectively organize language maintenance classes outside the official educational system; in London classes can be found taking place in Chinese, Polish, Greek and other languages, for children after normal school hours or at weekends. The Linguistic Minorities survey (1983) found that in Bradford 13 mother tongues were taught in maintenance classes to 3000 children for between one and 14 hours a week, only about a third of the classes being supported by the education authorities in any way.

The mainstream educational equivalent is educating minority children through their first language. At one extreme is the notion that children should be taught solely through the minority language – Bantustans in South Africa, or Turkish migrants' children in Bavaria – resulting in the minority speakers being a segregated enclave. More common perhaps is the notion that children have the right to access to their first language through the educational system. In Sweden, for example, there are playgroups run in minority languages for pre-school children and summer camps using minority languages for older children (Arnberg, 1987). Denmark has German schools in its German-speaking areas (Byram, 1986). The position of Maori in New Zealand has been revitalized in part through the provision of 'language nests' – pre-school playgroups in which Maori is used (Spolsky, 1989b). In Sweden in 1981, 10.6 per cent of immigrant children in primary schools were educated through their mother tongues, which ranged from Polish to Assyrian (Skutnabb-Kangas, 1981).

The assumption of maintenance classes is that minority language speakers have the right to continue with their own language and heritage, regardless of the official language of the country. To quote Tove Skutnabb-Kangas (1981), 'Bilingualism is no longer seen as a passing phase, but rather as something good and permanent, something to be striven for.' Transitional language teaching is neutral about the value of the minority language; bilingual teaching actively encourages a multilingual society. In England in the 1960s the talk was of 'English for Immigrants', in the 1970s of 'Multicultural Education', in the 1980s of 'Bilingual Teaching'. Such changes in slogans do not of course necessarily reflect changes in reality.

One form that this emphasis on bilingualism takes is the propagation of other official languages through the school system. In Indonesia 10 per cent of children speak Malay as a first language but 75 per cent learn it at school (Laponce, 1987). Canada has been famous for the experiment of 'immersion' schools where English-speaking children are educated through the medium of French. Whatever the hotly debated merits or demerits of immersion, it resembles bilingualism by choice where parents opt for the advantages that knowing a second language can bestow on their children rather than most minority language situations. Lambert (1990) indeed opposes its use with minority children as 'it fuels the subtractive process and places the minority child into another form of psycholinguistic limbo . . .'.

INTERNATIONAL GOALS OF TEACHING

Let us now turn to international goals, where language teaching has goals that go outside the society itself. The students are assumed to be speakers of the majority language, possibly quite wrongly, say when a person is teaching French in London. There are many types of international goals. Some illustrations will be taken from English syllabuses for Japan (Tokyo, Shoseki, 1990), where English has no official role, and Malaysia (Kementerian Pendidikan Malaysia, 1987), where it still has some residual value in the society, and from the UK National Curriculum for modern languages (HMSO, 1995).

Careers that require a second language

Without taking into account the situation facing immigrants practising their profession in another country, such as Polish doctors in England, there are many careers in which knowledge of another language is important. In the EC 29 per cent of young people want to learn second languages to increase their career prospects (Commission of the European Communities, 1987). For certain professions a particular language is necessary – for example, English for air traffic controllers. The *Angol Nyelv Alapfoken* English textbook in Hungary (Edina and Ivanne, 1987) has a plot line about travel agents and tourist guides, one kind of career that uses international languages. An important function of language teaching is indeed to train people for the international business world. The Malaysian syllabus points to English as 'an important language to enable

Malaysia to engage meaningfully in local and international trade and commerce'. Degrees in Japanese are popular among London University students because they lead to jobs in the City of London, as it is allegedly easier to teach a Japanese graduate finance than a finance graduate Japanese. Societies will always need individuals who are capable of bridging the gap between two countries for economic or political purposes, or indeed for the purposes of war, as in the American crash programme in foreign languages in World War Two which led to the audiolingual teaching method. But we should remember that this type of goal is not turning the student into an imitation native speaker. It preserves the Ll alongside the L2 so that the student can mediate between them – preparing an Ll report on a meeting held in the L2, for example.

Higher education

In many countries access to higher education is through another language or another country. This may be via universities sited in particular countries that use another language for higher education, say English in the National University of Singapore. Or it may be via universities in Britain or the United States or other English-speaking countries. The importance for the student is not the L2 itself but the information that is gained via the L2. Again the L1 is an important part of the situation.

Access to research and information

In schools the Malaysian syllabus encourages the students to 'read factual prose and fiction for information and enjoyment'. At a different level is the need for English to support various careers that are not primarily based on language – for scientists, doctors, or journalists. To keep up-to-date or to be well-informed, it may be necessary to use English. To quote the Malaysian syllabus, English 'also provides an additional means of access to academic, professional, and recreational materials'.

Travel

The motivation behind many students' L2 learning is to travel abroad. At one level this is the leisure activity of tourism: two weeks by the sea in Turkey does not require much Turkish. The assumption of the GCSE syllabus for French in England is that 'Communication is envisaged as taking place . . . in "face to face" contact . . . in a country where French is spoken (as short-stay visitor, family guest, or tourist, etc.)' (Southern Examining Group, 1995). One goal for my own beginners book *People and Places* (Cook, 1980) was international travel through English. Again the status of English makes this peculiar in that travel could be assumed in most places in the world to be possible through English. This assumption has still to let me down, whether in Latin America, North

Africa, or Eastern Europe. The goal of travel is included under international goals here as it involves contact with other countries, though in a sense it is an individual goal belonging in the next section.

INDIVIDUAL GOALS OF LANGUAGE TEACHING

Let us now briefly look at goals that are not related to the society itself or its external relations. Some of these have already appeared in earlier chapters, where we saw that 51 per cent of young people in the EC survey wanted to learn a second language for personal interest rather than for overtly instrumental or integrative reasons. Several goals can be recognized.

Understanding foreign cultures

The Japanese syllabus for English sets as one of its goals 'to heighten an interest in language and culture, thus increasing international understanding'. The UK National Curriculum for modern languages requires pupils to 'come in contact with native speakers in this country and, where possible, abroad' and 'identify with the experiences and perspectives of people in these countries and communities'. Regardless of the actual language that is being learnt, it is often held to be beneficial for the students to understand a foreign culture for its own sake.

Understanding language itself

An educated person should know something of how language itself works as part both of the human mind and of society. One of the four main goals of the UK National Curriculum is 'Language learning skills and knowledge of language' including such sub-goals as the ability to 'understand and apply patterns, rules and exceptions in language forms and structures'. This can be gained through foreign language study, or through language awareness training.

Cognitive training

The virtue of learning a classical language was held to be that it trained the brain. The logical and reasoning powers of the mind were enhanced through a second language. This has received support from psychological work that shows that children who speak two languages are more flexible at problem-solving (Ben Zeev, 1977), and are better able to distinguish form from meaning (Ianco-Worrall, 1972). Bialystok (1990), for example, asked children to say which was the biggest word in such pairs as *hippopotamus* and *skunk*; bilinguals were better able to keep the word size distinct from the object size and answer the question correctly. One aspect of any modern language in the curriculum is indeed the beneficial effects of L2 learning on using the first language. If children are deficient at listening for information or at taking 'long' turns at speaking, the skills involved can be developed through L2 teaching.

General educational values

Just as sport is held to train children how to work in a team and to promote leadership qualities, so L2 teaching can inculcate moral values. The first form in Malaysia covers 'courage, honesty, charity and unity' and the virtues of 'good citizenship, moral values and the Malaysian way of life'. From another angle many support 'autonomous' language learning, where the learners take on the responsibility for themselves because this is in tune with democracy. As Leslie Dickinson (1987) puts it, 'A democratic society protects its democratic ideals through an educational process leading to independent individuals able to think for themselves.' Another general value that is often cited is the insight that L2 learning provides into the L1 and its culture, or, in the words of the UK National Curriculum, helping the pupils to 'recognize cultural attitudes as expressed in language and learn the use of social conventions'.

Learning L2 as an academic subject

Language can also be learnt simply as another subject on the curriculum, another examination to be passed. Japanese teachers are not alone in complaining that they are in thrall to the examination system and cannot teach the English the students really need. The very learning of a second language can be an important mark of education. Traditionally it has been a mark of an educated person in some countries to know another language, another facet of 'élite' bilingualism. French had this kind of status in Western Europe, German in Eastern Europe. Skuttnab-Kangas (1981) paraphrases Fishman's account of bilingualism in the US as:

> If you have learnt French at university, preferably in France and even better at the Sorbonne, then bilingualism is something very positive. But if you have learnt French from your old grandmother in Maine then bilingualism is something rather to be ashamed of.

L2 learning as social change

The goals seen so far either accept the world as it is or benefit the student as an individual. But education and L2 teaching can also be seen as a vehicle of social change. According to Freire (1972), the way out of the perpetual conflict between oppressor and oppressed is through problem-posing dialogues between teachers and students which make both more aware of the issues in their lives and their solutions. Language teaching on a Freireian model would accept that 'authentic education is not carried out by A for B or by A about B but rather by

A with B mediated by the world, giving rise to views or opinions about it'. Language teaching can go beyond accepting the values of the existing world to making it better (Wallerstein, 1983). While the Freireian approach is included here under individual goals because of its liberating effect on the individual, it may well deserve a category all of its own of goals for changing society.

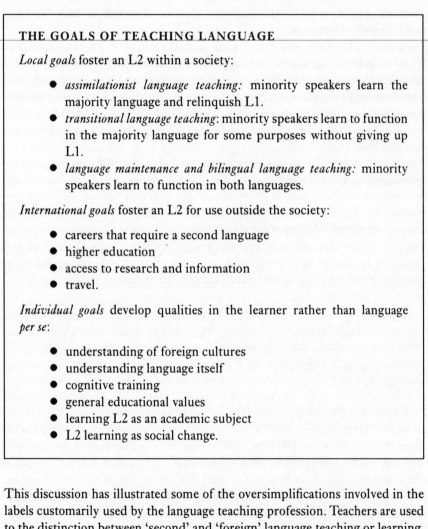

THE GOALS OF TEACHING LANGUAGE

Local goals foster an L2 within a society:

- *assimilationist language teaching:* minority speakers learn the majority language and relinquish L1.
- *transitional language teaching:* minority speakers learn to function in the majority language for some purposes without giving up L1.
- *language maintenance and bilingual language teaching:* minority speakers learn to function in both languages.

International goals foster an L2 for use outside the society:

- careers that require a second language
- higher education
- access to research and information
- travel.

Individual goals develop qualities in the learner rather than language *per se*:

- understanding of foreign cultures
- understanding language itself
- cognitive training
- general educational values
- learning L2 as an academic subject
- L2 learning as social change.

This discussion has illustrated some of the oversimplifications involved in the labels customarily used by the language teaching profession. Teachers are used to the distinction between 'second' and 'foreign' language teaching or learning. But this twofold distinction does not begin to cope with the complexities of most situations; foreign language teaching includes such different aspects as English as an International Language in Malaysia, and French literature at A level in England; second language teaching covers the teaching of Hebrew in Tel Aviv, the teaching of French in Quebec, and the teaching of English in London or Western Australia.

A second debatable term is 'communication', the buzzword of language teaching in the past twenty years. The idea of communication has never been far from language teaching in one way or another. Otto Jespersen back in 1904 was claiming that the purpose of L2 learning 'must be in order to get a way of communication with places which our tongue cannot reach', though this led him to something very different from communicative teaching. The modern emphasis has indeed led to a welcome shift in attention towards teaching practical uses of language.

However, the word 'communication' is dangerous if it distracts attention from the individual goals that aim at benefiting the student or the society. The purposes of language teaching described above cover a vast range of activities, from praying to using a telex, from taking an examination to becoming honest, from entering a new society to rebelling against its values to maintaining one's own values within a majority culture. Describing all these as communication tells one little, if anything.

Much of what has been said here about the goals of language teaching seems quite obvious. Yet it is surprising how rarely it is mentioned. Most discussions of language teaching take it for granted that everyone knows *why* they are teaching the L2. But the reasons for language teaching in a particular situation depend on factors that cannot be summed up just as 'communication' or as 'foreign' versus 'second' language teaching. Even if teachers themselves are powerless to change such reasons, an understanding of the varying roles for language teaching in different societies and for different individuals is an important aid in teaching.

One practical way in which this affects the classroom is through the actual content of the language lesson or textbook. I have argued elsewhere (Cook, 1983) that too much time is spent teaching 'imaginary' content about fictional people and places rather than 'real' content that tells the students something about the real world and real people, as we shall see in Chapter 8. Two solutions to this can be seen in the titles of two EFL textbooks, *South Africa – the Privileged and the Dispossessed* (Davies and Senior, 1983), a collection of annotated texts dealing with a deliberately controversial area, and *How to Improve Your Memory* (Wright, 1987), one of a series aiming to improve students' reading by teaching them a particular skill through English. In some places information about England or the USA will be specifically ruled out. In others it will be the most natural content of any lesson. We should not unthinkingly trivialize the content of teaching, when so much else is available. The choice of what the language of the lesson shall be about is as crucial as the choice of the language forms in which it is expressed, and both depend on the whole educational setting. Communication implies something to communicate and that is where the teacher's control of the lesson is crucial.

Teachers should be clear in their minds that they are usually teaching people how to use two languages, not how to use one in isolation. The person who can speak two languages has the special ability to communicate in two ways. The aim is not to produce L2 speakers who can only use the language when speaking to each other. Myhill (1990), for instance, points to the problems in using English materials for Aboriginals in Australia, such as *Tracks* (Northern Territory, 1979), that reflect their own lifestyle rather than that of the English-speaking community: what's the point in them speaking to each other in English? Nor is the aim to produce imitation native speakers, with the sole exception of those who are training to be spies. Rather the aim is people who can stand between two viewpoints and between two cultures, a multi-competent speaker who can do far more than any monolingual. Much language teaching has tried to duplicate the skills of the native speaker in the non-native speaker. Thus the functions of language or the rules of grammar known by the native speaker are taught to the students. The point should not be to manufacture ersatz native speakers but to equip people to use two languages without losing their own identity. The model for language teaching should be the fluent L2 user, not the native speaker: what Michael Byram (1990) calls 'intercultural communicative competence'. This enables language teaching to have goals that students can see as relevant and achievable rather than the distant chimera of native speaker competence.

This chapter has drawn on a different type of research from the others, often known as 'bilingualism' rather than 'L2 learning'. To apply SLA research properly to the classroom, this area is as vital as any of the others that have been dealt with. L2 learning varies according to the situation in which the L2 learner is placed. Teaching an L2 is tied into the political and ethical values of a society. At a practical level students will prosper when their teacher understands the multiple goals they are able to fulfil through the second language. At a more general level, teachers should be aware of the depth and range of the values embodied in their teaching and see what function L2 learning has for the individual students they teach and for the society in which they are placed.

In one sense, all of this chapter has been relevant to teachers, in another sense none of it. For the vital issues that are involved are seldom left to teachers to decide. The casting vote for or against bilingual education is more likely to be President Reagan's: 'It is absolutely wrong and against American concepts to have a bilingual education program that is now openly, admittedly dedicated to preserving their native language . . .' (cited in Wardhaugh, 1987). Vital as such decisions about language teaching are, they are not in the hands of teachers. Nevertheless, it is important for teachers to be informed about the different alternatives that are available for the aims and goals of language teaching so that they can contribute properly to the debate.

DISCUSSION TOPICS

1. What advantages do you feel you have had or might have had by being brought up bilingually?
2. How well do you think that countries function that have more than one

language, say South Africa, or Canada, or Singapore?

3. Would you prefer to be taught by a native speaker or a non-native speaker? Why?

4. As a language teacher, do you see yourself in the tradition of assimilationist, transitional or bilingual teaching, or none of these?

5. What goals do you think are present in the language teaching situation with which you are best familiar?

7. How can you reconcile the students' goals, the educational system's goals, and the teacher's goals?

8. How would you understand 'communication' as used in language teaching?

FURTHER READING

Apart from specific references in the text, this chapter draws on ideas and examples chiefly from: Grosjean (1982), *Life with Two Languages*; Skutnabb-Kangas (1981), *Bilingualism or not: The Education of Minorities*; Romaine (1994), *Bilingualism*; Wardhaugh (1987), *Languages in Competition;* Phillipson (1992), *Linguistic Imperialism*; Swales (1990), *Genre Analysis*.

8

General models of L2 learning

So far this book has illustrated the complexity and diversity of L2 learning and teaching, not from the heights of an overall theory that explains everything and therefore has mammoth global consequences for language teaching, but from the lowlands of particular areas of research and particular conclusions that apply to limited aspects of the language teaching operation. Some general models of L2 learning have, nevertheless, been proposed. The following discussion tries to give a flavour of these but cannot give them full justice, partly because many are offshoots of theories of linguistics, psychology, or sociology which cannot be treated at length here. This chapter highlights some of the general ideas underlying the more specific research looked at so far and relates them to language teaching. Rarely will the models correspond neatly to teaching methods. Nor, as we shall see, is any of them sufficiently powerful to act as the sole basis for teaching. Obviously this chapter also harks back to areas we have already discussed, this time from a different perspective.

We can recognize four overall types of learning model that represent extreme tendencies. The first type is knowledge models that emphasize the importance of the individual mind in L2 learning, such as the *Universal Grammar (UG) model,* which stresses language as part of the mind and sees learning as setting parameters from the actual sentences the learner encounters. The second type is language processing models, such as the *competition model,* which sees language learning as acquiring ways of processing. The third type is mixed models that recognize two sides to L2 learning, either permanently, such as the *monitor model,* or as a conversion from one side to another, as in the *competence/control model.* The last type is social models that stress the social aspects of L2 learning, such as the *socio-educational model* and the *acculturation model.*

1 Models of knowledge: Universal Grammar

Focusing questions

Is the sentence *Is Sam is the cat that black?* English? Why not?
Is the subjectless sentence *Speaks* English? Why not?
How much importance do you place on:

  (*a*) correction by parents in the L1?
  (*b*) correction by teachers in the L2?

KEYWORDS

Universal Grammar (UG): 'the system of principles, conditions, and rules that are elements or properties of all human languages . . . the essence of human language' (Chomsky, 1976, p. 29)
principles of language: abstract principles that permit or prohibit certain structures from occurring in all human languages
parameters of language: systematic ways in which human languages vary, usually expressed as a choice between two options

The Universal Grammar (UG) model, proposed by Chomsky in the 1980s, is a development of his earlier ideas into a new form called by him 'the second conceptual revolution'. UG has increasingly been used to explain how second languages are learnt, chiefly by those who approach L2 learning from a linguistics perspective. Its general claims about learning are based on the principles and parameters grammar briefly encountered in Chapter 2. A person who knows a language has acquired a grammar which consists of the universal principles of language that show why 'Is Sam is the cat that black?' is impossible in all languages (the structure–dependency principle) and the parameters that explain why *Shuo* (speaks) is a possible sentence in Chinese but *Speaks* is not possible in English (the pro–drop parameter). Much of the L2 research has been concerned with the question of whether Universal Grammar is still available to the L2 learner, some insisting vehemently that L2 learning goes by a different route. Here for purposes of discussion it will be assumed that UG is indeed available – after all no one has yet met an L2 learner who breaks structure–dependency. An account of this debate can be found in Cook (1993, 1994).

LEARNING AS SETTING PARAMETERS FROM EVIDENCE

The Universal Grammar model claims that these principles and parameters are built into the mind. Learners do not need to learn structure–dependency because their minds automatically impose it on any language they meet, whether it is English, Chinese, or Arabic. However they *do* need to learn that English must have subjects (non–pro–drop), while Chinese does not (pro–drop). It is the parameter settings that have to be learnt. All the learner needs in order to set the values for parameters are examples of the language. Hearing 'There are some books on the table' a learner discovers English is non–pro–drop because 'dummy' subjects such as 'there' and 'it' only occur in non–pro–drop languages.

It is common to conceptualize this is terms of a black box which cannot be opened so that its contents have to be deduced (Fig. 8.1).

Language input goes into the learner's mind and creates a knowledge of language consisting of principles, parameters, and lexical items. We cannot open up the black box of the mind itself but we can analyse the process through which the mind creates a grammar out of input.

Fig. 8.1 The black box in L1 learning

Learning in the UG model is a straightforward matter of getting the right input. In this theory, language input is the evidence out of which the learner constructs knowledge of language – what goes into the black box. Such evidence can be either positive or negative. Positive evidence consists of actual sentences that learners hear, such as 'The Brighton train leaves London at five'. The information in the sentence allows them to construct a grammar that fits the word order 'facts' of English that subjects come before verbs, verbs come before objects, and prepositions come before nouns by setting the parameters in a particular way. The positive evidence of the position of words in a few sentences they hear is sufficient to show them the rules of English.

Negative evidence has two types. Because learners never hear sentences without subjects in English, such as 'Leaves', they deduce that English sentences must have subjects – the same evidence as that advanced for curved bananas in the song 'I have never seen a straight banana'. The other type of negative evidence is correction: 'No you mustn't say "You was here" you must say "You were here."' Someone tells the learner that what they are doing is wrong.

Many linguists are convinced that the child learns the first language only by encountering actual sentences of the language; negative evidence could only help in marginal instances. But second language learning is different. The bulk of the evidence indeed comes from sentences the learner hears – positive evidence from linguistic input. But the L2 learner also has the first language available to them. Negative evidence can be used to work out what does not occur in the second language but might be expected to occur if it were like the first. A Spanish student listening to English will eventually notice that English does not have the subjectless sentences that happen in Spanish. The basis for the expectation is not just sheer speculation but the concrete knowledge of the first language the learners have in their heads.

Negative evidence by correction is also different in L2 learning. In the first language, it is not so much that it is ineffective as that it does not occur. In the second language, it can, and often does, occur with high frequency. The L2 learner has an additional source of evidence not available to the L1 learner. Furthermore, the L2 learner often has grammatical explanation available as another source of evidence. The usefulness and success of this can be debated. Nevertheless, it reflects an entirely different type of evidence for the learner that is absent from first language acquisition, at least up to the school years. Finally, the input to the L2 learner could be made more learnable by highlighting various aspects of it. James Morgan (1986) has talked of the need for 'bracketed input', sentences that make clear the phrase structure of the language. L2 teaching could try many ways of highlighting input in this fashion, again an opportunity unique to L2 learning.

A possible overall black box model for L2 learning is seen in Figure 8.2.

Fig. 8.2 The black box in L2 learning

This model presupposes that UG is totally available in L2 learning, and is known as a direct access model. Obviously it cannot be completely true, as the result of L2 acquisition seldom resembles completely that of L1 acquisition: something must be different if not everything.

L2 SETTING OF PARAMETERS

The L2 learner listens to input and sets the parameters accordingly. The question is whether *re*setting parameters is the same as setting them in the first place. Does the fact that there is already one setting in the L2 learner's mind affect learning? If L2 learning is the same as L1, Japanese learners of English will learn word order in the same way as French learners of English. On the other hand, if the L1 settings influence L2 learning, Japanese learners will differ from other learners wherever their L1 parameter settings are different.

Lydia White (1986) used the pro–drop parameter concerning the presence or absence of a subject in the sentence to investigate this issue, as outlined in Chapter 2. She found that the first language setting for the parameter was indeed carried over to the second. That is to say, Spanish learners of English initially assume that subjects are not needed, French learners assume that they are. Research on other areas of syntax has often produced similar conclusions. For instance, the acquisition of L2 word order is influenced by the L1, as is the acquisition of movement of elements within the sentence. There is some variation according to the area being tested. My own research into 'binding' – the relationship between 'John' and 'himself' in sentences such as 'Peter reported John's criticisms of himself' – found similar levels of difficulty and speeds of response between L2 learners of English who spoke Japanese, Norwegian, and Romance languages (Cook, 1990). Nevertheless, mostly L2 learners seem to start from their L1 setting rather than from scratch. This does not deny that UG is available. The learners still have access to the system of principles and parameters via their L1.

Because of such research evidence, most researchers prefer what is known as an indirect access model in which UG is only available via the first language (Fig. 8.3). Learners are not able to tap the resources of UG directly but can still use their UG-related knowledge of the L1.

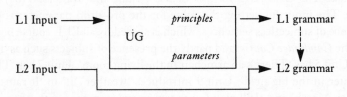

Fig. 8.3 The indirect access model

So L2 learners need to spend comparatively little effort on grammatical structure, since it results from the setting of a handful of parameters. They do, however, need to acquire an immense amount of detail about how individual words are used. The comparative simplicity of syntax learning in the UG model is achieved by increasing the burden of vocabulary learning. The learner needs to acquire large numbers of words, not only in the conventional way of knowing their dictionary meaning or pronunciation, but also in knowing how they behave in sentences. It is not just a matter of the beginner in English learning the syntax, function, and meaning of 'He plays football'; it is learning that in English the verb 'play' needs to be followed by a noun phrase. It has often been reported that learners themselves feel vocabulary to be particularly important. A questionnaire I gave to 351 students of English found that they placed the statement 'I want to learn more English words and phrases' second out of ten possible aims for their English course, after 'I want to practise English so that I can use it outside the classroom', and some way above structures, functions, or life in England. A major learning component according to the UG theory will indeed be vocabulary, if not perhaps in the way that either learners or teachers presently conceive of it. The future may see the reorganization of the role of vocabulary teaching, partly taking account of this, partly utilizing other notions presented in Chapter 3.

The syntactic basis of the UG model has been considerably revised in recent years within a theory known as the Minimalist Programme (Chomsky, 1993). All learning is now seen as vocabulary learning; even the acquisition of grammatical morphemes such as past tense '-ed' is considered as acquiring the phrases within which these morphemes can function and the parameters settings that go with them. Hence grammatical morphemes are, so to speak, attached to words before they are fitted into the sentence. An account of these developments can be seen in Cook and Newson (1996). However, their implications for second language acquisition research are as yet unknown, except for the even closer connection to vocabulary.

THE UG MODEL AND LANGUAGE TEACHING

What do parameters mean for teaching? In the case of the pro-drop parameter, UG theory suggests that teachers provide language input that allows the student to find out whether the setting should be pro-drop or non-pro-drop. Let us take *The Cambridge English Course* (Swan and Walters, 1984) as an example. The input for setting the value for the pro-drop parameter is partly the absence of subjectless sentences, which is shared by all EFL course books as well as the *Cambridge Course*, and partly the presence of subjects such as 'it' and 'there'. Unit 5 has 'There's an armchair in the living room'. Unit 7 has 'There's some water in the big field'. Unit 9 introduces 'weather' 'it' in 'It rains from January to March' and 'It'll cloud over tomorrow', together with 'there' as in 'There will be snow'. Unit 10 teaches dummy 'it' in 'It's a man'. Everything necessary to set the parameter is introduced within the first weeks of the course. It is hard to imagine language teaching not reflecting these two aspects of the pro-drop parameter, just as it is hard for any small sample of speech not to use all the phonemes of English. Almost any language input should provide the information on which the parameter setting depends fairly rapidly.

As the Universal Grammar in the student's mind is so powerful, there is comparatively little for the teacher to do. Few mistakes occur with the aspects of word order covered by the head parameter; I have never heard a student saying things like 'I live London in' for instance. Nevertheless some effects of the first language linger on. Quite advanced L2 learners still differ from native speakers when the L1 and the L2 have different settings for the pro-drop parameter. Thus the teacher's awareness of parameter resetting can be helpful. The useful book *Learner English* (Swan and Smith, 1987) provides examples of mistakes from students with L1s ranging from Italian to Chinese to Thai that linguists would attribute to the pro-drop parameter. Similarly, syllabuses for language teaching that use grammar need to accommodate such basic syntactic ideas, if only to indicate to teachers areas that they can refrain from teaching.

Many feel that the UG model is the most powerful account of L2 learning.

Its attraction is that it links L2 learning to current ideas about language and language learning. It has brought to light a number of apparently simple phenomena like the pro-drop parameter that appear to be relevant to L2 learning. Yet it would be wrong to draw conclusions from UG theory for anything other than the central area that is its proper domain, the core aspects of syntax. The UG model tackles the most profound areas of L2 acquisition, which are central to language and to the human mind. But there is rather little to say about them for language teaching. The UG principles are not learnt, the parameter settings probably need little attention. Any view of the whole L2 learning system has to take on board more than the UG model. Classroom L2 teaching must include many aspects of language that are not covered by the model. Nevertheless the UG model firmly reminds us that learners have minds and that one crucial question is the form that language knowledge takes in the human mind.

One particular theme in recent work, oddly enough, is the emphasis on acquisition of vocabulary. To make the syntax more powerful, much of the details of the grammar are now seen as part of vocabulary, as we saw in Chapter 3. Knowing the word 'give' means knowing that it usually has a subject that is animate and two objects, that is to say you cannot say 'The rock gave him a present' with a non-animate subject 'the rock' or 'The man gave a thousand pounds' without an indirect object saying whom it was given to. The grammar is seen as universal; the differences between languages come down to how words behave in sentences. Hence UG clearly indicates that language teaching should consider how vocabulary should be taught, not as tokens with isolated meanings, but as items that play a part in the sentence by saying what structures and words they may go with in the sentence.

THE UNIVERSAL GRAMMAR MODEL OF L2 LEARNING

Key theme:

- language is the knowledge in individual minds; the UG in the mind shapes and restricts the languages that are learnt.

Learning:

- is setting values for parameters and acquiring properties of lexical items, but not acquiring principles.

Teaching implications:

- no need to teach 'principles'.
- design optimum input for triggering parameters.
- emphasize the teaching of vocabulary items with specifications of how they can occur in grammatical structures.

2 Processing models: the competition model and the information processing model

Focusing questions

How would you decide what was the subject of the sentence, say in 'The old man likes bananas'?
How important do you think it is for students to know what is the subject?
Would you say that practice makes perfect in second language learning? Is it the same for all aspects of language?

THE COMPETITION MODEL

At the opposite pole from UG come models which see language in terms of dynamic processing and of communication rather than as static knowledge. These are interested in what happens in an actual language situation and in how people use language, rather than in knowledge in the mind. One model of this type is the *competition model* developed by Brian MacWhinney and his associates (Bates and MacWhinney, 1981; MacWhinney, 1987). This forms part of a psychological theory of language in which L2 learning forms only one component. The main key to language is communication: 'the surface connections of natural languages are created, governed, constrained, acquired, and used in the service of communicative functions.' Language has four main aspects: word order, vocabulary, word forms (morphology) and intonation.

Whatever the speaker wants to communicate has to be achieved through these four. But the speaker can do only a limited number of things at the same time. So the more a language uses intonation, the less it can rely on word order, the more emphasis it has on word forms, the less on word order; and so on. The amount of 'space' the mind has for using language is limited. The different aspects of language 'compete' with each other for the same space. The results of this competition for space favour one or other of these aspects in different languages. A language, such as Chinese, that has complicated intonation has no variation in morphology. English, with complicated word order, puts little emphasis on morphology. Latin, with a complicated case system for nouns, has little use for word order, and so on. The competition model suggests that there is a payoff between the four aspects of intonation, vocabulary, word order, and word forms (morphology). No language can pay equal attention to all of them because they would use up too much of the speaker's processing space.

The part of language that has been most investigated by the competition model is the subject of the sentence. Although subjects probably exist in all languages, there is a difference in what the subject actually consists of. Take the sentence 'He likes to drink Laphroaig.' What are the clues that give away the subject?

Word order

In many languages the subject occurs in a definite place in the sentence. In English it usually comes before the verb – 'he' comes before 'likes'; hence English is a subject verb object (SVO) language. Arabic and Berber are VSO languages and so the subject usually comes after the verb. In languages such as Baure and Tzeltal the subject comes after the object (VOS). Though they differ as to whether the subject comes in the beginning, the middle, or the end, in all these languages word order is a good guide as to which noun phrase is the subject. The competition for space is being won by word order.

Agreement

The subject often agrees with the verb in number: 'she' and 'plays' are both singular in 'She plays golf', as are 'il' and 'aime' in the French 'Il aime Paris' (He loves Paris). In some languages then the competition is won by agreement, which plays a subsidiary role in English.

Case

In other languages the subject noun has to be in the nominative case: 'He likes Laphroaig' rather than 'Him likes Laphroaig' in English: 'Ich liebe Bier' (I love beer) rather than 'Mich liebe Bier' in German. In some languages the competition is won by word forms, which play a lesser role in English.

Animacy

In languages like Japanese the subject of the sentence must be animate, that is to say, refer to someone or something that is alive. The sentence 'The typhoon broke the window' is impossible in Japanese because typhoons are not alive and so 'typhoon' cannot be the subject. However, in English it does not matter whether the subject refers to something alive or not. It is possible to say both 'Peter broke the glass' and 'The glass broke'. The competition is won in some languages by the factor of animacy. At least four clues potentially signal the subject of the sentence: word order, case, agreement between words, and animacy. The competition model claims that all four compete for space amongst themselves. The different clues to the subject are not equally important in each language. Rather the competition between them ends up with one dominating the others.

Children learning their first language are therefore discovering which clues are important for that language and learning to pay less attention to the others. Each of the four competing clues has a 'weighting' that affects how each sentence is processed. Experiments have shown that speakers of English depend chiefly on word order; speakers of Dutch depend on agreement

(Kilborn and Cooreman, 1987; McDonald, 1987); Japanese and Italian depend most on animacy (Harrington, 1987; Bates and MacWhinney, 1981). Learning how to process a second language means adjusting the weightings for each of the clues. L2 learners of English transfer the weightings from their L1. Thus Japanese and Italian learners select the subject because it is animate, and Dutch learners because it agrees with the verb. While their processes are not weighted so heavily as in their first languages, even at advanced stages they are still different. On the surface there need not be any sign of this in their normal language use. After all, they will still choose the subject correctly most of the time, whichever aspect they are relying on. Nevertheless their actual speech processing uses different weightings.

PROCESSING MODELS AND COGNITIVISM

The competition model addresses some of the performance processes discussed in Chapter 4. The model seems related to the behaviourist tradition which claims that language learning comes from outside – from input from others and from interaction and correction – rather than from inside the mind. An early version was Bloomfield's ideas that language learning is a matter of associating words with things (Bloomfield, 1933). The child who imitates an adult saying 'doll' is favourably reinforced by adults whenever a doll is seen and unfavourably reinforced when a doll is absent. The most sophisticated behaviourist account was provided by B.F. Skinner (1957) in the book *Verbal Behavior* that was savaged in a review by Chomsky (1959). Language to Skinner was learnt though 'verbal operants' that are controlled by the situation, which includes the social context, the individual's past history and the complex stimuli in the actual situation. One type of operant is the *mand*, which is the equivalent to a command (com+mand) and is reinforced by someone carrying it out; another is the *tact*, which is equivalent to a declarative (con+tact), and which is reinforced by social approval, etc. The child builds up the complex use of language by interacting with people in a situation for a purpose.

Other contemporary psychological theories of language learning are also affiliated to behaviourism. John Anderson (1983) has proposed a 'cognitive behaviourist' model called ACT*, which sees learning as building up response strengths through a twofold division into procedural memory (procedures for doing things) and declarative memory (what has here been called 'knowledge'). As declarative facts get better known they are gradually turned into procedures, and several procedures are combined into one, thus cutting down on the amount of memory involved. This model underlies the work of O'Malley and Chamot (1990) with learning strategies described in Chapter 5.

Rumelhart and McClelland (1986) and others have been developing the similar theory of 'connectionism', which sees learning as establishing the strengths between the vast numbers of connections in the mind and claims that language processing does not take place in a step by step fashion but that many things are being processed simultaneously. The methodology of connectionism consists of simulated learning by the computer; language data are fed into the computer's network of connections to see whether it will 'learn' the syntactic regularities. The L2 use then depends on the computer being first able to learn the L1 before looking at the L2. Blackwell and Broeder (1992) first got the computer to learn either Arabic or Turkish pronouns based on their frequency in language input to learners; then they added the second of the two languages. They found that the computer indeed duplicated the order of acquisition found in a naturalistic study of four L2 learners. Connectionism looks an important area for future research once it gets a wider coverage of specifically L2 syntax.

The main L2 model in this tradition is called the information-processing model (McLaughlin et al., 1983). In this learning starts from controlled processes, which gradually become automatic over time. When you first start to drive a car, you control the process of driving very consciously – turning the wheel, using the accelerator, and so on. Soon it becomes automatic and for much of the time you have no awareness of the controls you are using. To quote McLaughlin (1987) 'Thus controlled processing can be said to lay down the "stepping stones" for automatic processing as the learner moves to more and more difficult levels.' This is not necessarily the same as being conscious of language rules. A learner who starts by communicating hesitantly and gradually becomes more fluent is just as much going from controlled to automatic processes as is one who starts from grammatical rules and then tries to use them in ordinary speech.

Clearly some of the research discussed in Chapter 5 can be taken to support this model, for instance the increasing quickness of reaction time as learners make the language more and more automatic. However, the evidence for the information-processing model is mostly based upon ideas taken from general psychological theory or on experiments with the learning of vocabulary, rather than on L2 learning itself. It requires a continuum from 'higher' to 'lower' skills. Students who do not progress in the L2 are not making the lower level skills sufficiently automatic. Thus children learning to read an L2 may be held back by not having mastered the low-level skill of predicting what words come next. The information-processing model resembles the other processing models in assuming that language learning is the same as the learning of any other skill such as car-driving. All of them claim language is learnt by the same general principles of learning as everything else. They do not separate the mind into language faculties and non-language faculties but adopt the non-uniqueness position.

The main application to teaching is the emphasis on practice as the key to L2 learning. Practice builds up the weightings, response strengths and so on that determine how language is processed and stored. The UG model sets minimal store by practice; in principle a parameter can be set by a single sentence for ever more. Processing models see language as the gradual accumulation of preferred ways of doing things. Much language teaching has of course always insisted on this whether it is the practice of the audiolingual structure drill or the communicative information gap game. The processing models remind us then that language is also behaviour and skill. As well as the aspects of language that are abstract or under conscious control, there are skills learnt by doing them over and over again.

PROCESSING MODELS

Key theme:

- language is processing at different levels.

Learning:

- learning involves practising to build up the proper weightings, etc.

Teaching uses:

- exercises that build up appropriate strengths of response in students.
- the classroom should maximize practice by students.

---

3 Multicomponent models: the competence/control model and the input hypothesis

Focusing questions

Do you think you speak a second language 'better' or 'worse' in informal situations?
How does consciousness of what you are doing help in L2 learning?
Have you ever found that you were doing something you had learnt consciously without being aware of it?

So far the learning models have been at the two poles of those that emphasize language knowledge and those that emphasize language processing. UG and processing models reduce everything to variations on the same theme, whether abstract parameter settings or response weightings. Many current models within L2 learning research itself can be called 'mixed' because they try to accommodate both sides of this division. This is achieved either by keeping both sides separate, or by seeing one side as converting into the other – 'conversion' models.

Let us start with the *competence/control model* proposed by Ellen Bialystok and Mike Sharwood-Smith (1985), and named after its two main dimensions. This model is approached through the metaphor of a library. On the one hand, the books in the library are set out on the shelves according to a definite system; on the other hand, the user needs to know how to find a particular book. The arrangement of books is the learner's competence in the language ('the way in which the language system is represented in the mind of the learner'), the ways of finding them are control procedures ('the processing system for controlling that knowledge in actual performance').

Learning a second language involves two things: the knowledge that makes up competence and the control that is used in producing speech. The L2 learner may have problems with control procedures or with L2 knowledge. Inadequate procedures taken from the L1 will distort newly learnt L2 knowledge, or the L2 procedures may be adequate but the L2 knowledge is missing. For example, English learners of German often have difficulty with the fact that German has SVO order in main clauses but SOV in subordinate clauses. This might be because their English SVO *procedures* are still controlling their L2 *competence* and so leading to mistakes. Or it might be that their German L2 *competence* has incorrectly transferred the word order from English and their L2 procedures are perfectly adequate. Their interlanguage develops either because their underlying knowledge of the language improves or because their processes improve. Control is also important to variation. The reason why an L2 learner produces language that is not appropriate to the situation could be lack of control procedures – of knowing when to use what – rather than because they are not part of competence.

The question of variation was incorporated by Elaine Tarone (1988) into the concept of the interlanguage continuum. She suggests that learners vary their interlanguage for formal and informal situations. Japanese learners of English are better at pronouncing /z/ in more formal situations such as reading word lists than in less formal situations such as speaking spontaneously (Dickerson, 1975). Though they improve with time, nevertheless there is still a gap between their success in these two types of situation, the classroom and the informal. This observation will ring true for many language teachers. It can be interpreted in terms of the competence/control model as showing that the learners' control procedures are not working properly and are holding back their performance. However, Tarone's explanation is more consoling for teachers. She believes that the formal and informal varieties of speech are not equally important in L2 learning. Newly learnt items are mastered in the formal situation before they are carried over to informal situations. So it is not just that the learner possesses a range of ways of speaking but that the learner progresses through them from day-to-day along a continuum.

The chief difference between the formal and informal varieties on this continuum is in how much 'attention' speakers pay to their speech. Tarone claims that the formal variety is the most 'attended' – which, in a sense, is the same as saying the one in which the speaker is most self-conscious. The informal variety is the least 'attended'. So the new elements of the L2 are first acquired in the language variety in which the speaker pays most attention, and then slowly transferred to the variety which is less attended. The interlanguage continuum goes from most-attended speech to least-attended. Learners acquire aspects of the L2 in formal situations before they transfer them to the less formal. The classroom is usually a formal attended situation. The teacher is doing the students a disservice to pretend otherwise, since the point of entry for new information is only through this situation. Of course there are problems with this analysis in one sense. If the students' only encounter with the L2 is in the classroom, it is hardly surprising that new forms first manifest themselves in their classroom speech as they are not encountered outside.

Attention is one form of control; the more attention paid to speech, the more the speaker controls it. Much use of conscious understanding in L2 learning represents a type of conversion model in which one kind of information is turned into another. Is being conscious of the L2 structures and rules a help or a hindrance? The reader now knows from information supplied in the last section that Dutch is an SVO language in main clauses in which the subject of the sentence agrees with the verb. If given a Dutch noun 'vogel' (bird), a verb 'vliegen' (fly), and a singular ending for verbs '-zt', you could construct a Dutch sentence about a bird flying. You could consciously use explicit knowledge of language to construct a sentence, which might even be acceptable Dutch. But is consciousness-raising of this type useful in learning to actually speak Dutch? Consciousness is excluded from both the UG type models and the competition model. The models described in this section all take consciousness into account to some extent. The interlanguage continuum relies on attention, which at an extreme may be awareness of actual rules.

THE INPUT HYPOTHESIS

The model that was specifically developed to cover consciousness was the *input hypothesis model* of Krashen (1985). This started as an account of some aspects of language processing in the 1970s, and became an all-embracing theory in the early 1980s. However, it met with an extremely hostile reception from other researchers, mostly because it seemed too great a leap from a small base of evidence. The relevant aspects here are its attitudes to conscious use of grammatical rules. Krashen claims that there are two possible types of linguistic knowledge, acquired knowledge and learnt knowledge.

Acquired knowledge

One type of knowledge is that which is acquired by natural means in informal situations, a process termed acquisition. This is the form of all L1 knowledge and potentially of some L2 knowledge. It consists of rules, principles, etc. that are not available to conscious attention.

Learnt knowledge

The other type of knowledge is that which is learnt by conscious understanding of rules, a process termed learning. This is the form of much L2 knowledge acquired in formal classroom situations. It consists of explicit linguistic information that is consciously available to the speaker.

In one sense this division between acquisition and learning is obvious and familiar. The UG model, for instance, makes a distinction between the natural knowledge acquired through the faculty of language and the knowledge of language that could have been learnt by other faculties of the mind, say the reasoning faculty. Krashen's model differs over the relationship between the two types of knowledge. Figure 8.4 is found in variations in many books by Krashen (e.g. 1981a).

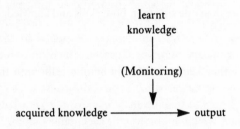

Fig. 8.4 The Monitor model

The process of speaking a second language depends primarily on acquired knowledge for all learners. Those who have a conscious learnt knowledge of the L2 are able to use it only as a Monitor of what they have already acquired. Thus someone who wants to say something in a second language will be able to Monitor what they are saying via the conscious grammatical rules they know – checking whether the tense is right, for instance. Krashen is not just saying that this is one of the uses of learnt knowledge. After all everyone probably checks out their knowledge from time to time by muttering, say, 'The mites go up and the tights come down' as a mnemonic for 'stalagmite' versus 'stalactite'. Rather Krashen is saying this is the *only* use of learnt conscious knowledge. Consciously learnt rules are never turned into acquired knowledge. Conscious learning *never* leads to anything more than the ability to Monitor what you want to say or write when the circumstances allow. His is the extreme non-conversion model in which the two sides do not mix. Hence it is sometimes called the 'dual competence' model.

Such models remind us of the range of language use. Different aspects of language are prominent in different situations. The L2 learner's speech is no more a single uniform variety than is the native speaker's. The conversion models in particular are the justification for giving explicit rules of language to the students. Teaching that asks the learner to convert conscious knowledge, for example, 'To be polite you use past tense auxiliaries in requests "Could you possibly . . ."', into appropriate use of requests in real situations relies on a conversion model. Krashen emphasizes the development of both sides. Acquisition in his terms is fostered by communicative 'natural' activities. Learning in his sense can be helped to some limited extent by the provision of appropriate 'rules of thumb'. Similarly, according to Bialystok (1990), L2 learning requires knowledge such as rules of grammar for the development of competence in her terms and needs practice in speaking, etc., to develop control processes.

CONVERSION MODELS AND MIXED MODELS

Key theme:

- L2 learning has more than one side to it, both skills and knowledge.

Learning:

- the two sides are either learnt separately or one leads into the other.

Teaching uses:

- exercises which exploit different aspects of learning, whether by conversion or separately.

---

4 Social models: the socio-educational model and the acculturation model

Focusing questions

How crucial to success do you see the attitudes that the students bring to the classroom?
What would you say was the best social relationship there could be between the students and the culture of the language they are learning?
What do you think are the origins of creoles and pidgins?

Many would say all the models described so far neglect the most important part of language: its social aspect. There are two interpretations of this. One is that L2 learning usually takes place in a social situation where people interact with each other, whether in the classroom or outside. The discourse and strategy elements in this have already been covered in earlier chapters. The second interpretation is that L2 learning takes place within a society and has a function within that society. This relates to the local and international goals of language teaching discussed in Chapter 7.

THE SOCIO-EDUCATIONAL MODEL

A complex view of L2 learning called the *socio-educational model* has been put forward by Robert Gardner (1985) to explain how individual factors and general features of society interact in L2 learning. He sees two main ingredients in the learners' success – motivation and aptitude – both of which were examined briefly in Chapter 5. Motivation consists of two chief factors: attitudes to the learning situation, i.e. to the teacher and the course, and integrativeness, which is a complex of factors about how the learner regards the culture reflected in the L2. These elements are put together to yield the model seen in Figure 8.5.

Fig. 8.5 Gardner's socio-educational model of L2 learning (simplified)

Success depends on motivation and aptitude; motivation depends on integrativeness and attitudes. Or, to put it another way, according to Gardner integrativeness and attitudes lead to motivation; motivation and aptitude lead to success. Each causes the other.

But where do attitudes and integrativeness come from? The answer according to Gardner is the social milieu in which the students are placed. The society sets a particular store by L2 learning; it has particular stereotyped views of foreigners and of particular nationalities, and it sees the classroom in a particular way. Hence one way of predicting if students will be successful at L2 learning is to look not at the attitudes of the students themselves but at those of their parents. The crucial factors are how the learner thinks of the speakers of a second language and how highly he or she values L2 learning in the classroom. The socio-educational model chiefly applies to language teaching for local goals, where the students have definite views on the L2 group whose language they are learning through everyday contact with them within the society, say the position of Japanese learners of English in Toronto. In teaching for international goals they may not have such definite opinions. For example, French teaching in England involves little contact with French-speaking groups.

THE ACCULTURATION MODEL

John Schumann (1978a) has proposed a complementary approach called the *acculturation model*. The most important influence on L2 learning for him is the relationship between the social group of the L2 learners and the social group of the speakers of the target language. Successful learning means acculturation, becoming part of the target culture. If the group of L2 learners thinks of itself as superior or inferior to the target language speakers, they will not learn the language very well. So in a colonial situation the rulers do not learn the language of their supposed inferiors as this would be 'going native'; the indigenous people on the other hand do not learn the language of their supposed superiors very well as this would be 'collaborationist'. An example from English history is that after 200 years when French was the official language of the ruling Normans in England and English was almost invisible, English re-emerged with hardly any effects of disuse. The Normans and the Anglo-Saxons were not very good at learning each other's languages because of the power relationship between them. In more modern days English, Russian, and French have all failed to be learnt successfully in various parts of the world because of their political overtones.

The relationship between the learner and the target groups exists on many different levels: social, artistic, political, technological, religious. Football is given as a reason by some English boys for preferring to learn German rather than French. Again it is hard to use the second/foreign language distinction. English learnt in South Africa is very different from English learnt in Canada though both can be called 'second' languages. English learnt in Argentina is very different from English learnt in Japan though both might be 'foreign' languages. It is the unique relationship between the learner's group and the target group that is crucial. One problem with this analysis is that international languages to some extent do not fit Schumann's scheme. The international use of languages such as English, for example, is often detached from the English-speaking peoples. Schumann does, however, have a further term, *enculturation*, to cover circumstances in which it is desirable to speak a second language within one's own culture, a form of élite bilingualism in which you gain status by having some knowledge of another language: at one stage any educated English person would claim to know French as part of their gentility.

One interesting insight from such theories is the similarity between L2 learning and the development of pidgin languages. A pidgin comes into being as a solution to the problems of two groups trying to communicate with each other without a shared language. As the contact is maintained, so the pidgin gets more developed; eventually children learn it as their first language and it becomes a creole language. Examples of pidgins are Tok Pisin spoken in Papua New Guinea, Hawaiian Pidgin, and Cameroon Pidgin English. Creoles are found everywhere from the English-based Krio of Sierra Leone, to French-based Louisiana creole, to Portuguese-based creole in Macao. Pidgins have certain characteristics in common regardless of the combinations of language involved, particularly their 'simplified' grammars. Schumann (1978b) originally drew people's attention to this through his study of a Spanish learner of English called Alberto whose speech had many of the simplified characteristics of pidgin, e.g. negation was expressed as 'no' + verb. Roger Andersen (1983) has developed the concepts of *nativization* and *denativization*. Nativization is progress towards universal underlying forms. This consists of adapting the language that is being acquired to built-in universal tendencies. Denativization, on the other hand, is movement in the opposite direction and involves changing the internal system to suit the language that is being learnt.

Oddly, the consideration of society has led back to the discussion of aspects of language built into the mind. Thus the sociolinguistic equivalent of Chomsky's Universal Grammar is Derek Bickerton's *Bioprogram* (Bickerton, 1981). Creole languages are created by children out of the pidgins spoken by their parents. The characteristics of creole languages may tell us about the essential features of the human language capacity.

The implications for teaching hark back to the discussion in the last chapter of the roles of language teaching in society. The total situation in which the students are located plays a crucial part in their learning. If the goals of teaching are incompatible with their perceptions of the world and the social milieu in which they are placed, teaching has little point. Teachers have to fit their teaching to the roles of language teaching for the person or the society, or attempt to reform the social preconceptions of their students. If they do not, the students will not succeed. These models also remind the teacher of the nature of the L2-using situation. The goal of teaching is to enable a non-native speaker to communicate adequately, not to enable him or her to pass as native. Hence pidgins and so on make us think once again of the central cross-linguistic nature of L2 use.

Each of these models of learning accounts persuasively for what it considers the crucial aspects of L2 learning; some, such as the acculturation model, are already looking a bit old-fashioned, others, such as connectionism, have hardly been tried out. What is wrong with them is not their claims about their own front yard so much as their tendency to claim that the whole street belongs to them. Each of them is at best a piece of the jigsaw. Do the pieces add up to a single picture? Can a teacher believe that language is mental knowledge gained by assigning weightings to factors by those with good attitudes towards the target culture without committing Orwellian doublethink? The answer is probably yes. The differences between the areas of L2 learning dealt with by each model mean that they are by no means irreconcilable. UG applies only to 'core' grammar; response weightings apply to speech processing; attitudes to behaviour in academic classrooms. Only if the models dealt with the same areas would they come into conflict. At the moment there is no overall framework for all the models. When they are fitted together, an overall model of L2 learning will one day emerge. At the moment there are many area-specific models, each of them providing some useful insights into its own province of L2 learning;

SOCIAL MODELS

Key theme:

- learning takes place in society.

Learning:

- learning depends upon motivation and aptitude, which in turn depend on integrativeness and attitudes (the socio–educational model).
- learning depends upon the perceived relationships between the target and the L2 groups (the acculturation model).
- L2 learning is related to processes in pidginization.

Teaching use:

- match the teaching with the social and personal roles of language teaching.
- remember L2 use is a multilingual situation.

---

there is not much point in debating whether a bicycle or an airplane is an easier way of getting from place to place; both have their proper uses. Hence there is not much sense in debating which overall model is best; rather each has to be developed to its logical limits to see where it might lead.

For the sake of their students, teachers have to deal with L2 learning as a whole, as we shall see in the next chapter. It is premature for any one of these models to be adopted as the sole basis for teaching, because, however right or wrong they may be, none of them covers more than a small fraction of what the students need. As Spolsky (1989a) wisely remarks, 'any theory of second language learning that leads to a single method must be wrong'.

It will have also been transparent to the reader that I have my own personal views on the desirable model, namely multi-competence. None of the current models starts from the normality of the mind that knows two languages. Whether it is UG or the competition model, the input hypothesis or the acculturation model, the starting point is knowledge of language, not knowledge of languages. Thus they all assume that L2 learning is inefficient because it never reaches the same goal as L1 learning. But why should it? By definition L2 learners are not native speakers and never can be, without time travel back to their time of birth. What we need is a model that recognizes the distinctive nature of knowing two or more languages rather than trying to measure L2 knowledge by a monolingual standard. As Sridhar and Sridhar (1986) point out, 'Paradoxical as it may seem, second language acquisition researchers seem to have neglected the fact that the goal of SLA is bilingualism.' Some evidence for multi-competence is presented in Cook (1992) and other papers can be found (Balcom, forthcoming), but far more is needed before it can be presented in a form as well worked out as those described in this chapter.

DISCUSSION TOPICS

1. Do you agree that there are parts of the second language that we do not need to teach, and parts that are based on transfer from our L1?
2. How could you teach vocabulary as related to grammatical structure?
3. What parts of the second language do you think can be built up by practice? What parts cannot?
4. How can you help students go from the formal language of the classroom to the informal language outside?
5. How helpful do you feel monitoring is to using a second language?
6. How much of your students' success would you attribute to the factors in the socio-educational model, how much to other factors?

FURTHER READING

Teaching applications of the UG model are discussed in Cook (1994), 'Universal Grammar and the learning and teaching of second languages'; its link to L2 learning is discussed in Cook and Newson (1996), *Chomsky's Universal Grammar*. An overall account of some L2 models by a psychologist can be found in McLaughlin (1987), *Theories of Second-Language Learning*. A useful synthesizing overview of L2 learning can be found in Spolsky (1989a), *Conditions for Second Language Learning*. The competition model and the input hypothesis model are discussed more critically in Cook (1993). Connectionism is surveyed in Broeder and Plunkett (1994), 'Connectionism and second language acquisition'.

9

Second language learning and language teaching styles

This chapter looks at some general questions of teaching methodology in the light of L2 learning research. It connects established methods of teaching to the research that has already been outlined, in a sense, reversing the direction of the last chapter in going from teaching to L2 learning.

'Teaching method' has been used in this book as a broad cover term for the diverse activities that go on in language teaching. Various suggestions have been put forward over the years for making the term 'method' more precise or for abandoning it. The traditional distinction is between overall 'approaches', such as the oral approach, 'methods', such as the audiolingual method, and teaching 'techniques', such as drills (Anthony, 1963). More recently Richards and Rodgers (1986) see 'approaches' as related through 'design' to 'procedures'. Marton (1988) on the other hand talks about four overall teaching 'strategies': the receptive strategy, which relies primarily on listening, the communicative strategy, in which students learn by attempting to communicate, the reconstructive strategy, in which the student participates in reconstructive activities based on a text, and the eclectic strategy, which combines two or more of the others. Allen *et al.* (1990) distinguish experiential 'activities' which rely on language use within a situation from analytic activities which use language study and practice.

To avoid the various associations and prejudices that these terms conjure up, let us use the more neutral terms 'teaching technique' and 'teaching style'. The actual point of contact with the students is the teaching technique, as we saw in Chapter 1. Thus a structure drill in which students intensively practise a structure is one technique; dictation is another, information-gap exercises another, and so on. A technique, as Clark (1984) puts it, is a 'label for what we do as teachers'. Teachers combine these techniques in various ways within a particular teaching style. Put a structure-drill with a repetition dialogue and a role-play and you get the audiolingual style with its dependence on the spoken language, on practice, and on structure. Put a functional drill with an information gap exercise and a role-play and you get the social communicative style with its broad assumptions about the importance of communication in the classroom. A teaching style is a loosely connected set of teaching techniques believed to share the same goals of language teaching and the same views of language and of L2 learning. The word 'style' partly reflects the element of fashion and changeability in teaching; it is not intended as an academic term with a precise definition but as a loose overall label that we can use freely to talk about teaching. A teacher who might feel guilty switching from one 'method' to another or in mixing 'methods' within one lesson has less compunction about changing 'styles'; there is no emotional commitment to a 'style'. Of course it is rare to encounter a classroom that is a pure version of one or other of these teaching styles as none of them fully satisfy all the needs of any real class of students; nevertheless they provide convenient reference points for the discussion of language teaching.

This chapter relates six teaching styles to L2 learning research: the *academic* teaching style common in academic classrooms, the *audiolingual* style that emphasizes structured oral practice, the *social communicative* style that aims at interaction between people, the *information communicative* style that stresses information transfer from one person to another, the *mainstream EFL* style which combines aspects of the first three, and, finally, other styles that look beyond language itself.

Before looking at these styles in detail, it is useful to assess one's own sympathies for particular styles by filling in the following questionnaire:

What is *your* style of language teaching?

Tick the answer that suits your *own* style of language teaching best (even if it is not the one you are supposed to be using). Try to tick only *one* answer for each question: then fill them in on the grid that follows.

1. WHAT IS THE CHIEF GOAL OF LANGUAGE TEACHING?

    (*a*) the students should know the rules of the language
    (*b*) they should be able to behave in ordinary situations
    (*c*) they should be able to communicate with other people
    (*d*) they should be able to understand and transmit information
    (*e*) they should both know the rules and be able to behave and to communicate
    (*f*) they should become better people, emotionally and socially

2. WHICH OF THESE TEACHING TECHNIQUES DO YOU VALUE MOST HIGHLY?

    (*a*) explaining grammatical rules
    (*b*) mechanical drills
    (*c*) communication games

(d) listening comprehension
(e) presentation and practice of functions, structures, etc.
(f) discussion of controversial topics

3. HOW WOULD YOU DESCRIBE THE LANGUAGE YOU ARE TEACHING THE STUDENTS IN THE CLASSROOM?

(a) rules about the language
(b) grammatical patterns
(c) language functions
(d) emphasizing content rather than form
(e) grammatical structures and functional elements
(f) a way of unveiling the student's own personality

4. DO YOU THINK THE STUDENTS ARE LEARNING LANGUAGE CHIEFLY BY:

(a) consciously understanding the language rules
(b) forming habits of using the language
(c) communicating with each other in the classroom
(d) trying to understand what is said to them
(e) understanding rules, forming habits, and communicating
(f) engaging in activities that are personally meaningful to them

Now fill in your answers on the following grid.

Answer	Q1	Q2	Q3	Q4	Teaching style
(a)					academic
(b)					audiolingual
(c)					social communicative
(d)					information communicative
(e)					mainstream EFL
(f)					others

It should now be possible to see which of the six teaching styles you are most in tune with by looking for the row with the most ticks. Question 1 tested the overall aims of language teaching; question 2 the slant on language teaching itself that you prefer; question 3 the language content used in the classroom; question 4 the ideas about language learning – of course these may now be rather different from when you started this book.

1 The academic style

An advanced foreign language lesson in an academic context often consists of a reading text taken from a newspaper or similar source, for example, the lead story on the front page of today's newspaper under the headline 'PM seeks new curbs on strikes'. The teacher leads the students through the text sentence by sentence. Some of the cultural background is elucidated – the context of legislation about strikes in England. Words that give problems are explained or translated into the students' first language by the teacher or via the students' dictionaries – 'closed shop' or 'stoppage', say. Grammatical points of interest are discussed with the students, such as the use of the passive voice in 'A similar proposal in the Conservative election manifesto in 1983 was also shelved'. The students go on to a fill-in grammatical exercise on the passive. Perhaps for homework they translate the passage into their L1.

Or take a secondary school. In one class the pupils are being tested on their homework. The teacher has written a series of sentence on the board: 'The child has (cross/crossed/crossing) the road', 'The boy was (help/helped/helping) his father', and so on. He asks them 'What's child?' 'A noun', 'What's cross?' 'A verb'; 'What's crossed?' 'Past participle'; 'So what do we say?' 'The boy has crossed the road'; 'Good'.

In the class next-door the pupils have a short text written on the board: 'In spring the weather is fine; the flowers come out and everybody feels better that winter is over . . .'. The teacher asks 'What is spring?' 'A noun', 'What's spring in Arabic?' 'Rabi'; 'So how do we translate 'in spring'?

The academic teaching style then is characterized by teaching techniques of grammatical explanation and translation, and so is sometimes known as the grammar-translation method. The style is similar in concept to Marton's reconstructive strategy or Allen *et al.'s* analytic activities. The academic style is a time-honoured way of teaching foreign languages in Western culture, popular in secondary schools and widespread in the teaching of advanced students in university systems around the world. The academic style may occur even when the teacher is ostensibly using other styles. A teacher explains how to apologize in the target language – 'When you bump into someone on the street you say "sorry"'; a teacher gives a quick grammatical explanation of the present perfect tense – ' "I have been to Paris" means that the action is relevant to the moment of speaking'; a teacher describes where to put the tongue to make the sound /θ/ in 'think' – all of these are slipping into an academic style where the pupils have to understand the abstract explanation before applying it in their own speech.

The academic style does not directly teach people to use the language for some purpose outside the classroom. Ostensibly it is language teaching with individual goals aimed primarily at the learning of the L2 as an academic subject, in other words at the creation of linguistic competence, language knowledge, in the students' minds. In addition it often claims to train the students to think better, to appreciate other cultures, and to foster other educational values.

But the academic style is nevertheless frequently intended as preparation for the actual use of language. By developing academic knowledge the student eventually becomes able to use the L2 in real-life situations outside the classroom. While the style does not directly practise language use in the classroom, it can provide a basis for language use when the student requires it. Hence the undoubted popularity of grammar books among students who, despite the lack of explicit grammar in most contemporary teaching methods, continue to believe that this will help them. Hence also the ways in which course books continue to feed in grammatical information explicitly to students; for instance, the grammatical appendix to book I of *COBUILD English* (Willis and Willis, 1989), ostensibly a lexically based course, is as good as many a full-size grammar book.

The view of learning in the academic style emphasizes the acquisition of grammatical competence as rules of a traditional type and as lists of vocabulary. It values what people know about the language rather than what they comprehend or produce. Students are seen as acquiring knowledge of language rather than communicative ability directly. It uses a 'conversion' model of L2 learning that sees the learner progressing from controlled conscious understanding of language to automatic processing of speech without thinking, as was described in the last chapter. The language teaching classroom is seen as similar to classrooms in other school subjects, with the teacher as a fount of knowledge and advice.

The academic style is appropriate for a society or an individual that treats academic knowledge of the L2 as a desirable objective and that holds a traditional view of the classroom and of the teacher's role. Its strengths are to my mind the intellectual challenge it can present some students, unlike the non-intellectual approach of many other styles, and the seriousness with which it views language: the pupils are not just learning how to get coffee in a café but how to understand important messages communicated in another language, particularly through its literature. One weakness is its description of language. The linguistic content is usually traditional grammar, rather than more recent or more comprehensive approaches, as we saw in Chapter 2; sometimes at advanced levels it ventures into the descriptive grammar tradition in English – as in, say, *A University Grammar of English* (Quirk and Greenbaum, 1973) . At the same time, while the treatment of vocabulary in text exercises is far-ranging, it is also unsystematic; the teacher has to cover whatever comes up in the text. Though the academic style laudably strives to build up relationships between vocabulary items encountered in texts, it has no principled way of doing so. Despite being concerned with linguistic forms, it pays little attention to components of language other than grammar and vocabulary and, occasionally, pronunciation. The same techniques could in fact be applied systematically to other areas, say listening comprehension or communicative function.

The academic teaching style caters for academically gifted students, who will supplement it with their own good language learner strategies, and who will probably not be young children – in other words, they are Skehan's analytic learners. But, while the style has often succeeded with such students, they represent the tip of an iceberg. Those who are learning language as an academic subject – the linguistics students of the future – may be properly served by an academic style. Indeed, at Essex University a descriptive grammar course is compulsory for all students learning modern languages. But such academically oriented students form a small fraction of those in most educational settings. Those who wish to use the L2 for real-life purposes may not be academically gifted or may not be prepared for the long journey from academic knowledge to practical use that the style requires.

When should the academic style be used? If the society and the students treat individual goals as primary, language use as secondary, and the students are academically gifted, then the academic style is appropriate. In a country where the learners are never going to meet a French-speaking person, are never going to visit a French-speaking country, and have no career needs for French, an academic style of French teaching may be quite appropriate. But the teacher has to recognize its narrow base. For the academic style to be adequate, it needs to include descriptions of language that are linguistically sound and descriptions that can be converted by the students into actual use. The academic style would be more viable as a way of L2 teaching within its stated goals if it changed the grammatical and vocabulary core to something that better reflects the ways in which language is described today: little teaching of English grammar, for example, in the academic style, makes use even of the elementary information from Chapter 2 about grammatical morphemes or principles and parameters. And it might succeed better if it searched for forms of grammar that related better to the processes of conversion from conscious to unconscious knowledge on which it relies; if it indeed intends the students to be able to use language at the end then the grammar it teaches has to be justified, not just by whether it is correct, but by whether it is assimilable by the student. Krashen as ever has the useful point that we should be teaching 'rules of thumb' that help the student even if they are not totally true, rather than fully accurate analyses. The quick generalization that English comparatives are formed with '-er' with monosyllabic words ('big/bigger', 'small/smaller', etc.) and with 'more' with words of more than two syllables ('intelligent/more intelligent', 'beautiful/more beautiful'), leaves the student only to puzzle out words with exactly two syllables. It may not satisfy the linguists but it may satisfy the students.

While the individual goals of the academic style are potentially profound, there is a danger that teachers can lose sight of them and see grammatical explanations as having no other role than imparting factual knowledge. The important other goals of language awareness, mental training, and the appreciation of other cultures may not be achieved spontaneously if the teacher does not give them particular attention in planning lessons and in carrying them out.

THE ACADEMIC STYLE OF LANGUAGE TEACHING

Typical teaching techniques:

- grammatical explanation, translation, etc.

Goals:

- directly, individual learning of the L2 as an academic subject, sometimes leading to communicative ability
- indirectly, ability to use language

Type of student:

- academically gifted, not young children

Learning assumptions:

- acquisition of conscious grammatical knowledge, conversion of knowledge to use

Processing assumptions:

- none

Weaknesses from L2 research perspective:

- inadequate use of grammar
- no position on other components of language knowledge or use
- inefficiency as a way of teaching use

Suggestions for teaching:

- use it with academic students with individual goals
- supplement it with other components of language and processes
- remember its individual goals

---

2 The audiolingual style

The name 'audiolingual' is attached to a teaching style that reached its peak in the 1960s, best conveyed in Robert Lado's thoughtful book *Language Teaching: A Scientific Approach* (Lado, 1964). Its emphasis is on teaching the spoken language through dialogues and drills. A typical lesson in an audiolingual style starts with a dialogue, say about buying food in a shop:

A: Good morning.

B: Good morning.
A: Could I have some milk please?
B: Certainly. How much?

The language in the dialogue is controlled so that it introduces only a few new vocabulary items, 'milk', 'cola', 'mineral water', say, and includes several examples of any new structural point: 'Could I have some cola?', 'Could I have some mineral water?' etc. The students listen to the dialogue as a whole, either played back from a tape or read by the teacher; they repeat it sentence by sentence, and they act it out: 'Now get into pairs of shopkeeper and customer and try to buy the following items . . .'. Then the students drill grammatical points connected with the dialogue, such as the polite questions used in requests 'Could I . . .'. The teacher writes on the board:

'Could I have some (milk, water, cola)?'

He says: 'milk'.

The students answer:

– 'Could I have some milk?',
– 'Water',
– 'Could I have some water',

and so on. The drill practises the structure repeatedly with variation of vocabulary. Many drills were not as nakedly structural as this but attempted to put the structure into a realistic conversational exchange:

– 'What about milk?'
– 'Oh yes, could I have some milk?'
– 'And cola?'
– 'Oh yes, could I have some cola?'
– 'And you might need some mineral water.'
– 'Oh yes, could I have some mineral water?'

Finally there are expansion activities to make the students incorporate the language in their own use: 'Think what you want to buy today and ask your neighbour if you can have some.' As Wilga Rivers (1964) put it, 'Some provision will be made for the student to apply what he has learnt in a structured communication situation.' Instead of homework, the students go to the language laboratory to practise dialogues and drills individually. Language is not only divided into the four skills of listening, speaking, reading, and writing, but these have to be *taught* in that order; spoken language always preceding written language, 'passive' skills preceding 'active' skills. Hence the audiolingual style stresses the spoken language rather than the written and the so-called 'active' skills of speaking and writing rather than the 'passive' skills of listening and reading.

There were two interpretations of the dictum that speech should come before writing. One was short term: anything the students learn must be heard before being seen; so the teacher always has to say a new word before writing it on the blackboard. The other was long term: the students must spend a period doing only spoken skills before they are introduced to the written skills; this might be a few weeks or indeed a whole year. This long-term interpretation in my experience led to most problems. Adult students who were used to the written text as a crutch did not know why it was taken from them; I used to present dialogues only from tape without any text until I caught the students writing down the text under their desks and decided that, if they were going to have a written text anyway, my correctly spelled version was far preferable to their amateur version.

Though few teachers nowadays employ a 'pure' audiolingual style, many of the ingredients are nevertheless common in today's classrooms: the use of short dialogues, the emphasis on spoken language, the value attached to practice, the emphasis on the students themselves speaking, the division into four skills, the importance of vocabulary control, the step-by-step progression, and so on. Virtually all pronunciation teaching uses the audiolingual techniques of repetition and drill when it does not employ the academic style of conscious explanation. Many teachers clearly feel comfortable with the audiolingual style and use it at one time or another in their teaching, even if most would challenge its assumptions about learning. In particular after reading Chapter 4 the reader may doubt whether listening is ever a passive skill!

Audiolingualism also happened to arrive in Europe at a time when the language laboratory became technically feasible. Many of its techniques indeed worked well with this equipment; repeating sentences and hearing recordings of your repetition, doing drills and hearing the right answer after your attempt, fitted in nicely with the tape-recorder. Recent styles that emphasize free production of speech and communication between people have found it far harder to assimilate language laboratories, apart from listening activities. Indeed any glance at commercial materials for computer assisted language learning (CALL) will show that they are essentially audiolingual in their emphasis on drill and practice, though paradoxically they depend primarily on the written language because of the computer's limitations in dealing with speech.

⤐ Of all the styles the audiolingual style most blatantly reflects a particular set of beliefs about L2 learning, often referred to as 'habit-formation'. Language is a set of habits, just like driving a car. Each habit is learnt by doing it time and again. The dialogues concentrate on unconscious 'structures' rather than the conscious 'rules' of the academic style. Instead of understanding every word or structure, students learn the text more or less by heart. Learning sentences means learning structures and vocabulary, which amounts to learning the language. Like the academic style, language is seen as form rather than as meaning, though its basis is more in structural than traditional grammar. Oddly enough, despite its emphasis on the spoken language, the structures it teaches are predominantly those of writing. The publishers of an intermediate audio-lingual course I co-authored, for example, took grave exception to the expression 'Good book that!', common as it may be in spoken English.

The goal of the audiolingual style is to get the students to 'behave' in common L2 situations, such as the station or the supermarket; it is concerned with the real-life activities the students are going to face. In one sense it is practical and communication-oriented. The audiolingual style is not learning language for its own sake but learning it for actual use, either within the society or without. While the appropriate student type is not defined, the style is not restricted to the academically gifted. Indeed its stress on practice can dis-advantage those with an analytical bias. Nor is the audiolingual style obviously catering for students of a particular age; adults may do it as happily as children.

Its views of L2 learning are closest to the processing models described in the last chapter: language is doing things, not knowing things. Partly this comes across in its emphasis on the physical situation. Most importance is attached to building up the strength of the student's response through practice. Little weight is given to the understanding of linguistic structure or to the creation of knowledge. It is not a conversion model in which knowledge of one type is turned into another. Rather, the ability to use language is built up piece by piece using the same type of learning all the time. Grammar is seen as 'structures' like 'Could I have some X?' or 'This is a Y' within which items of vocabulary are substituted. Courses and syllabuses are graded around structures; drills practise particular structures; dialogues introduce and exemplify structures and vocabulary in context. The style, however, has no particular views on language processing, apart from its interest in the production and comprehension of phonemes. It requires a classroom where the students are highly teacher-controlled except for the final exploitation phase when, as Lado puts it, the student 'has the patterns ready as habits but he must practise using them with full attention on purposeful communication'. Until the expansion phase of the cycle, students repeat, answer, or drill at the teacher's behest. Though they work individually in the language laboratory, all of them still use the same activities and teaching materials. The style demands students who do not expect to take the initiative. All responsibility is in the teacher's hands.

One virtue of the academic style is that, if it does not achieve its secondary goal of allowing the student to communicate, it might still have educational value via its goals of improving thinking, promoting cross-cultural under-standing, and so on. The audiolingual style has no fall-back position. If it does not succeed in getting the student to function in the L2, there is nothing else to be gained from it – no academic knowledge or problem-solving ability. Lado does, however, claim that it teaches a positive attitude of identification with the target culture. Furthermore, its insistence on L2 learning as the creation of habits is an oversimplification of the behaviourist models of learning that have been scorned as explanations for language acquisition for many years. Many of course would deny that the distinctive elements of language are in fact learnable by these means; the ability to create or understand 'new' sentences is not acquired by practising 'old' sentences. The principles of Universal Grammar, for example, are impossible to acquire through practice and reinforcement.

Syllabuses and textbooks in the audiolingual style mostly see structures, phonemes, and vocabulary items as the sum total of language. Though based on the four skills of listening, speaking, reading, and writing, the style pays surprisingly little attention to the distinctive features of each skill. The skill of listening, for example, is not usually broken up into levels or stages that resemble those seen in Chapter 4. More crucially, its view of language use now seems naïve. The communication situation is far more complex than the style implies. If communication is the goal of language teaching, its content needs to be based on an analysis of communication itself, which is not adequately covered by structures and vocabulary. Even if students totally master the content of an audiolingual course, they would still need much more to function in a real-life situation.

Yet many teachers fall back on the audiolingual style. One reason may indeed be that it provides a clear framework for teachers to work within. Teachers always know what they are supposed to be doing, unlike more flexible or improvisational styles. Students could relax within a firmly structured environment, always knowing the kinds of activities that would take place and what would be expected of them. Certain aspects of language may lend themselves best to audiolingual teaching. Pronunciation teaching has hardly changed its techniques in the past thirty years, unlike the rapid change in other areas of teaching, perhaps because of lack of imagination by teachers, perhaps because the audiolingual style is indeed the most effective in this area. Lado's 1964 pronunciation techniques of 'demonstration, imitation, props, contrast, and practice' seem as comprehensive as anything that has come since. The style reminds us that language is in part physical behaviour and the total language teaching operation must take this into account.

The teacher should be aware of the audiolingual source of many familiar teaching techniques. Though ostensibly out of fashion, its influence is still pervasive. Take for instance the emphasis on spoken language and on practice in speaking, which are found in many contemporary techniques; many people indeed see these as the core of communicative language teaching: communication is seen as primarily speaking and learning as doing things. Where do these ideas come from if not the audiolingual style? Or ideas such as vocabulary frequency, use of dialogues, and so on. It is important for teachers to be aware that, despite being adopted by the communicative styles of language teaching and other methods, they are based on the audiolingual view of language, which may well not be the one they consciously favour.

Indeed it sometimes seems to me that the germ of communicative teaching was the expansion phase, which was supposed to allow the students to incorporate the language into their own experience. As we have seen, this was regarded as essential by all the commentators on audiolingualism, whether

Lado or Rivers. It consisted of 'purposeful communication' (Lado, 1964) such as role-playing, and games – just the core activities of the communicative approach. Sadly, however, the audiolingual style failed to remember this vital stage in the practice of the classroom and the textbook, leaving it to the later styles to develop such activities.

THE AUDIOLINGUAL STYLE OF LANGUAGE TEACHING

Typical teaching techniques:

- dialogues, structure drills, etc.

Goal:

- getting students to 'behave' in appropriate situations

Type of student:

- non-analytical, non-academic

Learning assumptions:

- 'habit-formation' behaviourist theory

Processing assumptions:

- none

Classroom assumptions:

- teacher-controlled classroom

Weaknesses from L2 research perspective:

- inadequate form of grammar
- no position on other aspects of language knowledge or use
- inefficiency of habit-formation as way of teaching use

Suggestions for teachers:

- use for teaching certain aspects of language only
- be aware of the underlying audiolingual basis of many everyday techniques

---

3 The social communicative style

The beginning of the 1970s saw a shift towards teaching methods that emphasized communication. Initially this was largely a matter of redefining what the student had to learn in terms of communicative competence rather than linguistic competence: ability to use the language appropriately rather than the knowledge of grammatical rules implied in the academic style or the 'habits' of the audiolingual. The behaviour of native speakers was analysed and developed into syllabuses incorporating ideas of language functions, such as 'persuading someone to do something', and notions, such as 'expressing point of time', which were more sophisticated than those possible with the limited concepts of structure and situation of the audiolingual style. Recently, communication is often seen more in terms of the processes that people use to carry out specific communicative tasks; hence the syllabuses are designed around the processes or tasks that students use in the classroom.

The elaboration of communicative competence affected the specification of the teaching target but did not at first have direct consequences for teaching. The fact that the teaching point of a lesson is the function 'asking directions' rather than the structure 'yes-no questions' does not prevent it being taught through any teaching style, just as grammar can be taught in any style. Even a communicative function can be taught through academic style explanation or audiolingual style drills. The course *Function in English* (Blundell *et al.*, 1982) displays a list of alternatives for each function categorized as neutral, informal, and formal, and linked by codes to a structural index – clearly academic style. The textbook *Opening Strategies* (Abbs and Freebairn, 1982) makes students substitute 'bank', 'post office', 'restaurant' and so on into the sentence 'Is there a – near here?', clearly an audiolingual drill in all but name.

To many people, however, the end dictates the means: a goal expressed in terms of communication means classroom teaching based on communication. Hence a number of techniques developed that evolved into two styles, which we shall call here 'social communicative' style and 'information communicative' style. The social communicative style has its main emphasis on the joint functioning of two people in a situation, what Halliday (1975) terms the *interpersonal* function of language. The archetypal social communicative techniques are information gap exercises teaching how to give locations of people and places. Take an example from the textbook *Coast to Coast* (Harmer and Surguine, 1987). The students divide into pairs; one has a map of a street showing where Jim, Kathleen, and so on live, the other has a map of the same street showing where Kristy, Ben, and others live. They have to 'ask and answer questions to find where the people live' following a model exchange, and then write the names on the map. The students are given the vocabulary on the map and have an example question and answer. But they have to improvise the dialogue themselves to solve their communicative task. The second standard technique of the social communicative style is guided role-play. The students improvise conversations around an issue but do not have the same contrived information gap. *Headway Elementary* (Soars and Soars, 1993), for example, has an activity 'Work in pairs. Think of a problem you have had with officials. Act it for the rest of the class.' One student role-plays an official, the other their normal character. This reflects one of the main difficulties with role-playing such encounter situations between customer/patient/client/complainer and shop assistant/doctor/lawyer/manager: one student is playing himself or herself and is therefore learning something appropriate to their own interests and goals; the other is pretending to be something they are *not* and using language strategies and indeed vocabulary they may never have to employ in any future career; it is one thing to get a student to practise 'I've got a sore throat, doctor', another to get them to say 'Take a course of antibiotics four times a day before meals.'

In the social communicative style, language is defined as communication between people, rather than as texts or grammatical rules or patterns: it has a social purpose. Language is for forming relationships with people and for interrelating with them. Using language means meeting people and talking to them. Language is not so much rules or structures or texts as ways of talking to people. The aim is to give the students the ability to engage in conversations with people. The teaching syllabus is primarily a way of listing the aspects of communication the students will find most useful, whether functions, notions, or processes. It tries to develop the students' ability to communicate fluently rather than in grammatically flawless sentences.

The goals of the social communicative style are most often towards international use of the second language with people in another country rather than locally in multilingual societies. In general purpose language teaching the overall goals of the social communicative style have not usually been specified in great detail; they usually aim at the generalized situation of visitors to the target country with the accent on tourism and travel, without specific goals for careers, for education, or for access to information, as in the GCSE syllabuses cited in Chapter 7. In more specialized circumstances language has been taught for specific careers – doctors, businessmen, oil technicians, or whatever – and for higher education. In practice many communicative textbooks for beginners adopt what might be called 'travel agent communication' centred upon tourist activities, with the course book resembling a glossy holiday brochure and the teacher a jolly package-tour representative organizing fun activities. One entertaining if light-hearted method of evaluating courses is to measure the 'smile factor': the average number of smiling faces per page of the textbook. The higher the factor, the closer to 'travel agent communication'. *Headway Elementary*, for example, manages to pack fifteen smiling faces onto the first four pages (and seven unsmiling). *Cambridge English* (Swan and Walters, 1984) has sixteen smiles on the first four pages; *Reward* (Greenall, 1994) and *Hotline* (Hutchinson, 1992) a mere three each. Whether you consider this an advantage or not depends on whether it motivates the students to think of English as a jolly happy subject or as a trivialization of life. The smile factor certainly gives a quick insight into the attitudes being expressed by the textbook.

The classroom is a very different place in the social communicative style from the other two styles encountered so far. The teacher no longer dominates the classroom, controlling and guiding the students every minute. Rather the teacher takes one step back and lets the students take over the activities, making up their own conversations in pairs and groups, learning language by doing. A key difference from other styles is that the students are not required to produce substantially errorless speech in native terms, a consequence of the independent language assumption discussed in Chapter 1. Instead they use whatever forms and strategies they can devise themselves to solve their communication problem, ending up with sentences that are entirely appropriate to their task but are often highly deviant from a native perspective. While the teacher provides some feedback and correction, this plays a much less central part in his or her classroom duties. The teacher has the cofigurative role of equal and helper rather than the wise person of the academic style or the martinet of the audiolingual. This is a jump in cultural terms from the traditional teacher-led class and hence disconcerts or indeed alienates those from cultures who see education differently, as we have seen in Chapter 7. The adoption of a social communicative style, however ideal on other grounds, always has to recognize this cultural problem. Take a dialogue at a parents' evening featuring an Inuk parent and a non-Inuit teacher (Crago, 1992):

TEACHER: Your son is talking well in class. He is speaking up a lot.
INUK PARENT: I am very sorry.

To the teacher, it is obvious that it is a virtue to speak and contribute in class; to the parent, children who show proper respect for the teacher obviously stay silent in class. A communicative style with its emphasis on spontaneous production by the learners is unlikely to go down well with cultures that value silence and respect.

The style also is potentially limited to certain types of student. For instance, it might benefit field-independent students rather than field-dependent students, extroverts rather than introverts, and less academic students rather than academic students. Its cofigurative implications can also go against students' expectations of the classroom more than other styles; students in some countries have indeed been upset by its apparent rejection of the ways of learning current in their culture in favour of what they regard as a 'Western' view (though I would guess that there is no reason to think of the academic, audiolingual, or indeed 'humanist' other styles as intrinsically any more or less Western than the communicative – all came equally from educational traditions in the West).

Language learning in this style is the same as language using. Information gap exercises and role-play techniques imitate what happens in the world outside the classroom in a controlled form, rather than being special activities peculiar to language learning. Later on students will be asking the way or dealing with officials in a foreign language environment just as they are now doing in the classroom. Learning language means practising communication within the four walls of the classroom. You learn to talk to people by actually talking to them. L2 learning arises from meaningful use. This has been emphasized in recent developments which use the idea of communication as a dynamic process to stimulate communication in the classroom through task-based activities.

So the social communicative style does not hold a view about L2 learning as such but maintains it happens automatically provided the student interacts with other people in the proper way. Many of its techniques carry on the audiolingual style's preoccupations with active practice by the students, and with spoken language, elaborating the expansion phase of the audiolingual style, as we have seen. Indeed, like the audiolingual style, it often resembles behaviourist views of learning. I have sometimes introduced the ideas of 'mands' and 'tacts' mentioned in the last chapter to teachers without telling them they are verbal operants within Skinner's behaviourist model. Their reaction is normally that they sound a useful basis for a communicative syllabus! The main difference between the audiolingual style and the social communicative style is the latter's emphasis on spontaneous production and comprehension in pursuit of interpersonal communication.

In general, there is surprisingly little connection between this style and L2 learning research. It resembles to some extent the conversational analysis model described in Chapter 3 but differs in specifying abstract elements of communicative competence such as language functions and processes rather than the moves of discourse. Its nearest relations are functional theories of L1 acquisition, rather than the models of L2 learning described in the last chapter. As always, this is not to say that it is *wrong* – perhaps L2 learning research should pay more attention to this side of learning. It can be called a black box model of L2 learning because it assumes little about the learning process, apart from claiming that, if the right circumstances are provided to the students, something will happen inside their minds.

Historically there is a link between the social communicative style and the idea of interlanguage, which means that teachers should respect the developing language systems of the students rather than seeing them as defective. Indeed one might say that the major impact of second language acquisition research on language teaching so far has been the independent language assumption, which liberates the teacher from the carefully contrived grammatical progressions and allows them not to correct everything that the students do that differs from native speakers: learners need the freedom to construct language for themselves. The style uses techniques that change the teacher's roles to those of organization and support rather than direction and control, because it does not set the same store on the students consistently producing near-native sentences; it no longer matters if everything the student says is not exactly the same as that produced by natives. One element in this comes from ideas of Universal Grammar. If the students are using natural processes of learning built into their minds, the teacher can step back and let them get on with it by providing activities and language examples to get these natural processes going. This is related to the view of language learning as hypothesis-testing, an early version of the Universal Grammar theory, in which the learner makes a guess at the rules of the language, tries it out by producing sentences, and accepts or revises the rules in the light of the feedback that is provided. However, hypothesis-testing in this sense has been abandoned as it requires types of correction that L1 children never get and most L2 learners seldom encounter, particularly in a communicative classroom. This can be called *laissez-faire* teaching: learning takes place in the students' minds in ways over which teachers have no control, and so the students should be trusted to learn without the teacher's interference. It can lead to the dangerous assumption that any activity is justified that gives students the opportunity to test out 'hypotheses' in the classroom, with no criteria applied other than getting the students talking. However enjoyable the class may be, however much language is provoked from the students, the teacher always has to question whether the time is being well spent; are the students learning as much from the activity as they would from something else?

Chapter 7 suggested that the word 'communication' can blind us to individual goals of language teaching. The social communicative style covers only some of the relevant aspects of L2 learning, however desirable they may be in themselves, and has no techniques of its own for teaching pronunciation or vocabulary, little connection with speech processing or memory, and little systematic recognition of the possibilities available to the learner through the L1. Pairwork and groupwork among students with the same L1, for example, often leads to frequent codeswitching between L1 and L2, perhaps something to be developed systematically rather than seen as undesirable. In so far as the style recognizes grammar, it is often of a structuralist kind reminiscent of audiolingualism, as seen, for instance, in the substitution tables found in many communicative textbooks.

The social communicative style is highly appropriate for students and societies that value international goals of a non-specific kind. The teacher using it with a particular class has to remember that it will not appeal to students with other types of goal, say an interest in language structure or a desire for personal liberation. The unexpectedness of the classroom situation it employs may need selling to the students; the onus is on them to take advantage of the classroom, not on the teacher to spoonfeed them. It needs balancing with other styles to make certain that the coverage of language components is adequate even to achieve its own goal of communicative competence. But at least it sees communication as a dynamic social activity to be acquired by active participation by the students, marking a clear break in this respect from the academic and audiolingual styles.

THE SOCIAL COMMUNICATIVE STYLE OF LANGUAGE TEACHING

Typical teaching techniques:

- information gap, role-plays

Goal:

- getting students to interact with other people in the L2

Type of student:

- any

Learning assumptions:

- learning by communicating with *other* students in the classroom: *laissez-faire*

Processing assumptions:

- none

Classroom assumptions:

- teacher as organizer, not fount of wisdom

Weaknesses from L2 research perspective:

- lack of views on discourse processes, communication strategies, etc.
- black box model of learning
- lack of role for L1
- possible cultural conflicts because of its cofigurative basis

Suggestions for teachers:

- use with appropriate students in appropriate circumstances
- supplement with other components of language
- avoid trivialization of content and aims

4 The information communicative style

The social communicative and information communicative styles are in a sense two sides of the same coin. A conversation requires not only someone to talk to but also something to talk about. As de Saussure (1916) said, 'Speech has both an individual and a social side and we cannot conceive of one without the other.' Hence the two styles distinguished here as 'social' and 'information' communicative are not separated by teaching methodologists.

Nevertheless, communication can be seen as an exchange of ideas rather than as relationships with people – what Halliday (1975) calls the *ideational* function of language – since these result in rather different teaching styles. Teaching that emphasizes the information that is transferred rather than the social interaction between the participants can be called the information communicative style, equivalent to Marton's receptive strategy. A typical technique in this style is Asher's total physical response (TPR) method. Like other ways of using this style, it emphasizes the listening first approach mentioned, described in Chapter 3; listening is the crucial skill in providing the key to extracting information from what you hear. However, this is not logically the only form that information communicative teaching takes; teaching reading for gist may be just as much within this style, as may task-based approaches.

The information communicative style is hard to illustrate from teaching materials because it mostly depends on the individual teacher's preparation and improvisation during the class; one of the unfortunate consequences of the emphasis on functional social communication by publishers and institutions was that few attempts have been made to write materials within a purely information communicative approach; indeed it is regrettable that there is no published course available based on a listening first methodology.

Gary and Gary (1981a) have, however, published a specimen lesson from their listening-based materials *More English Now!*, which are designed for hotel staff in Egypt. The lesson starts with a 'Preview' section in which the language content of the lesson is explained and in which 'important words' such as 'last week' and 'checked out' are translated into Arabic. In the next section 'Let's Listen', students hear a tape giving the bookings for a hotel for next week and carry out a task-listening exercise, first filling in a form with the guests' names and details and then answering questions such as 'Who was in room 104?' in writing. Finally a 'Let's Read' section gives them the same tasks with a written text. Such listening first teaching requires the students to listen actively but not to produce sentences until they are ready. The point here is the information transfer. TPR students are listening to discover what actions to carry out; their social interaction with the teacher is quite unlike that found in any normal language exchange, except perhaps for the military drill square. Students following *More English Now!* are listening to get specific information to be written down in various forms. While this partly resembles their real-life hotel duties, it deliberately minimizes spoken production and natural social interaction, vital to their actual conversation with guests. The concentration is in both cases on the information to be obtained from language, not on the social relationship between listener and speaker. Working out information is the key factor: take care of the message and the learning will take care of itself. Hence the style is compatible with a large range of teaching techniques, united only by their emphasis on information.

The overall goal is to get students to use the language, first by comprehending, then by producing. Comprehension of information is not seen as a goal in its own right, but as a way into fuller command of the language in use. Sometimes the overall goal is more specific, as with the Cairo hotel staff. Mostly, however, it has a non-specific communicative goal, similar to that in the social communicative model. The information communicative style is used in both local and international circumstances. It implicitly plays down the individual goals of language teaching, making few claims to general educational values. In terms of classrooms, it is teacher-dominated, with the teacher supplying, in person or through materials, the language input and the organization of the students' activities and classroom strategies. The social communicative style is limited by physical factors in the classroom in that it becomes progressively more difficult to organize its activities with larger groups. The listening-based information communicative style, however, lends itself to classes of any size. Some versions of the style are therefore more compatible with the traditional teacher-dominated classroom than is the social communicative style. It caters for a range of student types, provided they do not mind having to listen rather than speak in the classroom. Again, the students need to be prepared for what the style is trying to do, since it differs from their expectations of the classroom.

The style makes two assumptions about learning. One that has already been encountered in Chapter 3 is the equation of decoding with codebreaking. Getting people to comprehend in the classroom is getting them to learn: comprehending is learning. The prime spokesperson for this point of view is then Steven Krashen, whose views were outlined in the last chapter: we acquire language by comprehending input. This shelves the issue of learning to some extent. The processes of learning are less important than the conditions for successful learning. The style again uses a black box model that does not concern itself with specific processes of L2 learning, but with the nature of the input. While the black box of the social communicative style draws on social interaction, the black box of the information communicative style draws on information exchange. It is another form of *laissez-faire*.

The second assumption links listening and speaking in a conversion model, as discussed in the last chapter. Listening is not just a separate skill from speaking, but forms the foundation for speaking. Learning how to listen helps the person with other skills as well as listening. Knowledge acquired by listening converts into knowledge of speaking. This ignores the distinctive features, memory systems and processes involved in each skill. The problem is also the obverse of the social communicative model in that listening first provides no guidance on how to construct discourse by putting sentences together for a particular purpose. It is hard to see how TPR gets the student to build up natural exchanges in the world outside the classroom since they are experiencing a particular style of classroom interaction rather than any simulation of non-classroom exchanges. TPR ignores the twofold nature of classroom language mentioned in Chapter 6. Listening tasks often train people to do listening tasks rather than to engage in interaction in the world outside.

As we have seen, there is no logical reason why the information communicative style should rely on listening at the expense of speaking; communication requires a speaker as well as a listener. The use of 'listening first' techniques represents an additional assumption about the importance of listening to the learning process, as discussed in Chapter 4. There has often been a kind of geographical division in the communicative styles: 'British-influenced' teaching has emphasized that from day one of the course students have to both listen *and* speak; 'American-influenced', or perhaps more strictly 'Krashen-influenced, teaching has emphasized listening without speaking. As a consequence, 'British' teaching seems to have concentrated more on the interpersonal function; the double role of listener and speaker immediately calls up interactive 'conversation' while the listener-only role resembles people listening to the radio.

As with the other teaching styles, L2 research points to the partial coverage of language content, components of language, and processes of language; to be successful the teacher will have to do far more than its precepts suggest. The information communicative style also has little connection with multilingual use of language but assumes an imitation monolingual speaker; it is communication defined as between natives or between teacher and students not as between functioning L2 users in the real world. The suggestions for the teacher are, as usual, to balance the style against other demands of teaching. It may be made more relevant to the students' goal by adapting the techniques in various ways. In particular, the listening tasks it employs can be chosen to correspond to those the students will meet in the world outside the classroom, as we saw in the Garys' materials, rather than being arbitrary tasks in which anything goes provided it carries a message. This step is a useful preparation for the later transition to non-classroom use of language, without sacrificing the principles of the style. Indeed the nature of listening itself could be built upon; systematic attention to teaching the listening processes of access to vocabulary, parsing, and relating the text to prior knowledge might be useful.

A final point that should be made is that information communication implies information to communicate. An important factor in the style is the choice of information. Many courses rely on 'imaginary' content (Cook, 1983): the lives of teenagers in England (*Hotline*), interviews with bank managers (*Cambridge English*), or For Sale ads for imaginary houses (*Headway*). In a survey I found that this type of content figured on nine pages out of ten in beginners courses, seven out of ten in intermediate. But it is also possible to have 'real' content based on actual information about the 'real' world: how people dress in different countries (*Reward*), the history of Stonehenge (*Meeting People*), the life of Buddy Holly (*The Beginner's Choice*). My own feeling is that imaginary content trivializes language learning; the message is conveyed that you do not gain anything significant from your language class. 'Real' content makes the language lesson have a point; the students have acquired information through the language. Different types of real information that might be conveyed include:

- *Another academic subject taught through English.* I have recommended students in England who complained they were stuck at a plateau to go to cookery classes rather than English classes.
- *Student-contributed content.* Getting the students to talk about their own lives and real interests, fascinating in a multilingual class, boring in one where everybody has known each other since primary school.
- *Language.* That is to say, information about the language they are studying, after all this is the one thing that all the students have in common.
- *Literature.* Despised for many years because of its inappropriate language but capable of bringing depth of emotion and art to the classroom.
- *Culture.* That is to say, discussing the cultural differences between languages, one of the goals of the UK National Curriculum.
- *'Interesting facts'.* These might not be connected to English but after the lesson the students can say they learnt something: how to treat a nosebleed, how to use chopsticks, how to play cards, how to make coffee, to take examples from an intermediate course of mine (*Meeting People*).

THE INFORMATION COMMUNICATIVE STYLE OF LANGUAGE TEACHING

Typical teaching techniques:

- information gap, role-plays

Goal:

- getting students to comprehend information in the L2

Type of student:

- any that want to handle information rather than interact socially

Learning assumptions:

- learning by comprehending information in the classroom leads to full ability to use language

Processing assumptions:

- black box – decoding is the same as codebreaking

> *Classroom assumptions*:
>
> - teacher-dominated; classroom type exchanges
>
> *Weaknesses from L2 research perspective*:
>
> - failure to specify the nature of learning itself
> - narrowness of components *and* processes covered
>
> *Suggestions for the teacher*:
>
> - adapt to goals of students and to less classroom-based language
> - develop specific processes of listening

5 The mainstream EFL style

The mainstream EFL style has developed in British-influenced EFL from the 1930s up to the present day. Till the early 1970s, it mostly reflected a compromise between the academic and the audiolingual styles, combining, say, techniques of grammatical explanation with techniques of automatic practice. Harold Palmer in the 1920s indeed saw classroom L2 learning as a balance between the 'studial' capacities by which people learnt a language by studying it like any content subject, that is to say, what we have called here an academic style, and the 'spontaneous' capacities through which people learn language naturally and without thinking, seen by him in similar terms to the audiolingual style (Palmer, 1926). Another name for this style in India was the structural–oral–situational (SOS) method, an acronym that captures several of its main features (Prabhu, 1987): the reliance on grammatical structures, the primacy of speech, and the use of language in 'situations'. Recently it has taken on aspects of the social communicative style by emphasizing person-to-person dialogue techniques.

Until the 1970s this early mainstream style was characterized by the term 'situation' in two senses. In one sense language was to be taught though demonstration in the real classroom situation; teachers rely on the props, gestures and activities that are possible in a real classroom. I remember seeing a colleague attempting to cope with a roomful of EFL beginners who had unexpectedly arrived a week early; his successful lesson was based on the only prop he had to hand, a wastepaper basket, real situational teaching. In the other sense language teaching was to be organized around the language of the real-life situations the students would encounter: the railway station, the hotel, etc. A lesson using the mainstream EFL style starts with a presentation phase in which the teacher introduces new structures and vocabulary. In the Australian course *Situational English* (Commonwealth Office, 1967), for example, the teacher demonstrates the use of 'can' 'situationally' to the students by touching the floor and trying unsuccessfully to touch the ceiling to illustrate 'can' versus 'can't'.

The next stage of the lesson usually involves a short dialogue. In this case it might be a job interview which includes several examples of 'can': 'Can you drive a car?', or 'I can speak three languages.' The students listen to the dialogue, they repeat parts of it, they are asked questions about it, and so on. Then they might see a substitution table such as Figure 9.1. They have to make

John	can	speak	German
Helen	can't		French
		ride	a bicycle
			a horse

Fig 9.1 A typical substitution table

sentences with 'can' by combining words from different columns – 'John can speak French', 'Helen can't ride a horse'. Palmer's studial capacities are involved in the conscious understanding of structures such as 'can', while the repetition and substitution activities use his spontaneous capacities.

A typical modern course book such as *Headway* (Soars and Soars, 1987), for instance, has elements of the academic style in that it explains structures such as the passive: 'Passive sentences move the focus of a sentence from the subject to the object of an active sentence.' It has elements of the audiolingual style in that it is graded around structures and the 'four skills'. But it has also incorporated elements of the social communicative style in pairwork exercises such as acting out conversations about choosing Christmas presents. A typical lesson such as Unit 9 focuses on conditional sentences. First it presents conditionals in a short dialogue; this develops into pairwork on 'imaginary fears'; then the three types of conditional sentence are explained, followed by a questionnaire on your life expectancy ('If you finished university add 1'); it goes on to an exercise of converting proverbs into conditionals and finishes with a task-listening exercise and a reading passage.

The pivot around which the lesson revolves is the grammatical point, couched in terms of structural or traditional grammar. The main difference from the early mainstream style is the use of groupwork and pairwork and the information orientation to the exercises. A mainstream EFL method is implied every time a teacher goes through the classic progression from presentation to dialogue to controlled practice, whether it is concerned with grammar or communicative function. It is the central style described in such TEFL manuals as *A Training Course for English* (Hubbard *et al.*, 1983), or *The Practice of English Language Teaching* (Harmer, 1994). It represents the mainstream EFL teaching of the past thirty years, if not longer.

The goals are in a sense an updated version of audiolingualism. What counts is how students use language in the eventual real-world situation rather than their academic knowledge or the spin-off in general educational values. The version of learning involved is similarly a compromise, suggesting that students learn by conscious understanding, by sheer practice, and by attempting to talk to each other. Some aspects of the knowledge models seen in the last chapter are reflected here, as are aspects of the processing models. Mainstream EFL teaching tries to have its cake and eat it by saying that, if the student does not benefit from one part of the lesson, then another part will help. In terms of student types as well, this broadens the coverage. One student benefits from the grammatical explanation, another from structure practice, another from role-play. Perhaps combining these together will suit more of the students more of the time than relying on a purer style. It does not usually encompass the information communicative style with its emphasis on listening, preferring to see listening and speaking as more or less inseparable. It has the drawbacks common to the other styles: the concentration on certain types of grammar and discourse at the expense of others. Is such a combination of styles into one mainstream style to be praised or blamed? In terms of teaching methods, this has been discussed in terms of 'eclecticism'.

Some have argued that there is nothing wrong with eclectic mixing of methods provided the mixing is rationally based. Others have claimed that it is impossible for the students to learn in so many different ways simultaneously; the teacher is irresponsible to combine incompatible models of language learning. Marton (1988) argues that only certain sequences between methods are possible. His receptive strategy, for instance, may precede, but not follow, the reconstructive or communicative strategies.

This book has illustrated some of the complexities of L2 learning. Each of the teaching styles captures some aspects of this complexity and misses out on others. None of the teaching styles is complete, just as none of the models of L2 learning is complete. Eclecticism is only an issue if two styles concern the same area of L2 learning rather than different areas. Hence it is, at the moment, unnecessary to speculate about the good or bad consequences of eclecticism. When there is a choice between competing styles of language teaching, each with a coverage ranging from grammar to classroom language, from memory to pronunciation, from motivation to the roles of the L2 in society, then eclecticism becomes an issue. At the moment all teaching methods are partial in L2 learning terms; some areas of language are only covered by one type of teaching technique; conversely some methods deal with only a fraction of the totality of L2 learning. The mainstream EFL style cannot be dismissed simply because of its eclecticism, as it is neither more nor less eclectic than any other overall teaching style in terms of L2 learning. My own feeling is that the mainstream style does indeed reflect a style of its own that is more than the sum of its parts.

THE MAINSTREAM EFL STYLE OF LANGUAGE TEACHING

Typical teaching techniques:

- presentation, substitution, role–play

Goal:

- getting students to know and use language

Type of student:

- any

Learning assumptions:

- understanding, practice, and use

Processing assumptions:

- none.

Classroom assumptions:

- both teacher-controlled and groups

Weaknesses from L2 research perspective:

- combination of other styles
- lack of L1 role
- drawbacks of mixture of styles

Suggestions for teacher:

- do not worry about the mixture of different sources
- remember that it still does not cover all aspects relevant to L2 teaching

---

6 Other styles

Other teaching styles have been proposed in recent years that mark a radical departure from those outlined earlier, either in their goals or in their execution. It is difficult to assign these a single name. Some have been called 'alternative methods', but this suggests there is a common conventional method to which they provide an alternative and that they are themselves united in their approach. Some are referred to as 'humanistic methods' because of their links to 'humanistic psychology', but this label suggests religious or philosophical connections that are mostly inappropriate. Others are called 'self-access' or 'self-directed learning'. In England the practice of these styles is still so rare that they are difficult to observe in a full-blooded form, although every EFL or modern language teaching class probably shows some influence from communicative teaching.

Let us start with *community language learning* (CLL), derived from the work of Curran (1976). Picture a beginners class in which the students sit in a circle from which the teacher is excluded. One student starts a conversation by remarking 'Weren't the buses terrible this morning?' in his L1. The teacher translates this into the language the students are learning and the student repeats it. Another student answers 'When do the buses ever run on time?' in her L1, which is translated once again by the teacher, and repeated by the student. And the conversation between the students proceeds in this way. The teacher records the translations said by the students and later uses them for conventional practice such as audiolingual drilling or academic explanation. But the core element of the class is spontaneous conversation following the students' lead, with the teacher offering the support facility of instant translation. As the students progress to later stages they become increasingly independent of the teacher's support. CLL is one of the 'humanistic' methods that include Suggestopedia, with its aim of relaxing the student (Lozanov, 1978), the Silent Way, with its concentration on the expression of meaning through coloured rods (Gattegno, 1972), and Confluent Language Teaching, with its emphasis on the classroom experience as a whole (Galyean, 1977).

In general, CLL subordinates language to the self-expression of emotions and ideas. If anything, language gets in the way of the clear expression of the student's feelings. The aim is not, at the end of the day, to be able to do anything with language in the world outside. It is to do something here and now in the classroom, so that the student, in Curran's words, 'arrives at a more positive view of himself, of his situation, of what he wishes to do and to become' (Curran, 1976). A logical extension is the use of language teaching for psychotherapy in mental hospitals. Speaking in a second language about their problems is easier for some people than in the first language.

The goal of teaching is to develop the students' potential and to enable them to 'come alive' through L2 learning, not to help them directly to communicate with others outside the group. Hence it sees language teaching in terms of individual goals. It stresses the general educational value for the individual rather than any local or international benefits. The student in some way becomes a better person through language teaching. The concept of 'better' is usually defined as greater insight into one's self, one's feelings and one's relationships with others. Learning a language through a humanistic style has the same virtues and vices as jogging; while it does you good, it is at the same time concerned with the individual self at the expense of other-related goals. This type of goal partly accounts for the comparative lack of impact of CLL on the mainstream educational system, where language teaching is often thought of as having more benefit outside the classroom, and where self-fulfilment through the classroom has been seen more as a product of lessons in the mother tongue and its literature. Hence the humanistic styles are often the preserve of part-time education or self-improvement classes. The goals of realizing the individual's potential are perhaps coincidentally attached to L2 teaching; they might be achieved as well through mother-tongue teaching, aerobics, Zen, assertiveness training, or motor-cycle maintenance. Curran says indeed that CLL 'can be readily adapted to the learning of other subjects'; Suggestopedia similarly is supposed to apply to all education; the Silent Way comes out of an approach to teaching mathematics.

A strong similarity between humanistic styles is that they see a 'true' method of L2 learning that can be unveiled by freeing the learner from inhibiting factors. L2 learning takes place if the learner's inner self is set free by providing the right circumstances for learning. If teachers provide stress-free, non-dependent, value-respecting teaching, students will learn. Hence a black box model of learning is again invoked. While no one knows what mechanisms exist in the students' minds, we know what conditions will help them work. So the CLL model of learning is not dissimilar to the communicative learning-by-doing. If you are expressing yourself, you are learning the language, even if such expression takes place through the teacher's mediating translation.

The other humanistic styles are equally unlinked to mainstream L2 learning research. *Suggestopedia* is based on an overall theory of learning and education. The conditions of learning are tightly controlled in order to overcome the learner's resistance to the new language. Georgi Lozanov, its inventor, has indeed carried out psychological experiments, mostly unavailable in English, which make particular claims for the effective learning of vocabulary (Lozanov, 1978). Again, where the outlines of an L2 learning model can be discerned, it resembles the processing models seen in the last chapter.

Oddly enough, while the fringe humanistic styles take pride in their learner centredness, they take little account of the variation between learners. CLL would clearly appeal to extrovert students rather than introverts. Their primary motivation would have to be neither instrumental nor integrative, since both of these lead away from the group. Instead it would have to be self-related or teaching-group related. What happens within the group itself and what the students get out of it are what matters, not what they can do with the language outside. Nor, despite their psychological overtones, do methods such as CLL and Suggestopedia pay much attention to the performance processes of speech production and comprehension.

An opposing trend in teaching styles is the move towards *learner autonomy*. Let us look at a student called Mr D, described by Henner-Stanchina (1986). Mr D is a brewery engineer who went to the CRAPEL (Centre de Recherches et d'Applications Pédagogiques en Langues) in Nancy in France to develop his reading skills in English. He chose, out of a set of options, to have the services of a 'helper', to have personal teaching materials, and to use the sound library.

The first session with the helper revealed that his difficulties were, *inter alia*, with complex noun phrases and with the meanings of verb forms. Later sessions dealt with specific points from this, using the helper as a check on the hypotheses he was forming from the texts he read. The helper's role faded out as he was able to progress through technical documents with increasing ease.

The aim above all is to hand over responsibility for learning to the student. The teacher is a helper who assists with choice of materials and advises what to do but does not teach directly. As Holec (1985a) from the CRAPEL puts it, 'By becoming autonomous, that is by gradually and individually acquiring the capacity to conduct his own learning program, the learner progressively becomes his own teacher and constructs and evaluates his learning program himself.' Using autonomous learning depends on devising a system through which students have the choice of learning in their own way. To quote Holec (1987) again, 'Learners gradually replace the belief that they are "consumers" of language courses . . . with the belief that they can be "producers" of their own learning program and that this is their right.'

At North-East London Polytechnic (now University of East London), we had a simple system in which students could make use of language teaching material of their own choice from the selection provided in a language laboratory at any time. One afternoon per week, helpers were available in all the languages on offer. These could be used by the students in any way they liked, say discussion of which materials to use, or assessment of progress, or straightforward conversation practice. Dickinson (1987) describes more sophisticated systems in operation at the Language Laboratory in Cambridge University, at Moray House in Edinburgh, and the system encountered by Mr D at the CRAPEL in Nancy. But self-direction can also be offered to children within the secondary school classroom. Leni Dam in Copenhagen uses a system of group-based tasks chosen by the students to suit their own needs and interests, what they want to learn, and how they want to learn.

A radical approach to learner autonomy is called the *process syllabus* (Breen, 1984). The idea is that what is covered in the classroom should not be decided by the teacher or the curriculum designer in advance but by a continuous process of negotiation between the teacher and the students. In a cycle, the teacher and students discuss what they want to know, choose the types of activities and tasks to carry it out, and then evaluate how successful they have been. My only practical experience with this approach was on a PGCE course where we asked the student-teachers what they wanted to know and then attempted to meet it. There turned out, however, to be a wide discrepancy between what we thought such a course should cover and what they wanted to learn: week 1 they requested 'Tips on keeping discipline in class', week 2 'More tips on keeping discipline in class', Week 3 'Even more tips on . . .'; they would have been quite happy if this had formed the whole content of the year; far from our idea of a course.

A process syllabus must then involve an element of compromise for both teachers and students, if only to bring in the other relevant parties to the discussion, namely parents, government inspectors, and examiners. It also necessarily requires well-trained and confident teachers who can handle this constant process of negotiation and students who are willing to take on what they may conceive of as the teacher's responsibility. Indeed, as we saw in Chapter 7, such a syllabus may have strong political and cultural overtones about the nature of society and of the classroom, which may render it inappropriate for many countries. In the terms of Chapter 7, it seems a classic expatriate Centre methodology imposed upon local culture rather than fitting into the local scene; true negotiation with the students might end up with them suggesting an extremely conservative teacher-dominated academic classroom, which might indeed be what is best for their specific situation.

Autonomous learning is not yet widely used, nor is it clear that it would fit in with many mainstream educational systems. One reason is the incompatibility between the individual nature of the instruction and the collective nature of most classrooms and assessment. Autonomous learning takes the learner-centredness of the humanistic styles a stage further in refusing to prescribe a patent method that all learners have to follow. It is up to the student to decide on goals, methods, and assessment. That is what freedom is all about. In a sense, autonomous learning is free of many of the criticisms levelled against other styles. No teaching technique, no type of learner, no area of language is excluded in principle. Nevertheless, much depends upon the role of the helper and the support system. Without suitable guidance, students may not be aware of the possibilities. The helper has the difficult job of turning the student's initial preconceptions of language and of language learning into those attitudes that are most effective for that student. L2 learning research can assist autonomous learning by ensuring that the support systems for the learner reflect a genuine range of choices with an adequate coverage of the diverse nature of L2 learning.

The diversity of L2 teaching styles seen in this chapter may seem confusing: how can students really be learning language in so many ways? However, such diversity reflects the complexity of language and the range of student needs; why should one expect that a system as complex as language could be mastered in a single way? Even adding these teaching styles together gives an inadequate account of the totality of L2 learning. Second language learning means learning in all of these ways and in many more. This chapter has continually been drawing attention to the gaps in the coverage of each teaching style. As teachers and methodologists become more aware of L2 learning research, so teaching methods will alter to take them into account and cover a wider range of learning. Much L2 learning is concealed behind such global terms as 'communication' or such two-way oppositions as 'experiential/analytic' or indeed such simplistic divisions into six teaching styles. To improve teaching, we need to appreciate learning in all its complexity.

But teachers live in the present. They have to teach now rather than wait for

---

OTHER STYLES OF LANGUAGE TEACHING

Typical teaching techniques:

- CLL, Suggestopedia, confluent language teaching, self-directed learning

Goals:

- individual, development of the potential, self-selected

Type of student:

- those with individual motivation, etc.

Learning assumptions:

- diverse, mostly learning by doing, or a processing model

Processing assumptions:

- none

Classroom assumptions:

- usually small groups with cofigurative or even prefigurative aims

Weaknesses from L2 research perspective:

- black box view of learning or partial idiosyncratic views
- little attention to learner variation in humanistic styles
- difficulties in generalizing to many educational situations

Suggestions for teachers:

- importance of students' feelings and involvement
- provision of student choice throughout
- open discussion with students over their needs and preferences

---

a whole new L2 learning framework to emerge. They must get on with meeting the needs of the students, even if they still do not know enough about L2 learning. A psychoanalyst treating an individual patient has to set aside theories in order to respond to the uniqueness of that particular person. Teachers also have the duty to respond to their students. To serve the unique needs of actual students, the teacher needs to do whatever is necessary, not just that which is scientifically proven and based on abstract theory.

And the teacher needs to take into account far more than the area of L2 learning research; in the present state of knowledge L2 learning research has no warrant to suggest that any current teaching is more than partially justified. This book has therefore made suggestions and comments rather than asserted dogmatic axioms. Practising teachers should weigh them against all the other factors in their unique teaching situation before deciding how seriously to take them. Considering teaching from an L2 learning perspective in such a way will, it is hoped, lead in the future to a more comprehensive, scientifically based view of language teaching.

REVISION ACTIVITY 1

Identify these people mentioned in the book, as my word processor interpreted them (answers on p. 206)

(*a*) Mannered Phenomena, Hams Decent, Panda Polices, Lied White
(*b*) Pit Corridor, Walleye Lambent, Hernia Holes, Steven Krishna
(*c*) Larry Slinkier, Head Dual, Vivid Cook, James Ashore
(*d*) Sue Gases, Simian Greenness, Jake Stealthier, Elaine Trainee
(*e*) Peter Shekel, Susan Fly, Kevin Greed, Sister Felon

Afterword: the proper uses of second language acquisition research in language teaching

After the first edition of this book was finished, reactions from different people suggested that it raised several issues about the application of second language acquisition research that had not been aired. This section is in the way of an afterword, trying to bring together some of the general threads and make certain that people have some idea of what is involved in applying second language acquisition research to language teaching, as we have been attempting throughout this book. It is based on conference talks and papers published since the first edition; some of the ideas in it have been incorporated in the EUROSLA (European Second Language Association) draft *Guidelines for the application of second language research*.

It has been obvious throughout that we do not yet possess a single overall theory of second language acquisition that can bring together the learning of syntax with phonology, of vocabulary with listening, that can look at all the diverse factors in the classroom, the learner, the teacher, and the educational setting, in short can begin to cope with the complex real world situation the teacher faces every day. Hence at one level any links are going to be partial: no second language acquisition research can provide a definitive answer to the real problems of second language teaching at this point in time.

Much of the research encountered seems on the face of it to put forward alternative explanations for second language acquisition: the competition model versus the monitor, the acculturation model versus learning strategies, Universal Grammar versus the rest. But these are rarely true alternatives to each other as they are not competing for the same territory. A model that is concerned with grammatical morphemes such as *past tense* '-ed' (the Monitor) scarcely contacts one concerned with such syntactic parameters as whether sentences have to have subjects (Universal Grammar); a model that relies on syntax (multidimensional model) has little overlap with one that emphasizes social interaction (communication strategies). Language students mostly need language as a whole: there is little point in teaching them the grammar of the language if they cannot pronounce it, do not know the vocabulary, and cannot join in conversations. Language teaching requires a wider coverage than any of the existing models; a 'framework' that allows alternative 'models' to coexist within a larger whole is needed rather than a 'model' or a 'theory', say the 74 conditions for language learning put forward by Bernard Spolsky (1989a). There is no predetermined correct theory of language teaching originating from second language acquisition research.

Throughout this book we have also seen the multiplicity of levels at which teaching could make use of second language acquisition research. Having decided that something is going to be useful, it is still necessary to decide what aspect of teaching it could be applied to. For example, in this book we have seen applications to:

- *goals of language teaching*: should the students be taught for international, local or personal reasons (Chapter 7)?
- *language teaching syllabuses*: should words be taught as wholistic items, or constellations of components or meaning, or related to prototypes (Chapter 2)?
- *overall teaching methods*: is communicative teaching justified by second language acquisition research (Chapter 9)?
- *interaction in the classroom*: how does the teacher combine natural types of classroom interaction with natural types of language interaction outside the classroom (Chapter 6)?
- *specific teaching techniques*: should repetition of phonemes in minimal pairs be used for teaching pronunciation (Chapter 3)?

The usefulness of a second language acquisition idea may then be at many levels.

But there are also dangers in applying research. When the research is based on an adequate coverage of the appropriate areas, all well and good. A precise insight into how people learn to use voice onset time can help us to design teaching techniques to help the student pronounce /k/ and /g/ better but not lead to a general theory of teaching. A theory about acquisition such as the multidimensional model can help us with the overall design of a sequence for teaching but not with a technique for teaching the present continuous tense. It is inexcusable to over-exaggerate the claims of a particular small research area for language teaching. For example, in Chapter 2 we dealt with the sequence of acquisition of grammatical morphemes; there is indeed some kind of order in which L2 learners acquire plural '-s', auxiliary 'be', and the others – perhaps important for thinking about the sequence of these items in the early stages of teaching. But it amounts to one small point about one small area of language and one small aspect of learning. It is hardly sufficient to form the basis of a theory of second language learning, namely the input hypothesis, or a theory of language teaching, as was ultimately done in the natural teaching method. This is slightly unfair as other components did get involved in the application. However, it is not so far from the truth. Dulay *et al.* (1983) present ten teaching guidelines based on the research surveyed in their book; this, however, makes no mention of vocabulary learning, discourse, or internal strategies or processes other than monitoring. The teachability hypothesis of Pienemann and Johnston (1987) similarly suggests that teaching affects certain aspects of SLA that are subject to variation but cannot affect other 'developmental' aspects. Attractive as their proposal may be, the examples they give are based on general proficiency or on syntax – that is to say, they do not encompass four out of five of the aspects listed above. Their 'multidimensional' model in fact only has two dimensions.

The danger is always that people will go too far. Second language acquisition research has developed rapidly over twenty years and made a number of interesting points. Compared to the complexity of the classroom and the accumulated wisdom of language teachers, second language acquisition research still has to be humble in applying its ideas to language teaching. Yes, there are genuine contributions to be made, many more of them in future. But at the moment we have to take great care to use the research appropriately. Provided that a proper account of appropriate SLA research is utilized, provided that an adequate framework of language teaching is employed, a whole new generation of language teaching concepts and methods can be derived from SLA research. We must not jump in prematurely with limited and partial ideas of either second language acquisition or language teaching.

ANSWERS TO REVISION ACTIVITY 1

    (*a*) Manfried Pienemann, Hans Dechert, Nanda Poulisse, Lydia White
    (*b*) Pit Corder, Wallace Lambert, Henri Holec, Steven Krashen
    (*c*) Larry Selinker, Heidi Dulay, Vivian Cook, James Asher
    (*d*) Sue Gass, Simon Greenall, Jacquie Schachter, Elaine Tarone
    (*e*) Peter Skehan, Suzanne Flynn, Kevin Gregg, Sascha Felix

DISCUSSION TOPICS

1. Think of what you did or saw done the last time you visited a class; would you say the terms to characterize it best were in terms of 'techniques', 'approaches', 'styles', or what?
2. To what extent does the academic style incorporate traditional values of education, say those held by the 'man in the street' or government ministries, compared to the values of other styles?
3. What aspects of the audiolingual style do you feel are still practised today, whatever they are actually called?
4. To what extent do you think students can carry over the ability to communicate socially from their first language to their second?
5. If communicative teaching is about transferring 'information', what useful information do you feel should be conveyed during the language lesson?
6. In what ways do you think language teaching has changed in the past seventy years so far as the average classroom is concerned?
7. Does teaching an 'alternative' style mean adopting an 'alternative' set of values?
8. Which aspect of second language acquisition research have you found most useful for language teaching? Which least?

REVISION ACTIVITY 2

Match the person and the concept

Here are some of the correct names from Revision Activity 1, plus some others (with the ideas they are associated with). Match the person with the idea.

interlanguage	Robert Gardner
additive bilingualism	Brian MacWhinney
information processing	Lydia White
parameter resetting	Vivian Cook
acculturation	Manfried Pienemann
integrative motivation	Wallace Lambert
multicompetence	John Schumann
developmental dimension	Steven Krashen
comprehensible input	Larry Selinker
competition model	Barry McLaughlin

FURTHER READING

An overall discussion from a slightly American perspective (i.e. no discussion of audiovisual methods, graded objectives, and other European movements) is Richards and Rodgers (1986), *Approaches and Methods in Language Teaching*; the balance is slightly redressed by Marton (1988), *Methods in English Language Teaching*. Other useful books: for the audiolingual style, Lado (1964), *Language Teaching: A Scientific Approach*; for self-directed learning, Dickinson (1987), *Self-instruction in Language Learning;* Nunan (1991), *Language Teaching Methodology*, provides useful summaries of many of the issues covered here.

EFL course books mentioned in text

ABBS, B. and FREEBAIRN, I. 1982: *Opening Strategies*. Harlow: Longman.
—— —— 1990: *Blueprint One*. Harlow: Longman.
BAKER, A. 1981: *Ship or Sheep?* Cambridge: Cambridge University Press.
BLUNDELL, J., HIGGINS, J., and MIDDLEMISS, N. 1982: *Function in English*. Oxford: Oxford University Press.
BOSEWITZ, R. 1987: *The Penguin English Grammar*. Harmondsworth: Penguin.
BOWEN, T., and MARKS, J. 1992: *The Pronunciation Book*. Harlow: Longman.
CAPELLE, G., PAVIK, C., and SEGAL, M.K. 1985: *I Love English, Level 1*. New York: Regents.
CARRIER, M., HAINES, S., and CHRISTIE, D. 1985: *Break Into English*. Sevenoaks: Hodder and Stoughton.
COMMONWEALTH OFFICE OF EDUCATION 1967: *Situational English*. London: Longman.
COOK, V.J. 1968: *Active Intonation*. London: Longman.
—— 1975: *English Topics*. Oxford: Oxford University Press.
—— 1979: *Using Intonation*. Harlow: Longman.
—— 1980: *People and Places*. Pergamon. Polish edition, Polish Scientific Publishers, 1987.
—— 1982: *Meeting People*. Pergamon. Polish edition, Polish Scientific Publishers, 1987.
DALZELL, S., and EDGAR, I. 1988: *English in Perspective*. Oxford: Oxford University Press.
DAVIES, E., and WHITNEY, N. 1979: *Reasons for Reading*. London: Heinemann.
DAVIES, G., and SENIOR, M. 1983: *South Africa—the Privileged and the Dispossessed*. Paderborn: Ferdinand Schoningh.
DESPOTOVA, V., SHOPOV, T., and STOYANKA, V. 1988: *English for the Fifth Class*. Sofia: Narodna Prosveta.
EDINA, B.A., and IVANNE, S. 1987: *Angol Nyelv Alapfoken*. Budapest: Tankonyvkiado.
ELLIS, G., and SINCLAIR, B. 1989: *Learning to Learn English*. Cambridge: Cambridge University Press.
GARTON-SPRENGER, J., and GREENALL, S. 1990: *Flying Colours 1*. London: Heinemann.
GRAF, G. 1983: *English for You*. Berlin:Volk and Wissen Volkseigener Verlag.
GREENALL, S. 1994: *Reward*. Oxford: Heinemann.
HARMER, J., and ELSWORTH, S. 1989: *The Listening File*. Harlow: Longman.
—— and SURGUINE, H. 1987: *Coast to Coast*. Harlow: Longman.
HUTCHINSON, T. 1992: *Hotline*. Oxford: Oxford University Press.
KLIPPEL, F. 1984: *Keep Talking*. Cambridge: Cambridge University Press.

MOHAMED, S., and ACKLAM, R. 1992. *The Beginners' Choice*. Harlow: Longman.

MOLINSKY, S.J., and BLISS, B. 1989: *Side by Side*. New Jersey: Prentice-Hall.

MURPHY, R. 1993. *Basic Grammar in Use*. Cambridge: Cambridge University Press.

NORTHERN TERRITORY DEPT. OF EDUCATION 1979: *Tracks*. Northern Territory.

OXFORD, R.L. 1990: *Language Learning Strategies*. Rowley, MA: Newbury House.

RUDZKA, B., CHANNELL, J., PUTSEYS, Y., and OSTYN, P. 1981: *The Words You Need*. London: Macmillan.

SOARS, J., and SOARS, L. 1987: *Headway*. Oxford: Oxford University Press.

SOARS, L., and SOARS, J. 1993: *Headway Elementary*. Oxford: Oxford University Press.

SWAN, M., and WALTERS, C. 1984: *The Cambridge English Course*. Cambridge: Cambridge University Press.

WILLIS, J., and WILLIS, D. 1987: *The COBUILD English Course I*. London: Collins.

—— —— 1989: *The COBUILD English Course II*. London: Collins.

WRIGHT, A. 1987: *How to Improve Your Memory*. Cambridge: Cambridge University Press.

References

ADAMS, S.J. 1983: Scripts and Second Language Reading Skills. In Oller, J.W., Jr. and Richard-Amato, P.A. (eds), *Methods that Work*. Rowley, MA: Newbury House.

ALLEN, P., SWAIN, M., HARLEY, B., and CUMMINS, J. 1990: Aspects of classroom treatment: toward a more comprehensive view of second language education. In Harley, B., Allen, P., Cummins, J., and Swain, M. (eds) 1990, *The Development of Second Language Proficiency*. Cambridge: Cambridge University Press.

ALLWRIGHT, D. 1988: *Observation in the Language Classroom*. Harlow: Longman.

ALPTEKIN, C., and ATAKAN, S. 1990: Field-dependence—independence and hemisphericity as variables in L2 achievements. *Second Language Research* 6(2), 139–49.

ALTENBERG, E.P., and CAIRNS, H.S. 1983: The effects of phonotactic constraints on lexical processing in bilingual and monolingual subjects. *Journal of Verbal Learning and Verbal Behaviour* 22, 174–88.

ANDERSON, J. 1983: *The Architecture of Cognition*. Harvard University Press.

ANDERSEN, R.W. (ed.) 1983: *Pidginisation and Creolisation as Language Acquisition*. Rowley MA: Newbury House.

ANTHONY, E.M. 1963: Approach, method and technique. *English Language Teaching* 17, 63–7.

ARNBERG, L. 1987: *Raising Children Bilingually: The Pre-school Years*. Clevedon: Multilingual Matters.

ASHER, J. 1986: *Learning Another Language Through Actions: The Complete Teachers Guidebook*. Los Gatos, CA: Sky Oaks Productions.

—— and GARCIA, G. 1969: The optimal age to learn a foreign language. *Modern Language Journal* 38, 334–41.

—— and PRICE, B. 1967: The learning strategy of total physical response: some age differences. *Child Development* 38, 1219–27.

ASSESSMENT OF PERFORMANCE UNIT 1986: *Foreign Language Performance in Schools: Report on 1984 Survey of French*. London: Department of Education and Science.

BACON, S. 1987: Differentiated cognitive style and oral performance. In VanPatten, B., Dvorak, T.R., and Lee, J.F. (eds) 1987, *Foreign Language Learning: A Research Perspective*. Rowley MA: Newbury House.

BADDELEY, A.D. 1986: *Working Memory*. Oxford: Clarendon Press.

BAHRICK, H.P. 1984: Semantic memory content in permastore: fifty years of memory for Spanish learned in school. *Journal of Experimental Psychology: General* 113(1), 1–30.

—— and PHELPS, E. 1987: Retention of Spanish vocabulary over eight years. *Journal of Experimental Psychology: Learning, Memory and Cognition* 13(2), 344–9.

BALCOM, P. (forthcoming) 'Verbal arguments and multi-competence'.

BATES, E., and MacWHINNEY, B. 1981: Second language acquisition from a functionalist perspective. In H. Winitz (ed.), *Native Language and Foreign Language Acquisition*. Annals of the New York Academy of Sciences. Vol. 379.

BEN ZEEV, S. 1977: The influence of bilingualism on cognitive strategies and cognitive development. *Child Development* 48, 1009–18.

BIALYSTOK, E. 1990: *Communication Strategies*. Oxford: Blackwell.

—— and SHARWOOD-SMITH, M. 1985: Interlanguage is not a state of mind: an evaluation of the construct for second-language acquisition. *Applied Linguistics* 6(1), 101–17.

BICKERTON, D. 1981: *Roots of Language*. Ann Arbor: Karoma.

BIKO, S. 1978: *I Write What I Like*. The Bowerdan Press. Reprinted in Penguin, 1988.

BLACKWELL, A., and BROEDER, P. 1992: Interference and facilitation in SLA: a connectionist perspective. Seminar on PDP and NLP, San Diego, UCSD, May. Reported in Broeder and Plunkett (1994).

BLOOMFIELD, L. 1933: *Language*. New York: Holt.

BRANSFORD, J.D., and JOHNSON, M.K. 1982: Contextual prerequisites for understanding: some investigations of comprehension and recall. *Journal of Verbal Learning and Verbal Behaviour* 11, 717–26.

BREEN, M.P. 1984: Process syllabuses for the language classroom. In Brumfit, C.J. (ed.) *General English Syllabus Design. English Language Teaching Documents* 118, 47–60.

BROEDER, P., and PLUNKETT, P. 1994: Connectionism and second language acquisition. In Ellis, N. (ed.), *Implicit and Explicit Learning of Languages*. London: Academic Press, 421–53.

BROSELOW, E. 1988: Prosodic Phonology and the Acquisition of a Second Language. In S. Flynn and W. O'Neil (eds), *Linguistic Theory in Second Language Acquisition*. Dordrecht: Kluwer.

BROWN, G., and YULE, G. 1983: *Teaching the Spoken Language*. Cambridge: Cambridge University Press.

——, ANDERSON, A., SHILLCOCK, R., and YULE, G. 1984: *Teaching Talk: Strategies for Production and Assessment*. Cambridge: Cambridge University Press.

BROWN, G.D.A., and HULME, C. 1992: Cognitive processing and second language processing: the role of short term memory. In R.J. Harris (ed.), *Cognitive Processing in Bilinguals*. Elsevier, 105–21.

BROWN, R. 1973: *A First Language: The Early Stages*. London: Allen and Unwin.

BRUNER, J. 1983: *Childs Talk*. Oxford: Oxford University Press.

BYRAM, M. 1986: *Minority Education and Ethnic Survival*. Clevedon: Multilingual Matters.

—— 1990: Foreign language teaching and young people's perceptions of other cultures. *English Language Teaching Documents*, 132.

CALL, M. 1985: Auditory Short-Term Memory, listening comprehension and the Input Hypothesis. *TESOL Quarterly* 19(4), 765–81.

CANCINO, H., ROSANSKY, E., and SCHUMANN, J. 1978: The acquisition of English negative and interrogatives by native Spanish speakers. In E. Hatch (ed.), *Second Language Acquisition*. Rowley MA: Newbury House.

CARAMAZZA, A., and BRONES, I. 1980: Semantic classification by bilinguals. *Canadian Journal of Psychology* 34(1), 77–81.

CARRELL, P.L. 1983: Three components of background knowledge in reading comprehension. *Language Learning* 33(2), 183–207.

—— 1984: Evidence of a formal schema in second language comprehension. *Language Learning* 34, 87–111.

CARROLL, J.B. 1981: Twenty-five years of research on foreign language aptitude. In Diller, K.C. (ed.) 1981, *Individual Differences and Universals in Language Learning.* Rowley, MA: Newbury House, 83–118.

CARTER, R. 1988: Vocabulary, cloze, and discourse. In R. Carter and M. McCarthy (eds), *Vocabulary and Language Teaching.* Harlow: Longman.

CASKEY-SIRMONS, L.A., and HICKERSON, N.P. 1977: Semantic shift and bilingualism: variation in the color terms of five languages. *Anthropological Linguistics* 19(8), 358–67.

CHAMOT, A. 1987: The learning strategies of ESL students. In Wendon, A., and Rubin, J. (eds), *Learner Strategies in Language Learning.* New Jersey: Prentice-Hall.

CHAUDRON, C. 1983: Research on metalinguistic judgements: a review of theory, methods, and results. *Language Learning* 33(3), 343–77.

—— 1988: *Second Language Classrooms: Research on Teaching and Learning.* Cambridge: Cambridge University Press.

CHOMSKY, N. 1959: Review of B.F. Skinner Verbal Behavior. *Language* 35, 26–58.

—— 1976: *Reflections on Language.* Temple Smith.

—— 1986: *Knowledge of Language: Its Nature, Origin and Use.* New York: Praeger.

—— 1988: *Language and Problems of Knowledge: The Managua Lectures.* Massachusetts Institute of Technology Press.

—— 1993: A minimalist program for linguistic theory. In K. Hale and S.J. Keyser (eds), *The View from Building 20.* Massachusetts Institute of Technology Press, 1–52; preliminary version in Massachusetts Institute of Technology, *Occasional Papers in Linguistics* 1992: No 1.

CLARK, E. 1971: On the acquisition of "before" and "after". *Journal of Verbal Learning and Verbal Behaviour* 10, 266–75.

CLARK, M.A. 1984: On the nature of techniques; what do we owe the gurus? *TESOL Quarterly* 18(4), 577–84.

CLEMENT, R., and KRUIDENIER, B.G. 1983: Orientations in second language acquisition: I. the effects of ethnicity, milieu, and target language on their emergence. *Language Learning* 33(3), 274–91.

COHEN, A. 1990: *Language Learning.* Rowley MA: Newbury House.

COLLIN, A., and HOLEC, H. 1985: Foreign language acquisition processes in a secondary school setting: negation. In Riley, P. (ed.) 1985, *Discourse and Learning.* London: Longman.

COMMISSION FOR RACIAL EQUALITY 1986: *Teaching English as a Second Language: Report of a Formal Investigation in Calderdale Education Authority.*

COMMISSION OF THE EUROPEAN COMMUNITIES 1987: *Young Europeans in 1987.* EC Commission.

COOK, V.J. 1973: The comparison of language development in native children and foreign adults, *International Review of Applied Linguistics* XI(1), 13–28.

—— 1977: Cognitive processes in second language learning. *International Review of Applied Linguistics* XV(1), 73–90.

—— 1979: Aspects of memory in secondary school language learners. *Interlanguage Studies Bulletin—Utrecht* 4(2), 161–72.

—— 1981a: Some uses for second language learning research. *Annals of the New York Academy of Sciences* 379, 251–8.

—— 1981b: Using authentic materials in the classroom. *Modern English Teacher* 9(2).

—— 1982: Kategorisierung und Fremdsprachenerwerb. *Gegenwartige Probleme and Aufgaben der Fremdsprachen-psychologie.* Leipzig: Karl Marx University.

—— 1983: What should language teaching be about? *English Language Teaching Journal* 37, 3.

—— 1985: Language functions, social factors, and second language teaching. *International Review of Applied Linguistics* 13(3), 177–96.

—— 1986: Experimental approaches applied to two areas of second language learning research: age and listening-based teaching methods. In Cook, V. (ed.), *Experimental Approaches to Second Language Learning*. Oxford: Pergamon.

—— 1988a: Technique analysis: a tool for the teacher. *Modern English Teacher* 16(1), 29–32.

—— 1988b: Language learners extrapolation of word order in phrases of Micro-Artificial Languages. *Language Learning* 38(4), 497–529.

—— 1989a: The relevance of grammar to the applied linguistics of language teaching. *Trinity College Dublin Occasional Papers* 22.

—— 1989b: Reciprocal language teaching: another alternative. *Modern English Teacher* 16(3/4), 48–53.

—— 1990: Timed comprehension of binding in advanced learners of English. *Language Learning* 40(4), 557–99.

—— 1992: Evidence for multi-competence. *Language Learning* 42(4), 557–9.

—— 1993: *Linguistics and Second Language Acquisition*. Basingstoke: Macmillan.

—— 1994: UG and the metaphor of access. In N. Ellis (ed.), *Implicit Learning of Language*. Academic Press.

—— 1994: Universal Grammar and the learning and teaching of second languages. In Odlin, T. (ed), *Pedagogical Grammar*. Cambridge: Cambridge University Press.

—— 1996: *Inside Language*. London: Arnold.

—— and NEWSON, M. 1996: *Chomsky's Universal Grammar: An Introduction*. Oxford: Blackwell.

CRAGO, M. 1992: Communicative interaction and second language acquisition: an Inuit example. *TESOL Quarterly* 26(3), 487–506.

CROOKES, G., and GASS, S.M. (eds) 1992: *Tasks in a Pedagogical Context*. Clevedon: Multilingual Matters.

—— and SCHMIDT, R.W. 1991: Motivation: reopening the research agenda. *Language Learning* 41(4), 469–512.

CRUZ-FERREIRA, M. 1986: Non-native interpretive strategies for intonational meaning: an experimental study. In James, A., and Leather, J. (eds), *Sound Patterns in Second Language Acquisition*. Dordrecht: Foris.

CUMMINS, J. 1981: Age on arrival and immigrant second language learning in Canada: a reassessment. *Applied Linguistics* 2, 132–49.

CURRAN, C.A. 1976: *Counselling-Learning in Second Languages*. Apple River Illinois: Apple River Press.

DE JONG, E. 1986: *The Bilingual Experience: A Book for Parents*. Cambridge: Cambridge University Press.

DE SAUSSURE, F. 1916: *Cours de Linguistique Générale*. Bally C., Sechehaye A., and Reidlinger, A. (eds). Paris: Payot.

DIAZ, R.M. 1985: The intellectual power of bilingualism. *Quarterly Newsletter of the Laboratory of Comparative Human Cognition* 7(1), 16–22.

DICKERSON, L. 1975: The learner's language as a system of variable rules. *TESOL Quarterly* 9.

DICKERSON, W. 1987: Explicit rules and the developing in interlanguage phonology. In James, A., and Leather, J. (eds), *Sound Patterns in Second Language Acquisition*. Dordrecht: Foris.

DICKINSON, L. 1987: *Self-instruction in Language Learning*. Cambridge: Cambridge University Press.

DOLLERUP, C., GLAHN, E., and HANSEN, C.R. 1989: Vocabularies in the reading process. *AILA Review* 6, 21–33.

DONALDSON, M. 1978: *Children's Minds*. London: Fontana.

DORNIC, S. 1969: Verbal factor in number perception. *Acta Psychologica* 29, 393–9.

DORNYEI, Z. 1990: Conceptualising motivation in foreign-language learning. *Language Learning* 40(1), 45–78.

—— 1995: On the teachability of communicative strategies. *Teaching English to Speakers of Other Languages Quarterly* 29(1), 55–83.

DOUGHTY, C. 1991: Second language instruction does make a difference. *Studies in Second Language Acquisition* 13, 431–69.

DULAY, H.C., and BURT, M.K. 1973: Should we teach children syntax? *Language Learning* 23, 245–58.

—— —— 1980: On acquisition orders. In Felix, S., (ed.), *Second Language Development: Trends and Issues*. Tubingen: Narr.

—— —— and KRASHEN, S. 1982: *Language Two*. Rowley MA: Newbury House.

EASTERN EXAMINING BOARD 1986: *French*. Colchester: Eastern Examining Board.

ECKMAN, F.R., BELL, L., and NELSON, D. 1988: On the generalization of relative clause instruction in the acquisition of English as a Second Language. *Applied Linguistics* 9(1), 1–20.

ECKSTRAND, L. 1978: Age and length of residence as variables related to the adjustment of migrant children with special reference to second language learning. In Nickel, G. (ed.), *Proceedings of the Fourth International Congress of Applied Linguistics*. Stuttgart: Hochschulverlag, 3, 179–97.

ELLIS, R. 1985: *Understanding Second Language Acquisition*. Oxford: Oxford University Press.

—— 1986: *Classroom Second Language Development*. Oxford: Pergamon.

—— 1990: *Instructed Second Language Acquisition*. Oxford: Blackwell.

—— 1994: *The Study of Second Language Acquisition*. Oxford: Oxford University Press.

FAERCH, C., and KASPER, G. 1984: Two ways of defining communication strategies. *Language Learning* 34, 45–63.

FALTIS, C.J. 1989: Codeswitching and bilingual schooling: an examination of Jacobson's new concurrent approach. *Journal of Multilingual and Multicultural Development* 10(2), 117–27.

FAVREAU, M., and SEGALOWITZ, N.S. 1982: Second language reading in fluent bilinguals. *Applied Psycholinguistics* 3, 329–41.

FELIX, S.W. 1981: The effect of formal instruction on language acquisition. *Language Learning* 31, 87–112.

FLEGE, J.E. 1986: Effects of equivalence classification on the production of foreign language speech sounds. In James, A., and Leather, J. (eds), *Sound Patterns in Second Language Acquisition*. Dordrecht: Foris.

—— 1987: The production of "new" and "similar" phones in a foreign language: evidence for the effect of equivalence classification. *Journal of Phonetics* 15, 47–65.

—— and HILLENBRAND 1984: Limits on phonetic accuracy in foreign language speech production. *Journal of the Acoustical Society of America* 76, 708–21.

FREED, B. 1980: Talking to foreigners versus talking to children; similarities and differences. In Krashen, S.D., and Scarcella, R.C. (eds), *Issues in Second Language Research*. Rowley MA: Newbury House, 19–27.

FREIRE, P. 1972: *Pedagogy of the Oppressed*. Harmondsworth: Penguin.

FRÖHLICH, M., SPADA, N., and ALLEN, P. 1985: Differences in the communicative orientation of L2 classrooms. *TESOL Quarterly* 19(1), 27–56.

GAIES, S.J. 1979: Linguistic input in first and second language learning. In Eckman, F.R., and Hastings, A.J. (eds), *Studies in First and Second Language Acquisition*. Rowley MA: Newbury House.

GALTUNG, J. 1980: *The True Worlds. A Transnational Perspective*. New York: The Free Press.

GALYEAN, B. 1977: A confluent design for language teaching. *Teaching English to Speakers of Other Languages Quarterly* 11(2).

GARDNER, R. 1985: *Social Psychology and Second Language Learning*. London: Edward Arnold.

—— and LAMBERT, W.E. 1972: *Attitudes and Motivation in Second Language Learning*. Rowley, MA: Newbury House.

GARY, J., and GARY, N. 1981a: Comprehension-based language instruction: practice. In H. Winitz (ed.), *Native and Foreign Language Acquisition*. New York Academy of Sciences.

—— —— 1981b: Caution: talking may be dangerous to your linguistic health. *International Review of Applied Linguistics* XIX(1).

GASS, S. 1979: Language transfer and universal grammatical relations. *Language Learning* 29(2), 327–44.

GATHERCOLE, S.E., and BADDELEY, A.D. 1993: *Working Memory and Language*. Hove: Lawrence Erlbaum.

GATTEGNO, C. 1972: *Teaching Foreign Languages in Schools: The Silent Way*. Educational Solutions: New York.

GENESEE, F. 1976: The role of intelligence in second language learning. *Language Learning* 26(2), 267–80.

GLICKSBERG, D.H. 1963: A study of the span of immediate memory among adult students of English as a Foreign Language. PhD, University of Michigan.

GOPNIK, M., and CRAGO, M.B. 1991: Familial aggregation of a developmental language disorder. *Cognition* 39, 1–50.

GRIFFITHS, R., and SHEEN, R. 1992: Disembedded figures in the landscape: a reappraisal of L2 research on Field Dependence/Independence. *Applied Linguistics* 13(2), 133–47.

GROSJEAN, F. 1982: *Life with Two Languages*. Boston: Harvard University Press.

—— 1989: Neurolinguists, beware! The bilingual is not two monolinguals in one person. *Brain and Language* 36, 3—15.

GROSS, M. 1990: Lexique–Grammaire LADL, paper given at the AILA Congress, Thessaloniki, April.

GRUNEBERG, M. 1987: *The Linkword Language System: French*. London: Corgi.

GUIORA, A.Z., BRANNAN, R.C.L., and DULL, C.Y. 1972: Empathy and second language learning. *Language Learning* 22(2), 111–30.

HAKUTA, K. 1974: A preliminary report on the development of grammatical morphemes in a Japanese girl learning English as a second language. *Working Papers on Bilingualism* 3(18), 38.

HALLIDAY, M.A.K. 1975: *Learning How to Mean*. London: Edward Arnold.

HANSEN, J., and STANSFIELD, C. 1981: The relationship of Field Dependent–Independent cognitive styles to Foreign Language Achievement. *Language Learning* 31(2), 349–68.

HANSEN, L. 1984: Field Dependence–Independence and language testing: evidence from six Pacific Island cultures. *TESOL Quarterly* 18(2), 311–24.

HARDING, A., PAGE, B., and ROWELL, S. 1981: *Graded Objectives in Modern Languages*. London: Centre for Information on Language Teaching and Research.

HARDING, E., and RILEY, P. 1986: *The Bilingual Family: A Handbook for Parents*. Cambridge: Cambridge University Press.

HARLEY, B. 1986: *Age in Second Language Acquisition*. Clevedon: Multilingual Matters.

—— ALLEN, P., CUMMINS, J., and SWAIN, M. (eds) 1990: *The Development of Second Language Proficiency*. Cambridge: Cambridge University Press.

HARMER, J. 1983: *The Practice of English Language Teaching*. Harlow: Longman.

HARRINGTON, M. 1987: Processing transfer: language specific processing strategies as a source of interlanguage variation. *Applied Psycholinguistics* 8, 351–77.

HATCH, E. 1978: Discourse Analysis and Second Language Acquisition. In E. Hatch (ed.), *Second Language Acquisition: A Book of Readings*. Rowley, MA: Newbury House.

—— and HAWKINS, B. 1987: Second language acquisition: an experiential approach. In S. Rosenberg (ed.), *Advances in Applied PsychoLinguistics*. Volume 2. Cambridge: Cambridge University Press.

HAWKINS, E . 1984: *Awareness of Language*. Cambridge: Cambridge University Press.

HAWKINS, J.A. 1983: *Word Order Universals*. New York: Academic Press.

HENNER-STANCHINA, C. 1986: From reading to writing acts. In Riley, P. (ed.), *Discourse and Learning*. London: Longman, 91–104.

HMSO 1995. *The National Curriculum*. London: HMSO.

HOLEC, H. 1985a: On autonomy: some elementary concepts. In Riley, P. (ed.) 1985, *Discourse and Learning*. London: Longman.

—— 1985b: You did say oral interactive discourse? In Riley, P. (ed.) (1985), *Discourse and Learning*. London: Longman.

—— 1987: The learner as manager: managing learning or managing to learn? In Wendon, A and Rubin, J. (eds), *Learner Strategies in Language Learning*. New Jersey: Prentice-Hall.

HOLLIDAY, A. 1994: *Appropriate Methodology and Social Context*. Cambridge: Cambridge University Press.

HOOTON, A.B., and HOOTON, C. 1977: The influence of syntax on visual perception. *Anthropological Linguistics* 19(8), 355–7.

HORWITZ, E.K. 1987: Surveying student beliefs about language learning. In Wendon, A and Rubin, J. (eds), *Learner Strategies in Language Learning*. New Jersey: Prentice-Hall.

HOWATT, A. 1984: A *History of English Language Teaching*. Oxford: Oxford University Press.

HUBBARD, P., JONES, H., THORNTON, B., and WHEELER, R. 1983: *A Training Course for TEFL*. Oxford: Oxford University Press.

HULLEN, W. 1989: Investigations into classroom discourse. In Dechert, H. (ed.), *Current Trends in European Second Language Acquisition Research*. Clevedon: Multilingual Matters.

HYAMS, N. 1986: *Language Acquisition and the Theory of Parameters*. Dordrecht: Reidel.

HYMES, D. 1972: Competence and performance in linguistic theory. In Huxley, R., and Ingram, E. (eds), *Language Acquisition: Models and Methods*. New York: Academic Press.

IANCO-WORRALL, A. 1972: Bilingualism and cognitive development. *Child Development* 43, 1390–400.

INSTITUTE OF LINGUISTS 1988: *Examinations in Languages for International Communication*. London: Institute of Linguists.

IOUP, G., and TANSOMBOON, A. 1987: The acquisition of tone: a maturational perspective. In Ioup, G., and Weinberger, S.H. (eds), *Interlanguage Phonology*. Rowley, MA: Newbury House.

JACOBSON, R., and FALTIS, C. (eds) 1990: *Language Distribution Issues in Bilingual Schooling*. Clevedon: Multilingual Matters.

JAMES, A., and LEATHER, J. (eds) 1986: *Sound Patterns in Second Language Acquisition.* Dordrecht: Foris.

JESPERSEN, O. 1904: *How to Teach a Foreign Language.* London: Allen and Unwin.

JOHNSON, J., and NEWPORT, E. 1989: Critical period effects in second language acquisition: the influence of maturational state on the acquisition of ESL. *Cognitive Psychology* 21, 60–99.

KEENAN, E., and COMRIE, B. 1977: Noun phrase accessibility and universal grammar. *Linguistic Inquiry* 8, 63-100.

KELLERMAN, E. 1986: An eye for an eye: constraints of the L2 lexicon. In Kellerman, E., and Sharwood-Smith, M. (eds), *Crosslinguistic Influences in Second Language Acquisition.* Oxford: Pergamon.

—— AMMERLAAN, T., BONGAERTS, T., and POULISSE, N. 1990: System and hierarchy in L2 compensatory strategies. In Scarcella, R.C., Andersen, E.S., and Krashen, S.D. (eds), *Developing Communicative Competence in a Second Language.* Rowley, MA: Newbury House.

—— BONGAERTS, T., and POULISSE, N. 1987: Strategy and system in L2 referential communication. In Ellis, R. (ed.) *Second Language Acquisition in Context.* London: Prentice-Hall.

KEMENTERIAN PENDIDIKAN MALAYSIA 1987: *Sukatan Pelajaran Sekolah Menengah: Bahasa Inggeris.* Malaysia: PPK.

KENWORTHY, J. 1987: *Teaching English Pronunciation.* Harlow: Longman.

KILBORN, K., and COOREMAN, A. 1987: Sentence interpretation strategies in adult Dutch–English bilinguals. *Applied Psycholinguistics* 8, 415–31.

KIRSNER, K., BROWN, H.L., ABROL, S., CHADHA, N.K., and SHARMA, N.K. 1980: Bilingualism and lexical representation. *Quarterly Journal of Experimental Psychology* 32, 585–94.

KRASHEN, S. 1981a: *Second Language Acquisition and Second Language Learning.* Oxford: Pergamon.

—— 1981b: The Fundamental Pedagogical Principle in Second Language Teaching. In Sigurd, B., and Svartvik, J. (eds), *AILA 1981.* CWK Gleerup.

—— 1985: *The Input Hypothesis: Issues and Implications.* London: Longman.

—— SCARCELLA, R., and LONG, M. (eds) 1982: *Child–Adult Differences in Second Language Acquisition.* Rowley, MA: Newbury House.

—— SFERLAZA, V., FELDMAN, L., and FATHMAN, A. 1976: Adult performance on the SLOPE test: more evidence for a natural sequence in adult second language acquisition. *Language Learning* 26(1), 145–51.

—— and TERRELL, T.D. 1983: *The Natural Approach.* Oxford: Pergamon.

LADO, R. 1964: *Language Teaching: A Scientific Approach.* New York: McGraw-Hill.

LAMBERT, W.E. 1981: Bilingualism and language acquisition. In Winitz, H. (ed.), *Native and Foreign Language Acquisition.* New York Academy of Sciences.

—— 1990: Persistent issues in bilingualism. In Harley, B., Allen, P., Cummins, J., and Swain, M. (eds), *The Development of Second Language Proficiency.* Cambridge: Cambridge University Press.

LANDRY, R.G. 1974: A comparison of second language learners and monolinguals on divergent thinking tasks at the elementary school level. *Modern Language Journal* 58, 10–15.

LAPONCE, J.A. 1987: *Languages and their Territories.* Toronto: University of Toronto Press.

LARSEN-FREEMAN, D. 1976: An explanation for the morpheme order of second language learners. *Language Learning* 26, 125–34.

LEATHER, J. 1987: F₀ pattern inferences in the perceptual acquisition of second language tone. In James, A., and Leather, J. (eds), *Sound Patterns in Second Language Acquisition*. Dordrecht: Foris.

LEE, D.J. 1981: Interpretation of morpheme rank ordering in L2 research. In Dale, P., and Ingram, D. (eds). *Child Language: An International Perspective*. Baltimore: University Park Press.

LENNEBERG, E. 1967: *Biological Foundations of Language*. New York: Wiley.

LEVENSTON, E.A. 1979: Second Language Acquisition: Issues and Problems. *Interlanguage Studies Bulletin-Utrecht* 4(2), 147–60.

LEWIS, M. 1993: *The Lexical Approach*. Hove: Language Teaching Publications.

LIEBERMAN, P. 1984: *The Biology and Evolution of Language*. Harvard University Press.

LIGHTBOWN, P.M. 1987: Classroom language as input to second language acquisition. In Pfaff, C.W. (ed.), *First and Second Language Acquisition Processes*. Rowley, MA: Newbury House.

—— and Spada, N. 1993: *How Languages are Learned.* Oxford: Oxford University Press.

LINGUISTIC MINORITIES PROJECT 1983: *Linguistic Minorities in England*. University of London Institute of Education, distributed by Tinga Tonga.

LITTLE, D., DEVITT, S., and SINGLETON, D. 1988: *Authentic Texts in Foreign Language Teaching: Theory and Practice*. Dublin: Authentik.

LITTLEWOOD, W. 1981: *Communicative Language Teaching*. Cambridge: Cambridge University Press.

LONG, J., and HARDING-ESCH, E. 1977: Summary and recall of text in first and second languages: some factors contributing to performance difficulties. In Sinmaiko, H., and Gerver, D. (eds), *Proceedings of the NATO Symposium on Language Interpretation and Communication*. Plenum Press.

LONG, M.H., 1983: Does second language instruction make a difference? A review of the research. *TESOL Quarterly* 17, 359–82.

—— and CROOKES, G. 1993: Units of analysis in syllabus design: the case for task. In Crookes, G., and Gass, S.M. (eds), *Tasks in a Pedagogical Context*. Clevedon: Multilingual Matters, 9–54.

LOZANOV, G. 1978: *Suggestology and Outlines of Suggestopedia*. New York: Gordon and Breach.

McDONALD, J. 1987: Sentence interpretation in bilingual speakers of English and Dutch. *Applied Psycholinguistics* 8, 379–413.

McDONOUGH, S. 1995: *Strategy and Skill in Learning a Foreign Language*. London: Edward Arnold.

MACKEY, W.F. 1967: *Bilingualism as a World Problem*. Montreal: Harvest House.

McLAUGHLIN, B. 1987: *Theories of Second-Language Learning*. London: Edward Arnold.

—— ROSSMAN, R., and McLEOD, B. 1983: Second language learning: an information-processing perspective. *Language Learning* 33, 135–58.

MacWHINNEY, B. 1987: Applying the Competition Model to bilingualism. *Applied Psycholinguistics* 8, 315–27.

MAGISTE, E. 1979: The competing linguistic systems of the multilingual: a developmental study of decoding and encoding processes. *Journal of Verbal Language and Verbal Behaviour* 18, 79–89.

MAJOR, R. 1986: The natural phonology of second language acquisition. In James, A., and Leather, J. (eds), *Sound Patterns in Second Language Acquisition*. Dordrecht: Foris.

MAKINO, T. 1980: Acquisition order of English morphemes by Japanese secondary school students. *Journal of Hokkaido University of Education* 30(2), 101–48.

MARSH, L.G., and MAKI, R.H. 1978: Efficiency of arithmetic operations in bilinguals as a function of language. *Memory and Cognition* 414, 459–64.

MARTON, W. 1988: *Methods in English Language Teaching*. Hemel Hempstead: Prentice Hall.

MEAD, M. 1970: *Culture and Commitment*. London: Bodley Head.

MILON, J.P. 1974: The development of negation in English by a second language learner. *Teaching English to Speakers of Other Languages Quarterly* 8(2), 137–43.

MORGAN, J.L. 1986: *From Simple Input to Complex Grammar*. Cambridge, MA: Massachusetts Institute of Technology Press.

MYHILL, M. 1990: Socio-cultural content in ESL programmes for newly arrived and NESB and Aboriginal school children in Western Australia. *English Language Teaching Documents* 132, 117–31.

NAIMAN, N., FROHLICH, M., STERN, H.H., and TODESCO, A. 1978: *The Good Language Learner*. Toronto: Ontario Institute for Studies in Education.

NATHAN, G.S. 1987: On second-language acquisition of voiced stops. *Journal of Phonetics* 15, 313–22.

NEUFELD, G. 1978: On the acquisition of prosodic and articulatory features in adult language learning. *Canadian Modern Language Review* 34, 163–74.

NUNAN, D. 1989: *Designing Tasks for the Communicative Classroom*. Cambridge: Cambridge University Press.

—— 1991: *Language Teaching Methodology*. Hemel Hempstead: Prentice-Hall.

O'MAHONEY, M., and MUHIUDEEN, H. 1977: A preliminary study of alternative taste languages using qualitative description of sodium chloride solutions: Malay versus English. *British Journal of Psychology* 68, 275–78.

O'MALLEY, J.M., and CHAMOT, A.U. 1990: *Learning Strategies in Second Language Acquisition*. Cambridge: Cambridge University Press.

—— —— and KUPPER, L. 1989: Listening comprehension strategies in second language acquisition. *Applied Linguistics* 10(4), 418–37.

—— —— STEWNER-MANZARES, G., KUPPER, L., and RUSSO, R.P. 1985a: Learning strategies used by beginning and intermediate ESL students. *Language Learning* 35, 21–46.

—— —— —— RUSSO, R.P., and KUPPER, L. 1985b: Learning strategy applications with students of English as a Second Language. *TESOL Quarterly* 19(3), 557–84.

ODLIN, T. 1989: *Language Transfer*. Cambridge: Cambridge University Press.

—— (ed.) 1994: *Pedagogical Grammar*. Cambridge: Cambridge University Press.

ORNSTEIN, P.A., and NAUS, M.J. 1978: Rehearsal processes in children's memory. In Ornstein, P. (ed.), *Memory Development*. Hillsdale, NJ: Lawrence Erlbaum.

OXFORD, R., CROOKALl, D., COHEN, A.D., LAVINE, R., NYIKOS, M., and SUTTER, W. 1990: Strategy training for language learners: six situational case studies and a training model. *Foreign Language Annals* 22(3), 197–216.

PAGE, N. 1986: *A Conrad Companion*. Basingstoke: Macmillan.

PALMER, H.E. 1926: *The Principles of Language Study*. London: Harrap.

PAPAGNO, C., and VALLAR, G. 1992: Phonological short term memory and the learning of novel words. *Quarterly Journal of Experimental Psychology* 44A, 47–67.

PAULSTON, C.B. 1986: Linguistic consequences of ethnicity and nationalism in multi-lingual settings. In Spolsky, B. (ed.), *Language and Education in Multilingual Settings*. Clevedon: Multilingual Matters.

PHILLIPSON, R. 1992: *Linguistic Imperialism*. Oxford: Oxford University Press.

PIENEMANN, M. 1984: Psychological constraints on the teachability of languages. *Studies in Second Language Acquisition* 6(2), 186–214.

—— 1986: Psychological constraints on the teachability of language. In Pfaff, C.W. (ed.), *First and Second Language Acquisition Processes*. Rowley, MA: Newbury House.

—— and JOHNSTON, M. 1987: Factors influencing the development of language proficiency. In Nunan, D. (ed.), *Applying Second Language Research*. Adelaide: NCRC, 45-141.

PITTENGER, R.E., HOCKETT, C.F., and DANBURY, J.J. 1960: *The First Five Minutes: A Sample of Microscopic Interview Analysis*. Ithaca: Paul Marteneau.

POPLACK, S. 1980: Sometimes I'll start a sentence in English y termino en español. *Linguistics* 18, 581–616.

PORTER, P.A. 1986: How learners talk to each other: input and interaction in task-centered discussions. In Day, R.R. (ed.), *Talking to Learn: Conversation in Second Language Acquisition*. Rowley, MA: Newbury House.

POSTOVSKY, V. 1974: Effects of delay in oral practice at the beginning of second language learning. *Modern Language Journal* 58.

POULISSE, N. 1987: Classification of compensatory strategies. *Second Language Research* 3(2), 141–53.

—— 1990: *The Use of Compensatory Strategies by Dutch Learners of English*. Berlin: Mouton de Gruijter.

PRABHU, N.S. 1987: *Second Language Pedagogy*. Oxford: Oxford University Press.

PRODROMOU, L. 1989: English as cultural action. *English Language Teaching Journal* 43.

QUIRK, R., and GREENBAUM, S. 1973: *A University Grammar of English*. Harlow: Longman.

RAMSEY, C., and WRIGHT, C. 1974: Age and second language learning. *Journal of Social Psychology* 94, 115–21.

RANNEY, S. 1993: Learning a new script; an explanation of sociolinguistic competence. *Applied Linguistics* 13(1), 25–50.

RICHARDS, J.C., and RODGERS, T.S. 1986: *Approaches and Methods in Language Teaching*. Cambridge: Cambridge University Press.

RILEY, P. 1985: Mud and stars: personal constructs, sensitization, and learning. In Riley, P. (ed.), *Discourse and Learning*. London: Longman.

—— (ed.) 1985: *Discourse and Learning*. London: Longman.

RINGBOM, H. 1982: The influence of other languages on the vocabulary of foreign language learners. In Nickel, G., and Nehls, D. (eds), *Error Analysis, Contrastive Linguistics and Second Language Learning*. Heidelberg: International Review of Applied Linguistics.

RIVERS, W.M. 1964: *The Psychologist and the Foreign Language Teacher*. Chicago: Chicago University Press.

ROLLER, C.M., and MATOMBO, A.R. 1992: Bilingual readers' use of background knowledge in learning from text. *Teaching English to Speakers of Other Languages Quarterly* 26(1), 129–40.

ROMAINE, S. 1994: *Bilingualism*. Oxford: Blackwell.

ROSCH, E. 1977: Human categorisation. In N. Warren (ed.), *Studies in Cross-Cultural Psychology*. New York: Academic Press.

ROSSIER, R. 1976: Extroversion–introversion as a significant variable in the learning of oral English as a second language. PhD, University of Southern California.

RUMELHART, D.E., and McCLELLAND, J.L. 1986: On learning the past tenses of English verbs. In J.L. McLelland, D.E. Rumelhart, and the PDP Research Group, *Parallel Distributed Processing: Volume 2 Psychological and Biological Models*. Cambridge, MA: Massachusetts Institute of Technology Press, 216–71.

RUTHERFORD, W.E. 1987: *Second Language Grammar: Learning and Teaching*. Harlow: Longman.

SAMPSON, G.P. 1984: Exporting language teaching methods from Canada to China. *TESL Canada Journal* 1(1).

SAUNDERS, G. 1982: *Bilingual Children: Guidance for the Family.* Clevedon: Multilingual Matters.

SCHANK, R., and ABELSON, R. 1977: *Scripts, Plans, Goals, and Understanding.* New Jersey: Lawrence Erlbaum.

SCHREUDER, R., and WELTENS, B. (eds) 1993: *The Bilingual Lexicon.* Amsterdam: Benjamins.

SCHUMANN, J. 1978a: The acculturation model of second language acquisition. In R.C. Gingras (ed.), *Second Language Acquisition and Foreign Language Teaching.* Georgetown: Centre for Applied Linguistics.

—— 1978b: *The Pidginisation Process: A Model for Second Language Acquisition.* Rowley, MA: Newbury House.

SELINKER, L. 1972: Interlanguage. *International Review of Applied Linguistics* X, 209–30.

SERVICE, E. 1992: Phonology, working memory, and foreign language learning. *Quarterly Journal of Experimental Psychology* 45A, 21–50.

—— 1989: *Phonological Coding in Working Memory and Foreign-Language Learning.* General Psychology Monographs B9, Dept. of Psychology, University of Helsinki.

SHARWOOD-SMITH, M. 1994: *Second Language Learning: Theoretical Foundations.* Harlow: Longman.

SINCLAIR, J., and COULTHARD, M. 1975: *Towards an Analysis of Discourse.* Oxford: Oxford University Press.

SINGLETON, D. 1989: *Language Acquisition: The Age Factor.* Clevedon: Multilingual Matters.

SKEHAN, P. 1986: Cluster Analysis and the identification of learner types. In Cook, V. (ed.), *Experimental Approaches to Second Language Learning.* Oxford: Pergamon.

—— 1988: Early lexical development and the prediction of foreign language learning success. *Polyglot* 9, fiche 2.

—— 1989: *Individual Differences in Second-Language Learning.* London: Edward Arnold.

SKINNER, B.F. 1957: *Verbal Behavior.* New York: Appleton-Century-Crofts.

SKUTNABB-KANGAS, T. 1981: *Bilingualism or not: The Education of Minorities.* Clevedon: Multilingual Matters.

SNOW, C., and HOEFNAGEL-HÖHLE, M. 1977: Age differences in the pronunciation of foreign sounds. *Language and Speech* 20, 357–65.

—— —— 1978: The critical period for language acquisition: evidence from second language learning. *Child Development* 49, 1114–28.

SOUTHERN EXAMINING GROUP, 1995: *GCSE French.*

SPOLSKY, B. 1989a: *Conditions for Second Language Learning.* Oxford: Oxford University Press.

—— 1989b: Maori bilingual education and language revitalisation. *Journal of Multilingual and Multicultural Development* 10(2), 89–106.

SRIDHAR, K.K., and SRIDHAR, S.N. 1986: Bridging the paradigm gap; second language acquisition theory and indigenised varieties of English. *World Englishes* 5(1), 3–14.

STREETS, L. 1976: *I Can Talk.* London: Down Syndrome Association. Reprinted 1991.

SWALES, J.M. 1990: *Genre Analysis.* Cambridge: Cambridge University Press.

SWAN, M., and SMITH, B. 1987: *Learner English.* Cambridge: Cambridge University Press.

TARONE, E. 1980: Communication strategies, foreigner talk, and repair in interlanguage. *Language Learning* 30(2), 417–31.

—— 1988: *Variation in Interlanguage.* London: Edward Arnold.

THOMPSON, G.G. 1952: *Child Psychology.* Boston: Houghton-Mifflin.

TOKYO, SHOSEKI 1990: *Course of Study for Senior High Schools, Foreign Languages: English.*

UNDERWOOD, M. 1989: *Teaching Listening*. Harlow: Longman.

VALDMAN, A. 1976: *Introduction to French Phonology and Morphology*. Rowley, MA: Newbury House.

VERMA, M.K., FIRTH, S., and CORRIGAN K. (1992): The developing phonological skills of Panjabi/Urdu speaking children learning English as a second language in Britain. In Leather, J., and James, A. (ed.), *New Sounds 92*. Amsterdam: University of Amsterdam.

WALLERSTEIN, N. 1983: The teaching approach of Paolo Freire. In Oller, J.W. Jr., and Ri⌐ ᵃrd-Amato, P.A. (eds), *Methods that Work*. Rowley, MA: Newbury House.

WARDHAUGH, R. 1987: *Languages in Competition*. Oxford: Blackwell.

WATSON, I. 1991: Phonological processing in two languages. In Bialystok, E. (ed.), *Language Processes in Bilingual Children*. Cambridge: Cambridge University Press.

WENDON, A., and RUBIN, J. (eds) 1987: *Learner Strategies in Language Learning*. New Jersey: Prentice-Hall.

WERKER, J.F., GILBERT, J.H.V., HUMPHREY, K., and TEES, R.C. 1981: Developmental aspects of crosslanguage speech perception. *Child Development* 52, 349–55.

WESCHE, M.B. 1981: Language aptitude measures in streaming, matching students with methods, and diagnosis of learning problems. In Diller, K. (ed.), *Individual Differences and Universals in Language Learning*. Rowley, MA: Newbury House, 83–118.

—— and READY, D. 1985: Foreigner talk in the university classroom. In Gass, S.M., and Madden, C.G. (eds), *Input in Second Language Acquisition*. Rowley, MA: Newbury House.

WHITE, L. 1986: Implications of parametric variation for adult second language acquisition: an investigation of the pro-drop parameter. In V.J. Cook (ed.), *Experimental Approaches to Second Language Acquisition*. Oxford: Pergamon.

—— 1989: *Universal Grammar and Second Language Acquisition*. Amsterdam: John Benjamins.

WIEDEN, W., and NEMSER, W. 1991: *The Pronunciation of English in Austria*. Tubingen: Gunter Narr.

WILLIAMS, L. 1977: The perception of consonant voicing by Spanish–English bilinguals. *Perception and Psychophysics* 21(4), 289–97.

WINITZ, H. (ed.) 1981: *The Comprehension Approach to Foreign Language Instruction*. Rowley, MA: Newbury House.

WODE, H. 1981: *Learning a Second Language*. Tubingen: Gunter Narr.

Index